THE CHALLENGE OF WEALTH

THE CHALLENGE OF WEALTH

A Jewish Perspective on Earning and Spending Money

Meir Tamari

JASON ARONSON INC.
Northvale, New Jersey
London

This book was set in 11 pt. Berkeley Old Style by Alpha Graphics of Pittsfield, New Hampshire, and printed by Haddon Craftsmen in Scranton, Pennsylvania.

10 9 8 7 6 5 4 3 2 1

Library of Congress Cataloging-in-Publication Data

Tamari, Meir.
The challenge of wealth : a Jewish perspective on earning and spending money / Meir Tamari.
p. cm.
Includes bibliographical references and index.
ISBN 1-56821-280-1
1. Economics–Religious aspects–Judaism. 2. Wealth–Religious aspects–Judaism. 3. Commercial law (Jewish law) 4. Ethics, Jewish. 5. Judaism and social problems. I. Title.
BM509.E27T36 1995
296.3'8568–dc20 94-22073

Manufactured in the United States of America. Jason Aronson Inc. offers books and cassettes. For information and catalog write to Jason Aronson Inc., 230 Livingston Street, Northvale, New Jersey 07647.

This book is dedicated to the chasidic master Shmuel of Sochochow, whose writings have had such a profound influence on my life.

CONTENTS

INTRODUCTION

PERSISTENCE OF MORAL ISSUES

The experience of the past seventy years, worldwide, has shown that free markets and planned economies, while each solving certain moral problems, seem to create others.

Planned economies have provided basic services for everybody, reducing mass hunger, ignorance, and economic insecurity. However, centralized economic power fosters corruption and restricts individual liberty. The economic inefficiency in supplying consumer needs leads the individual to pursue unethical methods to acquire them. Furthermore, such economies usually initiate policies contrary to economic logic. These policies make fraud, evasion, and falsehoods essential to the operation of the economy, and indeed the latter become intrinsic parts of everyday life.

In the real world, free markets do not always operate as efficiently as they are assumed to do. So, while they provide goods and services more efficiently than do the planned economies, nevertheless, when they break down or need readjustment, unemployment, shortages, and poverty occur. Furthermore they, as often as not, do not seem to be able to provide for the weak, inefficient, sick, and old members of society. They provide individual liberty, but are not always able to provide allover economic protection or a social safety net. Perhaps even more important than these shortcomings, free markets appeal to the egoism and selfishness of the human being, making the acquisition of wealth the primary ideal.

Irrespective of the type of economic system chosen, it seems clear that moral and ethical dimensions of economics in general, and of business in particular, remain. It is not surprising therefore that the 1980s and the early 1990s have shown a radical growth in awareness of this ethical dimension, in almost all of the major economies. In part this has been sparked by the scandals in the financial markets, at first in the United States, later in Europe and the United Kingdom, and more recently in Japan. These were expressed in the flagrant disregard of legislation regarding the use of insider information, in the phenomena of the corporate raiders and takeovers, and in the leveraged buyouts with the junk bonds that financed them.

However, of greater importance would seem to be the deregulating policies of the Reagan and Thatcher years, and the breakdown of Socialist and Communist economies, which led to a smaller role for government in the marketplace. These policies have laid a greater responsibility for an ethical market on the corporate sector and on the individuals operating in the marketplace. This responsibility covers the whole gamut of economic activity from consumer protection, to the property rights of intellectual goods, to redundancy, and to environmental protection.

More recently, the ethical dimension in business has acquired greater prominence as a result of consistent unemployment in the stagnant economies of the Western world and of the large numbers of people for whom there is no safety net providing for homes, health, education, and social services. This has happened not only in the West, but even more starkly in the former Communist countries of Eastern Europe, calling into question capitalism's ability to solve these moral issues.

The resultant awareness of economic moral issues has been strengthened in the Jewish world by the resurgence of learning and identification, which has characterized these decades. Unfortunately, this awareness has not been accompanied by commensurate literature and study material aimed at the general reader. Audience reaction to this author's lectures and seminars, almost worldwide, Jewish and non-Jewish alike, has ranged from astonishment that there should indeed exist Jewish perspectives on business, to a general feeling that such perspectives are irrelevant or impractical.

Such reactions are fueled by and, in turn, perpetuate the lack of attention paid to these perspectives in Jewish education at all levels. Somehow, despite the awareness that business morality and economic life present real, everyday, and persistent challenges to Jewish behavior and lifestyles, these challenges seldom are the subject of public discussions, sermons, or literature. This book has been written in order to assist in the stimulation and search for possible Jewish answers to the ethical issues facing the modern individual and society, in their involvement in the marketplace and in material goods.

Since so much time and effort are involved in business and in economics, and wealth is the cause of so much struggle, crime, and war, they have always represented a primary challenge to all religions and social philosophies including Judaism. The explosion of wealth over the past decades has left more people relatively wealthy than at any other time in human history; this simply heightens the challenge, since morality and ethics are issues that only those who possess wealth are called upon to face.

This challenge seems to be expressed in two forms, and the book is structured accordingly. There is the question of the means used to earn money and acquire wealth by individuals, which is dealt with in Part I of the book. There is, however, the no less problematic issue of what is done with that wealth, beyond satisfying the needs and wants of the owners. So in Part II of the book, charity, communal obligations, consumption, and so forth, are seen as part of the challenge of wealth.

The questions related to wealth—both earning and spending it—are universal ones, common to all societies, religions, and national groups. The answers, however, remain specific to the spiritual and cultural roots of each society. So this book attempts, using traditional Jewish sources, to provide guidelines for modern Jews to manage the ethical issues raised in the marketplace and by the possession of wealth. These guidelines are developed from written sources, ancient and modern, as well as the total economic behavior of Jewish individuals and communities throughout the ages.

Great care must be taken in such development to prevent projecting personal economic philosophies into these sources, thereby making them conform to current patterns of behavior based on non-Jewish thinking. Since works such as this book are of an interdisciplinary nature, it is easy to force subconsciously the Jewish legal, homiletical, and religious sources to sanction prevailing social concepts or ideologies. In the period between the two world wars, it was common for academics, rabbis, and laymen to equate Judaism with socialism. Prophets like Amos and movements within Judaism, such as the Pharisees of the Second Temple period or Chasidism of eighteenth- and nineteenth-century eastern Europe, were seen as forebears of modern Socialist thinking. More recently, free market economies and Judaism were considered to be almost synonymous. It would be more correct to argue that Judaism is an *ism* by itself. It possesses characteristics that in part are similar to those associated with socialism and yet others often similar to those of free-market operations. This is neither surprising nor problematical. After all, Judaism is not an economic system, but a spiritual and moral value structure, within which economic activity takes place and is formed into a pattern of holiness. Jews have lived, and continue to live, under many different economic systems, adapting their behavior to this spiritual and moral value structure.

Furthermore, in the popular imagination, there seem to be three major factors militating against the acceptance of these Jewish perspectives on the moral and ethical issues in modern business and economic behavior.

1. A general acceptance of the anti-Semitic slurs regarding Jewish avarice and business immorality, which are often reflected in the literature and culture of almost all of the Christian societies. The myth of Jewish capitalism and exploitation fostered both by Nazi Germany[1] and by the writing of Karl Marx[2] was built on age-old biases. These either saw in Jewish frugality, hard work, and entrepreneurship the implementation of a national materialistic obsession, or were based on jealousy, the desire to avoid contractual obligations, and the need for scapegoats to explain social or economic distress.

2. The association of biblical and talmudical regulation with a simple agrarian economy, far distant from the modern world of international finance, sophisticated patterns of merchandising, and constant technological changes. This seeming irrelevance of traditional Jewish teachings is based on the assumption that changes in economic systems are, in fact, changes in human nature, needs, or weaknesses.

3. An understandable yet unfortunate current overemphasis on spiritual behavior that, following primarily Christian religious patterns, has meant a disassociation of Judaism from such so-called secular

aspects of life as economics, political organization, and social change. The subsequent emphasis on ritual, traditional observance, the synagogue, and allied aspects was essential in order to preserve Jewish identity in the open societies in which Jews have increasingly found themselves since the end of the nineteenth century. Yet at the same time, it led to a search for non-Jewish secular answers, such as communism, liberalism, or social democracy, to economic dilemmas. This disassociation between Judaism and business was strengthened by the inability or unwillingness to construct Jewish communities, similar to those autonomous ministates in which Jews had lived for some 2,000 years in the various countries of the Diaspora. Much of the traditional Jewish economic morality was integrated into this communal structure, which involved both an independent judiciary and a separate fiscal system, so that the lack of such a structure inevitably weakened the application of specifically Jewish perspectives to the marketplace.

Widespread as these ideas are, nevertheless, they are all based on ignorance of the history of Jewish business activity throughout the centuries and in all the countries of the dispersion. Furthermore, they ignore the wealth of information contained in all the different types of Jewish written sources.

Physically, the economic conditions that existed both in the Land of Israel and in the surrounding countries at the time of the Mosaic Code were radically different from those of our own times. Nevertheless these differences should not be overemphasized in considering ethical perspectives. Basically, unlike the changes in physics or chemistry, economic activities have remained the same—production, distribution, transfer of wealth, money, and so on. However, while the techniques change over time, both the motivations and spiritual challenges remain similar. Both the experience of the 1980s in the Western world and the seventy years of communism have revealed clearly that mere changes in an economic system, of themselves, do not create moral solutions. This is simply because the promptings and drives of economic behavior—uncertainty, greed, wants, and jealousy—so deeply imbedded in human nature, do not basically change. Since Judaism is an ethical and moral value system rather than an economic philosophy, the Mosaic Code, which defines that system, is therefore as relevant to those underlying traits as it ever was.

HALAKHAH AND *AGGADAH*

Trust in Divine Providence, injunctions against theft, robbery, and exploitation, imposed mutual obligations for care of the poor, the oppressed, and weak, and the constant pursuit of justice remain as operative today as when they were first received.

Nevertheless, in the field of economic behavior as in all others, the Five Books of Moses provide only an outline for behavior that requires a more ramified and complex corollary, if it is to be transformed into a viable pattern for everyday living in all generations. The Oral Law, considered in Judaism to be of Divine Origin and as binding, comes therefore to implement the written Mosaic Code. Although partially redacted–first by Yehudah HaNasi (Land of Israel, c. 250 C.E.) in the *Mishnah*–the Oral Law has maintained its characteristics down to our own times. The six orders–*sedarim*–of the *Mishnah*, include *Nezikin*–literally, damages, which is in fact the repository of Jewish civil, criminal, and business law.

Some three centuries later, a further redaction took place, in the form of the *Gemara*. The *Mishnah* and *Gemara* together constitute the Talmud. The Babylonian Talmud was sealed by Ravina and Rav Ashi in Babylon in the fifth century, and the Jerusalem Talmud was concluded in Tiberias some decades later. Strictly speaking, however, the Talmud is not a codex, but a wide-ranging encyclopedia of Oral traditions stretching all the way back to Moses. Included in the Talmud were the *baraitot* (external teachings), representing those opinions not considered by Yehudah HaNasi as authoritative as the *Mishnah*, and the *Tosefta* (supplement), a more detailed discussion of the subject matter of the *Mishnah*. The rabbis of the *Gemara*, known as *Amora'im* to distinguish them from the *Tanna'im* of the mishnaic period, did not however restrict themselves to the *Halakhah* (literally, road or path)–the Jewish legal tradition. Equally important, both to them and indeed to all the sages down to the present, was the *Aggadah*, which thus forms an internal part of the Oral tradition. The *Aggadah* could probably be classified as the theological, philosophical, and moral literature of the tradition.

Part of this literature was included in the Talmud, but in part, it is represented by a parallel rabbinic literature in the form of homiletical works, translations, and commentaries on the Bible. They include the Aramaic translation cum commentary of Onkelos on the Torah and that on the Prophets, of Yonatan ben Uziel; the source book of Jewish mysticism, the *Zohar* (*Book of Splendor*) by Shimon bar Yochai; the *Midrash Halakhah*–literature in which *Halakhah* is deduced or supported from the words of the Torah, which constitutes a kind of legal commentary on the biblical material. Here were included the *Mekhilta* on Exodus (*Shemot*), the *Sifra* on Leviticus (*Vayikra*), and the *Sifre* on Numbers (*BaMidbar*) and Deuteronomy (*Devarim*). There were also other collections of *Midrashim*–interpretative commentaries and explanations–the major one being the *Midrash Rabbah*.

All these writings were, however, far more than a commentary. They represent the conceptual framework that lies behind the halakhic rulings. Any attempt, therefore, to try to separate these two streams of *Halakhah* and *Aggadah* will present a distorted view, not only of Jewish religious thinking, but, for that matter, even of its legal rulings. This distorted view has, unfortunately, become widely accepted in Jewish and non-Jewish circles, presenting Judaism simply as a ramified nonspiritual legal network.[3] More importantly, it ignores such spiritual, ethical, and moral rabbinic concepts as *lifnim mishurat hadin*–obligations going beyond the letter of the law–the necessity to be clean before God and man, and the idea of acts for which no legal consequences follow but which are nevertheless forbidden. Such concepts are an integral part of Judaism, and when they are overshadowed by the purely legalistic forms, we may be permitting economic acts forbidden by Judaism. A more correct perspective, therefore, would be to view them as twin strands, representing a tension between the legal framework, which even the most lofty concepts require if they are to be effective, and the spiritual dimensions, without which even the most perfect legal system becomes perverse and inhuman. This unity of *Halakhah* and *Aggadah* has been maintained throughout the ages, so that the halakhic personalities and codifiers were not only participants in the aggadic stream, but considered it as part of the overall process of Jewish legal thought. Maimonides, the great rationalist-codifier, ends each of his sections with spiritual insights and motives. Rabbi Yosef Caro was an important part of the circle of disciples of Rabbi Avraham Askenazi–the Ari–the leading personality of the influential mystics of Safed in the Land of Israel in the sixteenth century. The same Caro was the author of the *Shulchan Arukh*, the codex that gradually became the authoritative legal code for all Jews. The founder of the Lubavicher (*Chabad*) *chasidim*, part of the mystical movement that swept Jewry in the eighteenth and nineteenth centuries, Shneur Zalman of Lyady, in the eighteenth century authored a version of the *Shulchan Arukh*. Yet Eliyahu, Gaon of Vilna, the arch rationalist, teacher of the Lithuanian scholastic tradition and fierce opponent of Chasidism, was also known as a scholar of Kabbalah, Jewish mysticism.

The saga of the Oral Law continued even after the sealing of the Talmud. The Talmud has remained the major subject of Jewish study in all generations, not only for rabbis and judges, but, more importantly, for laymen of all ages. This ensured that the Jewish law and its aggadic spiritual dimensions became an integral part of all strands of Jewish societies. Each generation and each major center of learning produced its commentaries and its notes, many of which are printed together with the text itself. In this way both the spiritual traditions and the legal framework of the Mosaic tradition became the conceptual framework for all aspects of Jewish life, including the activities in the marketplace.

This framework, however, required accepted and authoritative legal rulings, which were provided over the centuries by codes. Chronologically, the first and easily the most comprehensive of all the codes is that of the Rambam, Rabbi Moshe ben Maimon (Maimonides), who lived most of his life in Egypt in the late twelfth century. His *Mishneh Torah* marks him almost as another lawgiver. The *Mishneh Torah* comprises fourteen volumes (hence its alternate name, *HaYad HaChazakah*, where the numerical value of the Hebrew letters in *Yad* equals fourteen). It covers every aspect of Jewish life, including those commandments temporarily in abeyance, such as those governing the Temple service and sacrifices. For the purpose of this book, the most relevant sections of the *Mishneh Torah* are *Nezikin* (Damages), *Mishpatim* (Judgments), and *Shoftim* (Judges). Within a half century of Maimonides, Yaakov ben Asher compiled the *Arbaah Turim* (*Four Rows*, referring to the jewels in the breastplate of the High Priest). Most of the later codes, commentaries, and rabbinic decisions adopted the following arrangement of the halakhic material of the *Tur*:

1. *Orach Chaim* (Way of Life)–primarily concerned with *Shabbat*, festival, and prayers.
2. *Yoreh De'ah* (Teacher of Knowledge)–dealing with the laws of forbidden and permitted things like kosher food, ritual purity, idolatry, and interest.

3. *Even HaEzer*–concerned with marriage, divorce, and family matters.
4. *Choshen Mishpat* (Breastplate of Judgment)–dealing with the commercial, civil, and criminal law, and property rights.

The *Tur* was restricted only to those commandments (*mitzvot*) obligatory at the present time. It is the fourth section of the *Tur* and later codes, together with their commentaries, that provide the source material for present-day halakhic decisions in the economic field. The main exception is the laws of interest, which are dealt with in *Yoreh De'ah*, a reflection perhaps of the Jewish treatment of interest as being a matter of spiritual purity rather than merely a function of borrowing and lending.

Yosef Caro, the author of the *Shulchan Arukh*, followed the pattern of *Tur*. The *Shulchan Arukh* (literally, Set Table) represents a synopsis of his earlier, monumental work, the *Bet Yosef* (House of Joseph), in which he not only commented on the *Tur*, but more importantly presented an analysis of his own decisions and the halakhic sources for them. Previously he had written the *Kesef Mishneh*, a classical commentary on Maimonides' codex.

Yosef Caro had not included in the *Shulchan Arukh* the halakhic decisions of the Ashkenazim (Franco-German rabbinic school). Rabbi Moses Isserles (Rama, sixteenth century) rectified this. He added his gloss to the *Shulchan Arukh*. By calling it the *Mappah* (Tablecloth), he indicated that the entire system of *Halakhah* was to be seen as one set table. He thus insured that the codex became accepted universally to the whole Jewish world–the descendants of the European-Ashkenazic Jews and the Spanish-Middle Eastern Sephardim alike.

At the beginning of this century, Rabbi Yechiel Michal Epstein produced the *Arukh HaShulchan*, a digest of the *Shulchan Arukh*, to which he added the rulings of subsequent *Achronim*, the later scholars who followed the generation of Yosef Caro.

Any legal system, especially a religious and moralistic one, cannot operate effectively without a philosophical and ethical framework. These come in Judaism from some of the following sources, as well as from the personal behavior of the Jewish religious leaders, who became the role models for the average layman. These were encouraged and obligated to study their works, as part of the unlimited personal obligation to devote time to religious study, irrespective of age or status.

Following the Rambam's system of thought is the *Sefer HaChinukh* (*Book of Education*), which sought to explain the ideological meaning of the 613 commandments as they appear in the Five Books of Moses. (It is commonly ascribed to Rabbi Aharon HaLevi of Barcelona in the thirteenth century.) The *Chovot HaLevavot* (*Duties of the Heart*) by Rabbenu Bachaya Ibn Pakuda of eleventh-century Spain, *Shaarei Teshuvah* (*Gates of Repentance*) by Rabbi Yonah ben Avraham of Gerondi, and *Mesillat Yesharim* (*Path of the Righteous*) by Moshe Chaim Luzzatto of eighteenth-century Italy are classic moralistic works that have become part of the curriculum of modern Torah scholars. These followed the great moralistic work *Sefer Chasidim*, of the medieval pietist Rabbi Yehudah HeChasid.

In the nineteenth century, Rabbi Israel Salanter founded the *mussar* (literally, instruction in right behavior) movement, geared toward improving the behavior of the graduates of the *yeshivot* (talmudic academies) of Lithuania, then the "university capital" of world Jewry. The writings of his disciples and the formation of special *mussar yeshivot* further entrenched the moral and ethical principles of Judaism in the mind and behavior of the ordinary Jew.

These sources all show that in fact, independent of the varied types of economies in which the Jew has found himself, there remains even down to this day a consistent pattern of economic behavior that reflects the moral teachings of Judaism and their implementations in everyday behavior.

Legal codes, rabbinic scholarship, and homiletical literature notwithstanding, it is quite possible that much of these principles could remain mere exhortations to piety, unobserved and irrelevant. There are however two sources showing that in actual fact, this was never so and that they are reflected in the economic behavior of the Jew in all the countries of the Diaspora. One of these sources is the ramified and extensive responsa literature and the second, the enactments of the various Jewish communities.

1. From the Geonic period, which followed the completion of the Talmud, until the present day, Jews both as individuals and as communities addressed questions—*she'eilot*—concerning all aspects of Judaism—ritual, legal, and philosophical—to the leading scholars of their time. These questions also included actual cases of litigation, arising out of the conduct of everyday business, as well as those concerning the com-

munal enactments regarding taxation, social welfare, and economic legislation. Since Jews generally did not have recourse to non-Jewish courts, the halakhic authorities represented, in fact, the arbitrators of economic disputes. The fact that there is no generation or country in which there is no such literature of questions and answers—*teshuvot*—shows that the responsa represent an ongoing application of Jewish law.

2. This application was facilitated by the existence of autonomous Jewish communities until the French Revolution. Since then, this autonomy has been increasingly eroded even though in various forms it still exists, even if only within parts of the Orthodox Jewish world. These autonomous communities were in fact mini-city-states with their own courts of law and power of taxation.[4] In addition, the communities retained the halakhic power to institute economic legislation regarding monopoly rights, competition, price control, and freedom of movement. They served therefore as an enforcement agency of the rabbinical courts and the decisions reflected in the responsa literature.

It is possible in this work to mention only a few of the most important of these autonomous units. For a period of about 400 years the Jews of medieval Franco-Germany like those of Spain were governed by synods called periodically in various centers.[5] So too, from the sixteenth century until the mid-eighteenth century, the Jews of Lithuania and Poland were governed by the Council of Four Lands (*Vaad Arba Aratzot*).[6]

A PATTERN OF ECONOMIC BEHAVIOR

The pattern of economic behavior encouraged and allowed to operate within the framework of all these Jewish sources may be summarized as follows:

1. Since the Divine blueprint for the world is such that economic wants are satisfied through human endeavor in normal nonmiraculous ways, there is nothing wrong or immoral with the possession of wealth and the acquisition of material goods. So, too, there is no spiritual value in poverty, nor is it a way to achieve spiritual redemption. The drive

for economic wealth is morally legitimate and an essential prerequisite for the existence and welfare of the human race.[7]

2. Yet at the same time, since greed is so powerful and all-pervasive, that drive can result in widespread unethical behavior and great economic immorality, leading to injustice and oppression. This greed is enhanced and empowered by man's perpetual fear of economic uncertainty. So we perpetually seek to protect ourselves against the risks involved in the market and in the human condition through legitimate means, but also by immoral ones.

3. In a world where men know that the full extent of their future needs and the source of satisfying them is assured, there would be no need for fraud, exploitation, or business immorality. Faith in Divine Providence and the assurance that God provides for all needs thus free man from the necessity to find unethical ways to protect himself from uncertainty or to deny private property rights of others for the same purpose. At the same time, it is this faith that allows people to take the risks needed for entrepreneurial development, thus maintaining the legitimate search for wealth within moral parameters.

4. The belief that all wealth originates from God and that His bounty –rather than luck, hard work, or ability–is the real source of our economic success is the only reliable means whereby greed is able to be channeled into morality.[8] Mere exhortations to morality or personal decisions based on changing individual concepts of ethics are only of limited value. At the same time, because economic drive is so powerful and pervasive a force, legislated morality is essential; otherwise society is left only with good intentions. The legislation needed to provide the ethical parameters for business activity cannot function, however, without a deep-rooted and commonly accepted normative morality.

5. The Divine origin of wealth mandates that it not be earned through immoral or unjust ways. Even where they are legal, therefore, exploitation, abuse of power, undisclosed conflicts of interest, and oppression through withheld information cannot coexist with a God-given morality.[9] So, Judaism rejects the concept of "let the buyer beware" and places the primary onus for full disclosure on the seller, who is usually more knowledgeable. The biblical injunction against placing a "stumbling block in the path of the blind" is understood as forbidding giving advice or selling goods and services that are to the physical or spiritual detriment of the other party.[10]

Moreover, most economic crimes are committed in secret, and so are a rejection of God's ability to see and know all. In this perspective, robbery is taken out of its context of violent crime and is seen as including acts such as the denial of debts incurred, the private use of another's property or money placed in one's trust, and withholding wages. The social or personal pressure on people to agree to transactions to which they are opposed, as sometimes happens in hostile takeovers, is considered to be coercion and therefore tantamount to robbery. Above all, the spiritual damage to the performer of unethical acts has always to be considered, over and above the financial damage suffered by the victim. This makes avoidance of immoral acts, even when they are legally possible, essential to one who considers himself a God-fearing person.

6. God as the Provider and Father of all men is the source of the brotherhood of man. The world consists, therefore, not only of vertical relationships between man and God but also horizontal relationships between man and man. Mankind is not just a mass of unrelated beings, but a large family linked by their Creator. The wealth provided therefore by Him, although meant primarily for the satisfaction of the needs and wants of the private owner, is also meant to be used to satisfy the needs of the poor and the inefficient—the old, the weak, and even the lazy. Just as business morality needs to be legislated, so too does this mutual assistance. If left to the philanthropy of the individual and to his acts of kindness, human nature and the lust for wealth would limit this act of sharing. So society acquires a property right in the wealth of the individual to provide, through compulsory acts of taxation, the social and charitable needs of its members. These funds are either *tzedakah* (charity) or *tzedek* (justice). Voluntary sharing of wealth in response to claims of the poor and weak is charity, but compulsory participation in the communal funds to provide these needs is an act of justice. Nonparticipation in such funding becomes tantamount to theft, either from the recipients of the funding or from the other participants who now have to provide a greater share. This Divine insistence on using part of private wealth for the needs of others makes it holy money, which also demands that it be neither wasted nor abused.

7. Mankind is the pinnacle of creation; hence all natural resources exist to provide for the human race. This makes the use of these resources legitimate and necessary, yet at the same time, it limits their exploitation. Since they are granted to us in a custodial relationship,

they may not be frivolously dissipated or wantonly destroyed, even where the legal ownership is unquestioned. So the Rabbis likened one who wastes his property or destroys it in anger to an idolator, for both deny the Divine source of wealth. Man as a custodian of natural resources needs to husband them, so that in addition to being used, they remain for future generations. In this, he becomes, as it were, a partner in the Divine process of creation. Society may need to limit its economic development in order to allow for that and to earn the spiritual and social benefits of environmental health.

8. The wide-ranging Jewish framework for moral economic behavior that flows from recognition of the Divine source of wealth ultimately leads to an "economics of enough." Every Jew, irrespective of his age, social status, wealth, or intellect, is obligated to study Torah, the revealed law of God. This obligation is one unlimited by time, so that it severely curtails the "free" time available for economic activity and, therefore, for the accumulation of wealth. In addition, both the religious milieu of Judaism and its communal living pattern have contributed, over the ages, to an ingrained modesty in demand. If adhered to, this modesty substantially dampens the individual's demand for a spiraling standard of living and leads thereby to a reduced pressure to find immoral ways to satisfy it. To the classical economic axiom that "more is better than less," Judaism would provide the rejoinder of the patriarch Jacob: "I have all I need."[11]

THE JEWISH ROLE MODEL

The purpose of this moral framework is the creation of the Jewish role model, the *talmid chakham*, Torah scholar. The economic behavior of the *talmid chakham* is summarized by Maimonides in a way to dispel all anti-Semitic prototypes as well as to be applicable in all economic systems or institutions.

> The commerce of the *talmid chakham* (the Jewish role model) has to be in truth and in faith. His yes is to be yes and his no, no; he forces himself to be exact in calculations when he is paying, but is willing to be lenient when others are his debtors. One is not to buy on credit when one has the wherewithal to pay cash, nor should one be a surety for a loan (getting involved in potential conflicts that are not of one's concern) or serve as a representative to collect others' debts [in both these cases, according to the Raivad and the Kesef Mishneh, the Rambam is not referring to acts of charity or

assisting in collecting debts from recalcitrant debtors, which are primarily judicial functions.] He should keep his obligations in commerce, even where the law allows him to withdraw or retract, so that his word is his bond, but if others have obligations to him, he should deal mercifully, forgiving and extending credit. One should be careful not to deprive one's neighbor of his livelihood [even where this is legal] or cause hardship and anguish to others [either bodily or financially]. He who does all these things is the one referred to by the prophet Isaiah, when he said, "You, Israel, are My [God's] servant, with whom I am exalted."[12]

I

"Eat of the Fruit of Your Labor— It Shall Be Well with You."

Psalm 128:2

1

UNCERTAINTY, GREED, AND BUSINESS MORALITY

INTRODUCTION

The world operates in such a way that economic wants are satisfied only through human endeavor, rather than by direct Divine intervention. This applies also to all other needs of man, such as continuation of the species, social hierarchy, sex, communal organization, and so forth. Given the complexity of human nature, the satisfaction of all these needs has since time immemorial created a tension between morality, spirituality, and righteousness and the more mundane, materialistic, and selfish aspects of everyday existence. The marketplace (and all associated with it) constitute only a specific forum for this tension, even if perhaps the single most important one. Here more than in any other aspect of human endeavor, the demands of materialistic human nature clash constantly with the call of a higher dimension, with the godlike nature of people and with the claims of justice and morality.

It is in the light of such an ideological tension that the issues flowing from business activity, from the pursuit of wealth, and from the very existence of the marketplace must be viewed. Irrespective of the solution suggested by different religious, cultural, or social systems, the questions can inevitably be seen primarily in this clash of materialism and spirituality in the tension between matters of this world and the challenge of some higher world. Pagan societies, seeing only the existence of this tangible materialistic existence, unplanned and often buffeted by mere chance or fate, opt for constant gratification of wants, at best, restrained only by human logic and the moral imperative not to cause damage to others. On the other hand, it is possible to have a society in which the search is for ultimate spirituality or the fixation with a superior heavenly other world. All too often this leads to complete abandonment of this world and everything concerned with it—economics, politics and justice—to secular powers. Monotheistic religions, with their concept of a Creator who demands accountability and supervises, as it were, man's actions in this world, provide solutions based in varying degrees on the sanctification of the here and now, through divinely inspired norms of behavior. Even modern socialism and the free-market philosophies each in their own way can be shown to be deeply rooted in this spiritual tension, drawing from the previously mentioned religious philosophical ideologies.

In order to be able to supply answers, rather than mere questions, any analysis, Jewish or otherwise, of economic morality must concern itself with an understanding of the causes of economic immorality or unethical behavior. Only then can any of the ideological systems develop an educational system geared toward handling these issues, promoting role models in the marketplace, and encouraging legislation aimed at protecting society from immoral individuals. The causes of immorality and the solutions must be seen as relevant not only to captains of industry, to framers of government policy, or to businessmen and economists. Since everybody desires and needs wealth, earns it, spends and saves it, in reality everybody is intimately and consistently concerned with both the causes of unethical behavior and the solutions suggested.

Trite as it may seem, it is nevertheless true that the major cause of immoral economic behavior is greed and the unlimited desire for unearned wealth, present in all people. Further consideration, however, will show that there is a second major cause, namely the fear of uncertainty in general and of economic uncertainty in particular. This fear of uncertainty is, unlike greed, not always an obvious cause, since it is often shrouded in legitimate concern. It is the treatment of these two factors, human greed and the fear of economic uncertainty, that provides the overall conceptual framework for a Jewish perspective on the moral challenges of wealth.

GREED

When one inquires as to what it is that leads men to exploit their workers, or to defraud their competitors or their customers, and to pollute or rape the environment, it is easy to point to greed as the culprit.

From a Jewish perspective, this answer would suffice were it not for the fact that greed itself is an essential part of human economic activity. In talmudic times, we are told, the Sages captured the evil inclination of man, the *yetzer hara*, the source of his greed, his lust, and desire. They rejoiced, believing that thereby they could now eradicate all evil actions. They discovered, however, that in the whole country they could not find even one single fertilized egg.[1] So, much to their sorrow, they released the evil inclination, understanding that this is what leads to human activity.

Without greed, without the need and desire for material wealth, nobody would work, nobody would plant trees, nobody would construct homes. Furthermore, this inclination or lust exists in all men, irrespective of the level of their spiritual development, their education, or their age, so that there is no Jewish problem with the question, "How come people of high status or occupying important positions or those considered to be paragons of virtue actually commit misdeeds and crimes?" Israel Baal Shem Tov, the founder of Chasidism, the mystical movement that swept eastern European Jewry in the late seventeenth century, taught that there is only one man who does not have such an inclination—a dead man. Still, acceptance of the necessity of the *yetzer hara* did not blind our Sages to its potential for evil. They only emphasized that it can be sanctified and become converted into positive acts.

The story of Shimon bar Yochai, author of the Zohar, *Book of Splendor*, the fountainhead of Jewish mysticism, is perhaps the most typical of Judaism's view of the positive aspects of all the inclinations of man. In the second century of the Common Era, in a rabbinic discussion of the achievements of Roman civilization, bar Yochai presented all their evil effects. "They build markets to be able to sell slaves, they build bathhouses to satisfy their attraction to sexual immorality and they build roads and bridges in order to move their armies rapidly in the subjection of other peoples."[2] For this he had to flee before the wrath of the Roman conquerors of the Land of Israel. Together with his son, he hid in a cave in the Galilee, their time spent in great spiritual endeavors and their material needs supplied miraculously. When they left the cave, their anger at seeing people engaged in the ordinary everyday things of economic life—ploughing, sowing, and harvesting—rather than in the elevation of their religious characters caused death and havoc. Divine displeasure forced them back into the cave, since they were destroying God's world.

After another prolonged period in the cave, covered in sand to their necks to obviate even the need for clothing, bar Yochai and his son emerged once again into the world. Realizing the religious and spiritual importance of the real world, bar Yochai said, "A miracle has been performed for me, so I will go and do something practical and useful for the world." Such actions, being in effect human participation in the completion of the world, are a partnership in the Divine creation. Bar Yochai was only repeating the actions of the patriarch Jacob. When Jacob returned from his exile to the Land of Israel, his first stay was in the town of Shechem. The *midrash* tells us that there the patriarch improved the marketplaces, established proper weights and measures, and purified the metallic coinage, seeing all these actions as befitting a spiritual leader of his stature. This is merely one example of the many that could be brought to show the absence of any anticommercial or antiwealth creating activity in Judaism. Business, economics, and the marketplace are not necessarily to be equated with evil, being essential to human existence and development.

God created the *yetzer hara*, so it must be good, or alternatively, and perhaps preferably, this inclination, although it has a potential for evil, can be sanctified and become converted into positive acts. Rashi (Rabbi Shlomo Yitzchaki, Franco-Germany, 1040–1105), the medieval classic commentator on the Bible, clearly reveals this attitude. Quoting the *Midrash* on the verse in Genesis, "The Lord saw [the creation] and it was very good," he writes, "This refers to the *yetzer hara*."[3] Rabbi Akiva (mishnaic, *Eretz Yisrael*) explains, "You shall love God with all your heart" (Deuteronomy 6:55), that is, with both inclinations—the good and the bad.[4] Thus, while Judaism teaches that all men have this inclination and that it is an essential part of the human condition, nevertheless, the revealed Divine Law has both the purpose and possibility of purifying and educating economic greed and lust, so that they may become morally positive and contribute to the human welfare.

It must be made quite clear, however, that this understanding of the importance and legitimacy of wealth creation and the efficient distribution of goods and services through the marketplace is not a total endorsement of capitalism or a free-market ideology. Since there is nothing unlimited in Judaism, wealth creation too is limited. It cannot be viewed as anything other than the satisfaction of the normal needs of sustenance, housing, clothing, and social development. There is no place for the creation of wealth for its own sake, nor can it seen as the major goal in life, nor are all means permissible for its achievement. Wealth creation is limited in time by the unceasing obligation placed on all Jews to devote time to studying Torah and improving themselves spiritually. The *Shabbat*, the Festivals, prayer, and righteous acts place further limitations on the time allocated to the creation of wealth. Even macroeconomic limitations exist, for example, the Sabbatical year—*Shmittah*—and the Jubilee—*Yovel*. The claims of society and of the less fortunate to a share of our wealth, place economic activity in a special perspective. Since despite its positive aspects, the needs for material and economic goods are still a function of the *yetzer hara*, it leads, if unchecked and uncontrolled, to immorality, selfishness, conflict, and jealousy. So like all other types of *yetzer hara*, this one too is limited both by the halakhic obligations devolving on the individual and the communal legislation, aimed at achieving economic justice and social morality.

This attitude of Judaism to the *yetzer hara* in economics, as one that can be sanctified, stands in contrast to the attitudes found in Christianity, Buddhism, and even socialism. Their understanding of the economic drive as being the cause of hate, jealousy, theft, and murder was a correct one and one that is perfectly acceptable. It is, however, their method of handling the economic drive that differs from that of Judaism, since primarily they aimed at trying to eradicate it.

The attitude of Christianity to the evil inclination, including that concerning wealth, flows primarily from the sense of overwhelming sin that can only be corrected by Grace or avoided by Divine guidance rather than acts. This led to attempts to eradicate the *yetzer hara* in sex through celibacy and, in materialism, through the "virtue of poverty."[5] In Catholicism this took the form of monastic movements, and in Protestantism it led to the abolition of church law in the marketplace, substituting the guidance of Grace in individual choices for acts.[6]

In socialism, the evil effects of property and wealth led to various forms of abolition of private ownership, ranging from communism with its state ownership of the factors of production, through socialism with the centrally planned economy, through to communalism with its voluntary rejection of private ownership. All these were aimed at destroying private property and handing it over to the group. The latter was seen as producing a classless society, and since people did not have property, there would be no point or no reason to steal or to act immorally. The experience of seventy years of communism in the Soviet Union and of socialism in many countries has shown, however, that merely changing the economic system does not eradicate the moral issue. It is true that these movements solved certain aspects of economic immorality, such as child labor, widespread poverty, and the exploitation of weak and unprotected groups. At the same time, however, the changes in the economic system created other moral issues. Dishonesty in many forms became a way of life in order to compensate for the weaknesses of a system built contrary to economic realities. For example, the egalitarian wage structure created irrespective of the demand for skills or services, was not viable and brought to certain groups a wide variety of benefits, such as access to special housing, stores, trips abroad, and so forth, so that despite the facade of equality, great social differences emerged. This facade of equality involved many rampant forms of lying, stealing, extensive black markets, and individual allocation by favoritism, in order to obtain the benefits.

Even of greater immoral force was the curtailment or abolition of private property and the transfer of economic activity from the market to that of the state. Since it severed the relationship between the activity of the individual and the return that society was paying him, this raised other moral issues of a fair return for an honest day's work. Furthermore, by placing economic decisions in the hands of state officials and bureaucrats, these were given the power of life and death over individuals, thus creating a widespread system of coercion and bribery.

It is the intensity and pervasiveness of the economic *yetzer hara* that make changing the economic system of itself insufficient to eradicate economic immorality or to make poverty a viable alternative. Economic lusts are more powerful than any of the others with which the human being is faced. Ill health, old age, or abundance usually lead to a decline in most of the lusts that people have. However, the need for more money, for more property, and for more wealth is not related to these weakenings. The Rabbis express the difference between economic hunger and the other lusts that afflict us very simply. "The less food one has, the more one wants, the more food one has, the less one wants. The more sex one has, the more sex one wants. The less sex one has, the less one wants. Money however is different. The less money one has, the more one wants. The more money one has, the more one wants."[7]

The power of this economic lust and its continuation throughout all periods of our lives are perhaps the explanation why the Torah surrounded those activities with more *mitzvot* and laws than any other. A review of the 613 commandments, *taryag mitzvot*, incumbent on Jews will show that over 120 are related to the way we earn our living, save our money, and spend it. Kosher food, recognized by all as intrinsic to Judaism, is only surrounded by 26 such laws. On the holiest day of the Jewish year, *Yom HaKippurim*, Jews fast, make confession of their sins, and await Divine forgiveness. Of the detailed acts confessed publicly, 16 refer to sins associated with commerce, money, and wealth.

It is recognition of the power of this economic lust that led Christianity to extol poverty and socialism to deny the role of private property. Both of these, however, are contrary to the Jewish model. Judaism is the only religion in the world whose founders were wealthy men. The Bible tells us that Abraham the patriarch was heavy in flocks, sheep, goats, gold, and silver. The same was true of Isaac and later Jacob. Buddha, however, the founder of Buddhism, while a young prince fled his father's palace in order to pursue poverty since this was the only way that he could handle the challenge of wealth. So too, Jesus and his apostles were propertyless people and foresaw a heaven into which rich men could only enter as could a camel enter through the eye of a needle. In the *Shema*, containing the basic laws and concepts of Judaism, however, the Lord promises that obedience to His commandments will lead not to an ethereal hereafter, but to material assets like timely rain, flocks, and bountiful crops. The punishment for not obeying will be drought and communal economic destitution.[8]

It is not the possession of material goods per se that is seen in Judaism as being evil. Rather, it is the method of obtaining them and the use thereof that represent an almost unlimited challenge to morality. In the *Ethics of the Fathers* (*Pirkei Avot*), the man who sees his economic aims as being achieved through "What's mine is yours and yours is mine" is not regarded as an evil person, but as an *am haaretz*, an ignorant one, since the rejection of the concept of private property can lead only to further or different types of immorality. The *chasid*, the righteous man, is viewed as the one who is able to relinquish part of his legal property voluntarily saying, "What's yours is yours and what's mine is yours," thus demonstrating that the property has other purposes beyond the satisfaction of one's own personal wants.[9] It is interesting that Rabbi Yehudah HaNasi in redacting the Sinaic Oral Law in the six orders of the *Mishnah*, placed the *Ethics of the Fathers*, Judaism's moralistic and ethical treatise, not in one of the tractates dealing with ritualistic matters, but rather in the tractate of *Nezikin* (literally, "damages," but in effect the business, civil, and criminal code of the Jews). The Rabbis, seeing in the way men held, obtained, and used their economic wealth a method of spiritual redemption, provided an alternative name to *Nezikin*, *Sefer HaYeshuot*, the *Book of Redemption*.[10]

None of this obviates the power of the challenge of wealth, the power of the evil that can flow from acquiring material goods, or from their use. It is not in ignorance of this power or in the minimizing of this power that Judaism rejects the social forms or religious concepts that promote poverty or militate against the institution of private property. It is clearly understood that these challenges must not be avoided but rather can be met and transformed through those business acts permitted by Judaism and by avoiding those forbidden by it.

UNCERTAINTY

Understanding the power of greed and pervasiveness of this economic lust, and even accepting the possibility of sanctifying and educating it are still not sufficient to explain the real causes of economic immorality. There is evidence to show that the real cause is the fear of uncertainty.

At all stages of social history, man has been faced with the necessity of providing himself with scarce goods and services. It is the very scarcity of these goods and services that really gives them their economic worth. Providing them is what creates economic activity and the marketplace, but this of itself does not constitute a moral challenge or pose ethical dilemmas. These only arise because of the fear of not being able to overcome the scarcity. If the world were constructed in a way in which there was no uncertainty regarding the future and no risk of man being in need, then normal legitimate economic acts would be sufficient to eradicate or diminish scarcity. In the real world, however, no such guarantees exist. There is constant uncertainty, with a real possibility of a shortage of food, goods, and services. It is this uncertainty that leads us to devote ourselves so completely to accumulate wealth by all and any means, legal or otherwise. The source of the uncertainty is not really relevant. Drought, fluctuations in the business cycle, inefficiency, war, and theft all contribute equally to creating and perpetuating the uncertainty, and so stimulate our efforts to achieve a risk-free life.

Men who have a net equity of such size that neither they, their children, nor their children's children can ever consume it, nevertheless, continue to create and hoard additional economic assets. All of us, irrespective of our wealth, are unable, in our economic training and activity, to create a mental framework or a social situation where we will be content with satisfying only our own essential needs. Rather we try to provide all our envisaged needs, even for 120 years. The society surrounding us resounds constantly and stridently, "more is better than less," so that wants, real or imaginary, become transformed into needs. Then we force ourselves to find ways to protect ourselves against the uncertainty and risk of not being able to satisfy them. This envisaged protection is meant to provide for the wants of our own lives, and even for those of our children and our children's children.[11]

This fear of risk leads us to adopt many different methods to secure ourselves against the uncertainty of economic life. Some methods are legitimate, being simply an extension of normal business practices. Some, however, are aimed at distorting the economic process, while yet others are immoral and unethical. Theft, robbery, fraud, deceit, and war are as much methods of protecting ourselves against uncertainty as are the legitimate and healthy ways open to us.

When we take out insurance policies, save money, and expand our business, we are investing instead of eating up our income. This is in effect separating part of our wealth to protect ourselves in the future. This is legitimate. After all, it is simply diverting part of economic wealth from the satisfaction of present wants and needs in order to provide for the future. This is a means of buying security from risk and uncertainty with our wealth just as we would buy other needs. The problem becomes a moral issue, however, when the efforts we make against uncertainty are exaggerated or unethical ones.

Socialism can be seen in essence as a method that came to remove the fear of economic uncertainty seen to be inherent in the Capitalist system. Planned economies would, it was argued, protect people against the effects of the business cycle. The public purse would provide for old age when economic income would be less, and also protect the inefficient and the weak members of society against the uncertainties of economic life. This was done by transferring part or all of the factors of production to the state, which would in turn protect the citizens against uncertainty. The economic and political freedom of the individual was traded for the economic security provided.[12]

The feudal system that arose in Europe after the breakdown of the Roman Empire was a similar method of protection against uncertainty. Because of the constant barbaric invasions and the consequent breakdown of law and order arising from the lack of a unified state and a viable legal system, farming, industry, and trade became hazardous undertakings. People moved toward a closed economy in which the feudal lords provided physical security in exchange for a share of the economic wealth of the serfs.[13]

Slavery too provides the slave with protection against economic uncertainty. The slave works for his master for the rest of his life, while his master guarantees to provide for him. This security explains why slaves often preferred their situation to the risk involved in being free men.

In the late nineteenth century similar forms of protection evolved in England and the United States in the form of company towns. The workers promised industrial peace and a docile labor force, while the company provided housing, shopping, and other facilities such as schooling.

The present-day Japanese policy of lifelong employment has many overtones of this and of all these systems of protecting people against uncertainty.

Crime in the economic sphere is also primarily a method of protecting ourselves against uncertainty. If people could be guaranteed that their present standard of living would remain forever or that it would be always possible to achieve an economic standard of living that they consider essential for their use, there would be no point in economic immorality. It is only the fear of not being able to achieve or retain economic safety or security that leads to economic crime at all its various levels.

Sometimes this uncertainty flows from the very nature of the market economy. Capitalism and the free market are characterized as profit systems, but Milton Friedman has pointed out on numerous occasions that capitalism is a profit or loss system. In the free market, there is always a risk involved of sometimes earning profits, but also of sometimes not. The awarding of the Nobel Prize for economics to Wolf Markowitz for his portfolio theory, which has become a cornerstone of financial management, is an acceptance of this problem of uncertainty, since basically it envisages an investment policy that minimizes risk even if this also minimizes profits.

The recent breakdown of the economies of eastern Europe has, for the first time, presented the people of those countries with the realities of economic life. It is true that with the abolition of communism, they can have the benefits of an efficient market. Now they may eventually be able to buy consumer goods that they lacked before, and they can avail themselves of a standard of living that could conceivably approach that of the western countries. For the first time in many years, however, there is now also a risk of unemployment and the risk of shortages. Furthermore there has already emerged a form of rogue capitalism morally more similar to the rapacious nineteenth-century model than to that of the more humane version of the late twentieth century. It is quite conceivable that this increased risk and man's need for economic security could lead some of them to regret the breakdown of the Communist system. The changeover from a centralized Socialist economy in Israel is hampered by exactly that same fear of uncertainty.

The lack of security and the fear of risk can also flow from the human desire to enjoy not a self-determined standard of living, but rather one that other people have, or one to which we are taught to aspire. Economic needs and wants are very difficult to define or to measure, since there are no absolute parameters to them. As often as not, there is also no clear demarcation between economic wants and needs. Wants are developed as a result of measuring up to what others have, or say we should have, so they usually have no relationship to actual needs. The risk or the uncertainty of not being able to achieve that same economic goal can lead us to defraud, to steal, and to other forms of immorality. It does not require much research or flights of imagination to discover just how much of our own economic living is prompted by the possessions of others. It is coveting that leads us, on the one hand, to emulate them and to strive to earn enough for what we consider desired objects primarily because they belong to other people. It is, however, also the same coveting that leads us to commit crime, if we are unable or unwilling to obtain them through legitimate means.

The last of the Ten Commandments in the Book of Exodus (22:17) is an injunction against coveting. The Ten Commandments are repeated in the Book of Deuteronomy (5:18), but the tenth commandment there forbids lusting after another's property. Both lusting and coveting are the only prohibitions in the Ten Commandments that are not action oriented. Since Judaism is an action-oriented religion, the Rabbis had a problem; how is a Divine commandment that does not obligate man to do anything to be understood? Coveting as a sin of the mind could be understood. After all, there are such things as evil thoughts, and Judaism teaches that all men have evil thoughts. However, the problem is how can men be punished for one of those thoughts, and how could the Torah legislate against them? The Rabbis came to the conclusion that it is a process: lusting after another's property leads to coveting. Coveting leads to stealing, and stealing can lead to bloodshed when the owner wishes to protect himself against the thief.[14]

This is demonstrated in the biblical story of the vineyard of Naboth. Achav, king of Israel, was a neighbor in the town of Jezreel of a man called Naboth, who had a vineyard. The king, in the words of the Bible, lusted after the vineyard of Naboth and he wished to buy it from him. The owner, however, refused to sell the vineyard, so the king went home to Jezreel frustrated, turned his face to the wall, and refused to eat or drink. His foreign wife, Jezebel, failed to understand that in Israel the king did not have the right simply to take whatever he wanted, in this case the vineyard of Naboth. Nevertheless, she undertook to give the king the vineyard and obtained false witnesses who testified that Naboth had blasphemed God and king. Since the punishment for this was capital punishment, Naboth was put to death and his property, as that of a rebel, was transferred to the king. Now Achav had obtained his vineyard. When he went down to take possession of it, the king was met by the prophet Elijah, who commented bitingly, "Hast thou murdered and also taken possession?"

The Rabbis said, "It was the lust and coveting of the vineyard of Naboth that led to his murder and to the theft of the vineyard."

The biblical story of the twelve spies can serve to illustrate further the tension between spiritual aspirations and the economic immorality that flows from the human desire to find protection against uncertainty. As we are told in the Books of Numbers (13-14) and Deuteronomy (1:22-45), the spies were sent by Moses prior to the entry into the Land of Israel to investigate the Promised Land. They returned with a false report about the Land, emphasizing the inability of the Jews to conquer the powerful nations that lived there. The biblical commentators have a wide variety of explanations as to what the actual sin of these spies was. Over and above that, there remains the question of what led them to commit this sin. After all, they were leaders of the Jewish people—they were all *nesi'im*, princes of the community. Each one was handpicked and selected by Moses.

The chasidic *Admor*, Shmuel of Sochochow (Poland, early twentieth century), explained their dilemma as follows:

> They lacked a confidence in their spiritual ability to handle the everyday challenges of earning an economic existence in a normal way. As long as they lived in the desert, God provided them daily with Manna from heaven. Their water came from the miraculous spring of Miriam, and they were sheltered from the blazing sun by the Divine Clouds of Glory [and, as we are told in the farewell address of Moses, their clothes did not rot on them nor did their shoes disintegrate nor did they lack for anything]. Wealth was no spiritual challenge to them. However, going into the Land of Israel, where their livelihood would have to be earned through the normal processes of agriculture, industry and trade, meant that they would be faced with the challenge of economic morality. They feared their own ability to meet that challenge. They preferred the sanctity of the Divine provider in the desert to the danger of the challenge of wealth and it was this that caused them to bring back the false reports which would keep them in the desert.[15]

Religion and Uncertainty

Irrespective of the source of the fear and uncertainty regarding the economic future, any religious, social, or philosophical system that would try to provide guidelines for a framework for educating toward greater economic morality or to stimulate the creation of ethical standards for handling wealth must of necessity address itself to this lack of security as a source of economic immorality. This immorality must not be seen as restricted merely to the criminal activities of the cat burglar or armed robber, which would severely curtail its importance. Taking money that does not really belong to one in a transaction, whether in buying or selling, borrowing or lending, through overcharging or through coercion, and exploiting ignorance or weakness, constitutes an immoral act. The wanton destruction of natural resources, even those that legally belong to one, and causing damage to another's person or property, either through one's body or economic assets, are similarly immoral acts. Economic immorality is really a potential danger in the whole gamut of the market activities. The more sophisticated those activities become, the more discerning one has to be regarding the ethical dangers involved. Rabbi Israel Meir HaKohen, the *Chafetz Chaim*, the major Torah scholar of twentieth-century eastern European Jewry, taught that most people see themselves as honorable people, yet owing to the powerful peer pressure of economic wants permit themselves all sorts of unethical actions.[16]

The Rabbis of the Talmud maintained that the majority of people fail to resist dishonesty, and Rashi explains that this is because they find justification and legitimization for immoral actions in their commerce, which leads them to profit illegally at the expense of their fellows.[17] The *Midrash* tells us that the quarrel between the shepherds of Lot and those of the patriarch Abraham flowed from the refusal of the former to muzzle their flocks in order to prevent them from grazing in the fields of others. The rationale behind the shepherds of Lot is both modern and instructive, being typical of much of the justification for economic immorality. They explained they were not, God forbid, stealing when they grazed their unmuzzled cattle. This was their legal right. God had promised the land of Canaan to Abraham, and Lot was Abraham's sole heir, so that this promise actually belonged to Lot. Rationalizing away the fact that the promise would only be realized 400 years later, they permitted themselves to steal.[18]

Irrespective of the form or nature of the immorality involved, there exists a major chasm between the three monotheistic religions on the one hand and the secular-humanistic approach on the other regarding the question of the uncertainty that causes it. Judaism, Christianity, and Islam, irrespective of the differences among them, all believe in a Creator of heaven and earth, of man, and of all else within that world. They all believe that the Creator provides for the needs of the world that He created, ranging from the plant kingdom through that of the animal, and finally reaching its peak with regard to human beings. They all believe in the nurture and care with which the Lord Creator provides for the needs of His creatures. This belief in the Creator, His goodness, and His caring provides the security and strength necessary to face the awesome fear of uncertainty, poverty, and hunger.

With the security provided by this belief in Divine Providence, man can afford to take the risks necessary to create economic assets. The belief in this security means that they may also devote themselves to other noneconomic pursuits, thus limiting the amount of time and energy devoted to their creation of wealth. At the same time, this security enables them to conduct their economic affairs in a moral and ethical fashion, since they understand that over and above their own activities, there is the greatness of the God Provider, so that it is not necessary to steal, to rob, or to achieve wealth in other criminal ways.

It is unnecessary, one would assume, to stress that the belief in the Divine source of wealth and God's greatness in providing that wealth introduces Divine demands as to the way that wealth is earned and the use to which it may be put. Faith in God the Provider not only assuages man's anxiety and fears regarding uncertainty and the risks inherent in his economic future, it also confronts him with moral and ethical demands regarding his wealth. The Divine source of wealth therefore constitutes a partnership between the Provider and His creatures in which the Lord provides their needs and they subject their lusts and desires to His will.

In the Book of Genesis we read that the punishment of the snake was to eat of the dust of the earth. It is not at all clear why this was a punishment. After all, almost the only thing in the world that is unlimited and always available is dust. This means that the snake would have no need to fear uncertainty or scarcity regarding his source of food. The snake is the only creature on the earth to be in this situation. It would seem that this is something we would all like to be blessed with, absolute economic security. The chasidic master Menachem Mendel of Kotsk taught that the curse lay exactly in that: God provided him with a livelihood and then told him to get out of His sight. While the whole of creation depends for their livelihood on Him and so has access to the Divine Presence, such a relationship was no longer to exist between God and the snake. The same idea was used by Menachem Mendel's grandson, Shmuel of Sochochow, to explain why the first Jewish exile had to be in Egypt, though this was not spelled out in the Divine Revelation to Abraham in the Book of Genesis (15:13). It was the way the Egyptians regarded their wealth that made it necessary for the Jewish exile to take place there. In the land of Egypt all economic bounty depends not on rain, but on the Nile. The flooding of the waters of the Nile provides Egypt with its sustenance, while it is rain that supports most of the rest of mankind. The eyes of the Egyptians therefore would always be turned to the ground. Everywhere else, however, rain comes from Heaven, so men lift their eyes to Heaven, send their praise to God, and God sends down rain to provide for them. In Egypt, there was no spiritual relationship between man and God in the economic sphere. In order to construct a proper ethical society, the Jews had to learn this lesson. Perforce, their exile was to be in Egypt.[19]

In the ancient pagan world, and for that matter including present-day Buddhism, Hinduism, and other similar nonmonotheistic religions, the absence of a single Creator can be shown to negate any form of Divine morality. The multiplicity of gods is translated into a multiplicity of moral and ethical standards that, in the last resort means an absence of morality. The lack of a Creator who demands an accounting of our actions removes a powerful element in a man's policing of himself.[20] Moreover, in respect to economic morality, the nonbelief in a single Creator, or often even in the fact of Creation, reemphasizes the uncertainty and makes the satisfaction of needs and wants solely dependent on man's actions or on the whims of the gods. This severance, from daily life, of the divine obligation to provide for His creatures further militates against economic morality.

It is true that all societies have created a legal framework for economic activity, yet this is based not on absolute moral standards but primarily on the requirements of law and order in the marketplace. After all, it is simply impossible to conduct an economy where fraud, theft, robbery, and immorality are rife. This may be seen in almost all the problems of the underdeveloped modern countries. Investment is not possible in many of them, since the investor not only takes the normal risks of business, but also faces the complete destruction of his equity, through the lack of a stable political and legal environment. That, however, is not morality but a technical arrangement to enable people to operate together. Brigandage can be put down by the forces of law and order. It is in the complex and sophisticated white-collar crime, carried out in the dim secrecy of privacy, that this pragmatic and legalistic framework for morality does not operate successfully. It does not provide for spiritual supervision or for the fear of retribution in the case of the secret crimes that make up most economic immorality. When God is a partner, however, the Partner demands and is able to receive a different pattern of behavior.

This normative pattern of ethical behavior stands in contrast to many commonly held views on business ethics. There is a cost-benefit concept of morality based on the idea that the cost of economic misdeeds, namely, jail, fines, and shame, is greater than the benefits thereof. However, it is quite obvious that contrary to the common adage, crime actually pays. People only steal, lie, and rob when it is profitable. It is only then that morality becomes an issue. If there is no economic gain to be earned or no potential loss to be suffered, then everybody can and would be moral.

Furthermore, it is commonly argued by free marketeers that the enlightened self-interest of people will provide a brake on economic misdeeds and a moral policing of the marketplace. Workers, it is argued, who are well treated will provide greater productivity. Customers who learn to appreciate the moral status of their suppliers will remain loyal. The trust earned from colleagues and competitors alike will enable a person to turn his high moral code into economic benefits; moral business is good business. This, however, while true, is the same specious argument for morality as the one that crime doe not pay. It also has nothing to do with morality, but is primarily good business practice. When, however, the time comes for good business practice to demand immoral acts, and there are many such scenarios, then the power of self-interest to prevent such misdeeds is broken. Even though the argument of the morality of enlightened self-interest is commonly ascribed to Adam Smith's *Wealth of Nations*, closer examination will show that he was aware of its spiritual shortcomings. A leading modern scholar has shown adequately that the father of free-market economics realized the necessity to police and contract the self-interest of participants in the market.[21]

Judaism, however, it may be argued, would maintain that the self-contained, dual nature of the *yetzer hara* as both a potential power for evil and an essential ingredient for people's positive existence makes it practically impossible for people on their own to educate and control it.

People do not *a priori* decide to do evil deeds, but do so primarily when their rational minds are overcome, as it were, by the power of their lust or in despair at overwhelming pressure. In such states, the ethical training provided by the everyday performance of the *mitzvot* in all spheres of life provides spiritual strength to prevent or limit immoral acts.[22] The *mitzvot* are reminders of the Divine authority that commanded them, and that authority is in the final analysis the bulwark against crime and immorality. In this way Judaism has provided legal and communal frameworks in order to force people to be moral, irrespective of whether it is profitable or not, irrespective of whether that is what people want, and even irrespective of whether the surrounding society considers it to be immoral.

Perhaps instead of Jewish business ethics, the discussion should revolve around permitted or forbidden acts. Just as kosher food is food that is permitted and just as certain acts are forbidden on the *Shabbat*, so certain economic acts are permitted and others forbidden. The profit or loss involved, the individual agonizing as to whether the act is moral or not, and the influence of social consensus are all subjected to a normative legislated morality.

THE ECONOMIC RIGHTS AND OBLIGATIONS OF SOCIETY

The legislative and obligatory motive of Jewish morality is reinforced by the important role that society plays in all spheres, relative to the individualistic emphasis of Christianity and to a lesser degree Islam. In contrast to the idea of the individual salvation of these other monotheistic faiths, Judaism is a group- or national-oriented religion. Abraham is not just the father of monotheism. After all, there were others before him who understood that there was only one God. Abraham and Sarah, however, are the parents of the Abrahamic family. It is among that family, the House of Israel, and God that the covenant at Sinai was made and not among the individual followers of a religion. The legislated and spiritual Jewish economic morality, therefore, applies both between individuals and individuals, as well as between the individual and society.

The idea that there are social and moral issues that have to be handled by society is often rejected on the grounds that this is simply "passing the buck," because relying on society to do something really means that nobody has to do it. This is, however, contrary to Jewish teaching. In Judaism, society, or the community, is a real personality with power, rights, and obligations. The individual has obligations to the community, and he also has the right to expect the community to assist him. The community has an obligation to assist and therefore has rights in the wealth of the individual to fund such assistance.

Throughout history, this has provided the moral basis for the Jewish society to tax its members, thereby taking of the wealth of some individuals and giving to others. At the same time, this provides the moral obligation for society to tend to the welfare of the poor, the weak, the aged, and inefficient, not as individual acts of charity but rather in fulfillment of a communal obligation.

This communal nature of Judaism is different from the social contract between men and their government envisaged by Hobbes, which so influenced much Protestant thought. There the idea is that men should give up their sovereign powers out of self-interest. It was only by the governor possessing more power than each individual that he would have the ability to protect them. Here the unity is phrased in egocentric and utilitarian terms. Since the only reason for the social contract was the benefit that the individual received, the major motivation remained the ego, seen in utilitarian terms.[23]

The Jewish communal concept however is neither utilitarian nor ego centered. Torah was given in order to create a Kingdom of Priests, a Holy Nation, through which knowledge of the Lord could be translated into the reality of the everyday world. That envisaged kingdom may be symbolically represented by the human body. There, while each organ has its own specific function, they all contribute to each other—so they constitute a cohesive entity. Sanctity is achieved not by contracting out some of one's rights to others but by doing or sharing with others, irrespective of the utility or reciprocity.

This is shown by the saying of the Rabbis that "he who does not do his fellow a favor, is not of the sons of Abraham." At the same time, bearing in mind that good intentions alone tend to remain just that, the same Rabbis taught that "we force one to act contrary to the selfishness of Sodom."

The Rabbis of the Talmud thus taught, "He who acts because he is commanded is more commendable than he who acts without being commanded."[24] This is because the latter is obeying his own intelligence and biases rather than the Divine Will, which transcends his relative or self-determined morality.

The emphasis on the community found in Judaism is of vital importance, since the whole ethical issue of economic immorality and business crime revolves around the clash between the perceived benefits accruing to the individual and the welfare of other individuals or society. It would seem that in all business decisions, the tension between these two interests pertains. The unethical behavior occurs when the individual benefits only from harm to others. Theft and robbery are the most blatant examples of this, yet the issue is far more complex. Coercion, fraud, exploitation of ignorance or weakness, environmental damage, and tax evasion are perhaps less obvious yet prevalent examples of this clash.

Judaism, considering the pervasiveness of the moral issues flowing from the economic tension between individual and group, places them in a fundamental role in the scheme of religious living, as may be seen from the rabbinic understanding of the biblical verse in Exodus "and will do that which is right in His eyes, and will hearken to His commandments and observe all His statutes" (Exodus 15:26). "That which is right in His eyes" refers to the business dealings of people. This is to teach us that one who deals honestly in his business affairs and enjoys moral relationships with people is regarded as having observed the whole Torah.[25]

This Torah aims at making the Jew *kadosh*—holy, as distinct from *tahor*—pure. *Tahor* refers to one who has had no contact with impure things or has undergone a ritual of purification. Holiness, however, is the transformation of ordinary and material human actions into the elevated and sanctified.

The *Admor* of Sochochow taught that while angels lacking this ability of transformation can only be pure, men, however, can become holy. His master, Menachem Mendel of Kotsk, however, asked:

> How is it possible for frail human flesh and blood to become holy, which is a Divine state? The biblical verse (Leviticus 19:1-2) "And the Lord spoke to Moses, saying: Speak unto all the congregation of the Children of Israel, and say unto them: Ye shall be holy, for I, the Lord your God, am holy," is couched in the plural. Here we learn that the individual on his own cannot achieve holiness. This becomes possible only through his integration with the congregation of the Children of Israel. Whenever he removes or distances himself from the community, he loses his holiness.[26]

The spiritual infuence creating holiness flows from the community to the individual and vice versa, so that business immorality of either of them diminishes or destroys the holiness.

In the Mosaic Code (Exodus 21:1-6), a thief who could not afford to pay back the costs of the stolen goods had to be sold as a slave (actually an indentured servant since his labor covered that cost). For that slave, the Torah uses the phrase *eved ivri*, which is not employed anywhere else to denote a Jew or Israelite. Only Abraham is known as an *Ivri*, derived from the Hebrew word for "over" or "across," since he came from across the river, the Euphrates, to Canaan. The Rabbis interpreted this also metaphysically, saying, "Abraham stood *mi'ever* [on one side], and the rest of the pagan world stood on the other side." Now that the thief has broken his link with the Abrahamic family through his theft, he moves back across to the world of idolatry from which Abraham had come, an *eved ivri*.[27]

Many of the *mitzvot* given to the Jews come to educate and to intensify the spiritual dimension of the economic actions of the individual and the community. Primarily this is done by stressing the social responsibility that comes with wealth. Perhaps the best example is that of the *Yovel*, the Jubilee year. In this year all land had to be returned to its original owner, in effect substituting leaseholding for actual permanent sale. Many social thinkers and biblical scholars have seen the *Yovel* as a Mosaic means of reducing social tensions between rich and poor, redistributing land every fifty years.[28] There seems, however, to be in Jewish thought another educational aspect beyond this. The *Sefer HaChinukh* sees *Yovel* as an institution that comes to counteract economic injustice, through the molding of people's character.

"The Deity, blessed be He, wished to teach His people that all wealth belongs to Him and that ultimately all would be transferred [from the present owners] to those to whom He had wished to give it in the first place. This *mitzvah* [*Yovel*] by requiring the counting of the years [in the *Yovel* cycle, thus permeating the individual's conceptual framework,] will prevent people from coveting their neighbour's land and from stealing it."[29]

Rabbi Avraham HaKohen Kook (the first chief rabbi of Israel) understood the *Yovel* as the release of communal spirituality, which is able to remedy the moral faults and shortcomings that have led to the inequalities and inequities in the marketplace.

> The individual recovers from the influence of the material and the mundane at regular frequent intervals every *Shabbat* day. What the *Shabbat* achieves for the individual [breaking the influence of man's involvement with his material possession] the *Yovel* achieves for the society as a whole. This temporary, periodical suspension of the normal economic routine raises the Nation spiritually and morally . . . a year of peace and quiet

> without oppressor or tyrant. There is no private property and no privilege and the peace of God reigns. Sanctity is now not profaned by the search for the private accumulation of all the year's produce, while the covetousness of the wealth stirred by business, is now forgotten.[30]

Both of these views of the *Yovel* year represent Judaism's attitude that business immorality is first and foremost a communal-ideological problem, so that any legal framework concerned with restraining or preventing it has to be accompanied by a spiritual dimension. Concentrating on the material damage done to others, important and necessary as this is, is not sufficient to prevent abuses in the market. Unless people are aware of the spiritual damage that the criminal suffers and are sensitized to the unacceptability of economic immorality, legislation can achieve only minimal results. In the long term, such legislation will usually crumble before the widespread acceptance of unethical behavior, leading to what the Rabbis called *naval bireshut HaTorah*—dishonesty within the parameters of the Law.

Beyond the Community

The important role played by the economic rights and obligations of the community is not restricted to Jews. Just as there exists a covenant between Israel and God, so there exists an additional covenant between God and man. This differs in extent and in depth from that of the Israel-God covenant, with greater scope for human legislation and input. Nevertheless, being created in God's image, all men constitute a brotherhood, with mutual spiritual obligations, promulgated by the Creator, as ethical guidelines in all spheres of life. In the covenant made first between God and Adam, and later with Noah and his sons, the Seven Noachide laws were made obligatory on all men, just as the Divine Revelation of Sinai imposed the 613 *mitzvot* on the Jewish people. These Noachide laws are concerned with idolatry, cursing the Lord, murder, sexual immorality, robbery, eating of living-animal flesh, and establishing a judicial system.[31]

The *Chatam Sofer* (Hungary, nineteenth century) remarks, "Both Nachmanides [Spain and *Eretz Yisrael*, thirteenth century] and Maimonides [Egypt, twelfth century] agree that a Noachide incurs the death penalty for transgressing the laws applicable to them. Furthermore they both agree that the Noachide laws include those applicable to the Jews regarding monetary matters."[32] Nachmanides explains that Noachides—all people—are obligated under the injunction to appoint judges, to observe the laws of the Torah regarding *onaah* (price oppression), removing a neighbor's landmark (infringing property rights), bailees, theft, oppression, protecting wages, causing damage to property, person, health or environment, buying and selling, and those regulating money lending and borrowing.[33] This legal obligation would logically seem to apply to providing for the stranger, the needy, the weak, and the inefficient members of society, since this is one of the purposes of the divinely provided wealth. Indeed, many rabbinic authorities ruled that Noachides are also obligated to give charity as part of the requirement to establish an equitable judiciary. It was the failure of the people of Sodom to do just that that led to the destruction of the Cities of the Plain in Genesis 19:24-26.[34] So too the destruction of the men of Shechem was required, since they had witnessed the rape of Dinah (Genesis, chapter 34) and had done nothing to punish the perpetrator.[35]

2

Clean before Man and God

INTRODUCTION

The ramified legal framework created by the *Halakhah*, rabbinic courts, and communal enactments may easily overshadow the spiritual demands and ethical strivings that are an integral part of the Jewish economic perspective. In all societies where such a separation occurs between the moral parameters of a society and its legislation, the results are at best mechanical compliance with the demands of the law, but more often than not, large-scale evasion of these demands. For example, any fiscal system will give rise to tax evasion and the creation of an underground economy. The higher the tax rate, the greater the evasion. People simply resist having part of their wealth taken from them. However, where there is widespread support for the social philosophy for the taxation, then the evasion is smaller. A present-day comparison between Italy and Sweden, both operating with high rates of taxation, will show that the underground economy in the latter is substantially smaller owing to public support of the social aims.[1] Similarly, Margaret Thatcher's poll-tax policy was rejected in England in the early 1990s because of the widespread opposition to what was regarded as a regressive and unfair tax. All aspects of economic legislation, control, or regulation that are not accompanied by moral and ideological support will simply be ineffective. Human ingenuity devoted to the single-minded pursuit of wealth inevitably leads to strategies justifying and permitting actions diametrically opposed to the moral basis of the legal framework. The Rabbis understood that one could be a *naval bireshut HaTorah*—evil within the parameters of Torah.[2]

It is essential, therefore, that any discussion of the halakhic provisions for monitoring and preventing dishonesty in creating wealth be preceded by a presentation of the spiritual and ethical perspectives that underlie these provisions. Such perspectives demanding that one be "clean before man and God" include concepts like *lifnim mishurat hadin*—beyond the letter of the law, *kiddush HaShem*—sanctification of God's name, and *lifnei iver*—the prohibition of placing a stumbling block in the path of the blind.

RATIONALIZING DISHONESTY

The Talmud comments that most people who normally lead moral lives are often guilty of dishonesty.[3] Rashi, the great medieval biblical and talmudical commentator, explains that they rationalize their business behavior to benefit immorally at the expense of their fellowmen. This rationalization at first seeks out methods within the law but ultimately involves illegal actions as well. Primarily, the rationalization would seem to flow from viewing theft and robbery as referring solely to the actions of the burglar, the pickpocket, or the armed robber, but not actions in the marketplace that, similarly, lead to unethical transfers of wealth from one party to another. Halakhic sources, even though they clearly distinguish between the various forms of dishonesty for purposes of determining the scope and nature of the recourse to the rabbinic courts, see as theft and robbery a wide spectrum of actions encompassing the whole gamut of activities in the marketplace. So there are theft, robbery, *onaah* (fraud), *geneivat daat* (literally, stealing another's mind), *lifnei iver* (literally, putting a stumbling block in the path of the blind), destroying another's livelihood, and false weights and measures. There is even the opinion that the biblical injunction against taking interest indicates that it is a form of theft.[4] Indeed any transfer of wealth from one individual to another without their knowledge or consent is regarded by Rabbi Israel Salanter, the founder of the eighteenth-century *mussar* movement, as Torah theft.[5]

The rationalization that leads to business dishonesty applies to many practices that are often regarded as normal business behavior. A simple illustration of this is to be found in the ruling of the Magen Avraham, a major commentator on the *Shulchan Arukh* (Rabbi Avraham Gombiner, eastern Europe, seventeenth century). He defines a thief as one who buys on credit even though he has no knowledge of how he will be able to repay his debt.[6] A later commentator developed this idea further to include the acts of one who borrows money without any idea or calculation of repayment.[7] The person who borrows money without any idea of how he will pay it back or involves himself in other forms of credit with the same lack of planning is as often as not tempted not to repay it or to steal in order to be able to pay. In this way he now becomes guilty of immorality. It sounds simplistic, yet lawyers who handle clients' trust money, guardians of the funds of minors, and other people whose job is to oversee temporarily the funds of other people are often tempted to borrow the funds for their own use on the assumption that the owners will not become aware of it. Since they are not doing any lasting harm, their actions become perfectly legitimized in their own minds. The problem arises, however, when for a variety of reasons, they are not able to put that money back where it belongs.

More sophisticated, yet closely related, is the ease with which bankruptcy is entered into as a means of escaping debts and obligations. In some cases, the future bankruptcy was actually planned at the beginning of the venture. This would be deliberate fraud, and so perhaps constitutes only a marginal phenomenon. Far more common is the use of bankruptcy to solve severe financial difficulties irrespective of their causes. Over and above the purely commercial and financial issues, there exists here the moral question of the debtor not being able to repay money given to him by his creditors, whether they represent bankers, suppliers, or family members.

Legislation in recent decades in the United States to protect the interests of the debtors and to enable corporations to operate even though they are economically bankrupt is a statement enabling the debtor to avoid such a moral obligation. It stands in clear contradiction to a Jewish moral imperative.

Jewish communal censure of the immoral behavior of bankruptcy may be clearly seen in the following enactment in Lublin in 1624 by the *Vaad Arba Aratzot* (Council of the Four Lands). Actually, the minute books of the council contain a large number of similar enactments of which this is only a sample. (The *Vaad Arba Aratzot* was a supranational council of Jewry in Great Poland, Little Poland, East Galicia and Podolia, and Volhynia between the end of the sixteenth century and the middle of the eighteenth century.)

> If a bankrupt debtor should offer to make a settlement for his debts [instead of paying them in full] then the *cherem*, ban of excommunication, is to be published against him. . . . He is to be considered to be unfit to give testimony or to take an oath. He is to be imprisoned for a whole year and shall not be appointed to any religious position . . . and he shall not be called up to the Torah for a whole year [or] until he repays his creditors. The creditors may take away all the clothes which the bankrupt has made [even] for his wife within the year that he became bankrupt. He shall lose the rights of citizenship in the community [which limited his right to remain and do business in that town].
>
> When the *cherem* is pronounced in the synagogue the bankrupt person's wife and children must be present [so as to a priori educate against fraud through the fear of such shame].[8]

The imprisonment referred to in the enactment is in direct contradiction to rabbinic law, which makes no provision either for it or for bodily mutilation for any form of theft. This and similar provisions in central and eastern Europe primarily during the seventeenth century must be seen as a lay reaction to increased fraud through bankruptcy and the inability of the communal institutions to limit it in other ways.

So we learn from this responsum of the Rivash (Rabbi Yitzchak bar Sheshet, Spain, fourteenth century) to Rabbi Yitzchak Alrinasi, concerning the Jews of Aragon, Spain:

> "Reuven had borrowed money from Shimon with all the legal requirements and further accepted on himself, indentured service in case of default, should there not be enough unsecured movables to pay the debt. This is in accordance with the laws of Aragon which provided for debtor imprisonment. Now we find that Reuven cannot pay and Shimon claims the right of imprisonment. Reuven, however claims that this is not according to the Torah, since no man of Israel can be imprisoned for his debts. We need to know what is the law." The Rivash answered that "the law is with Reuven that a man cannot be sold for his debts. It is true that it is a *mitzvah* to pay one's debts and the *bet din* has the obligation to enforce it. So we will impound all his assets and even flog him to make payment. These measures however only apply to one who has assets but refuses to reveal them to pay his debt. Here, however, Reuven cannot pay, so we have no power to punish him. After all, the Torah says, 'Thou shall not be to him a creditor.'

This includes even forbidding the creditor to pass before a debtor who he knows cannot pay."[9]

TWIN STRANDS

Most legal systems restrict themselves to forbidding certain actions and providing legal protection for those injured by them. This creates a mentality that easily equates moral actions with only those permitted by law. The Jewish spiritual system, however, aimed at creating a holy nation and educating toward it, cannot be satisfied only with the prosecution of criminals and obtaining the restitution of damage done. Measures have also to be taken to prevent or to minimize fraud both by providing absolute ethical standards and by educating against immoral behavior even where such behavior cannot be prosecuted in a court of law. Unless this is done, the effect on the perpetrator is ignored, which permits an ever-spreading circle of economic immorality until the whole of society becomes affected.

There does indeed exist a clear halakhic system in which such rulings militating against unethical actions are paralleled by the duty of the religious courts to provide protection for those suffering from these factors and punishment for the perpetrator. Furthermore the personalities of the Sages and the study of religious texts create Jewish role models for the individual to emulate, thus further strengthening the moral imperative.

It is clear that the rabbinic courts have a religious obligation to implement the halakhic rules regarding a thief and a robber, and to ensure that the wrong done to one person by another is remedied accordingly. This obligation applies to all people, Jews and non-Jews, as discussed in the following chapter.

Maimonides codifies the halakhic obligation regarding theft when he rules, "He who steals money [or property] worth a small copper coin (*shaveh prutah*) or more, transgresses the negative commandment, 'Thou shall not steal'" (Leviticus 19:11).

Maimonides continues:

> This is irrespective of whether he steals the property of another Jew or of an idolator [based on the *Talmud Bavli* 113a-b which forbids robbing a gentile, and Maimonides applies it to theft as well], of an adult or of a minor. However, this transgression does not carry with it the legal punishment of

flogging [which is mandatory in the case of an action which violates a negative commandment]. After all, the thief is obligated [by the Torah] to pay monetary compensations. [Halakhically, such compensation for transgressing forbidden action, annuls the flogging.]

However, in the following subsection, Maimonides goes on to state categorically.

> It is forbidden by the law of the Torah to steal anything [even less than a *shaveh prutah*] so too one is forbidden to steal in jest or [to merely anger the owner] with the intention to return it [so that the thief does not even have a material benefit, thus reinforcing the spiritual concept of theft as negating a Divine injunction]. All these acts are forbidden so that one should not be accustomed to stealing. [The *Shulchan Arukh* rules that a minor, a boy below *bar mitzvah* age or a girl who has not reached twelve years and a day, is punished physically even though they are not of age to become legally liable in order to prevent them becoming accustomed to theft. This is contrary to the procedure in other negative acts, such as eating nonkosher food, where the purpose is merely to educate them toward observance, so that no physical punishment is mandatory].[10]

The Jewish insistence on preventing dishonesty as distinct from merely punishing wrongdoers finds further expression in the prohibition of buying stolen goods. Such goods include not only items known to be stolen but also purchasing them from a known thief or robber, or even in circumstances that suggest that the goods do not belong to the seller. All the codes rule against buying such goods on the basis of the following *mishnah*:

"One may not buy wool, milk, or kids from the shepherds [who in those days were primarily hired workers who watched over flocks or herds belonging to other people]. Nor may one buy trees or fruit from the hired watchmen of orchards. . . . Wherever the seller asks that the goods be hidden [on leaving] it is forbidden to buy them."[11]

One who nevertheless does buy such goods is considered as strengthening the "hands of evildoers" and so putting a stumbling block in the path of the blind, contrary to the biblical injunction of *lifnei iver*. The thief is blind, so to speak, to the moral consequences of his actions, and the buyer, by providing the market without which theft would be unprofitable and useless, is causing him to stumble.

Defaulting on a contract or noncompliance is easily viewed as unethical when it is illegal or when it causes loss to other parties. Halakhic enforcement of such contracts is therefore neither surprising nor worthy of much comment. It is, however, important to recognize the Rabbis' view of the spiritual damage flowing from noncompliance even where no monetary loss is involved and their steps to express the association with godliness of keeping one's word, whether given verbally or reduced to legal contracts.

Commenting on the biblical verse "Just weights and just measures ye shall have," the *Sifre* uses the Hebrew *chein tzedek*, actually "just measures," to also denote the Hebrew word *chein*, for "yes," saying, "Let your yes be yes and your no be no."[12] The injunction in the Ten Commandments "You shall not take the name of the Lord in vain" is understood inter alia in relation to oaths.

Sometimes it is sufficient for the terms of the envisaged contract to be merely implied by one's conduct as in the talmudic story of Rabbi Safra. Rabbi Safra was standing in prayer when a buyer approached him to purchase his goods. When the buyer received no reaction to his original offer, he raised the price, taking the rabbi's silence for rejection. As the prayer continued, so the bidding rose, until finally Rabbi Safra showed that he had finished. Hastily, the merchant counted out the coins of his last offer only to find that Rabbi Safra returned to him the difference between that and his first offer.[13]

A modern responsum dealing with price changes shows how this idea was integrated into applied rabbinic thinking. A storekeeper had displayed the prices on the articles in his store. When the market price on these goods rose, the question of changing his prices without canceling the advertisement was addressed to a rabbinic authority in New York, who wrote the following:

> According to the ruling of the *Shulchan Arukh* (*Choshen Mishpat* section 23, subsection 20) when prices in the market move higher, the storekeeper may similarly raise his own. Here too the storekeeper may do so. However, in this case the further question of keeping his word is involved. By displaying the prices in his store, he has signified his agreement to these prices, even though the agreement was made in writing [rather than verbally which is considered to be more binding]. Now by changing his prices, he shows himself to be lacking in trust in the Divine Providence [to provide him with his livelihood even if he maintains his promise of the lower price level]. This is in contrast to the actions of Rabbi Safra described in the Talmud.[14]

These spiritual underpinnings of the injunction to fulfill one's promises even at the cost of a financial loss to oneself find their symmetry in the disapproval of unfulfilled contracts, even where no loss is suffered by the other party or even in those circumstances under which legally both parties may retract. In both cases the moral problem of breaking one's word still remains. Unchecked and unhindered, this behavior creates a cultural and spiritual framework within which obligations can be ignored or evaded by the mere payment of money. Such a framework is conducive to a general dissipation of the individual moral and social obligations, encouraging a wide spectrum of immoral actions. So halakhic disapproval of voided contracts and the public disgrace of those practicing such policies become a bulwark against the general spread of unethical business practices.

In this light it is easy to understand the statement of Rabbi Eliezer in the Talmud "that he who changes his mind [alters his undertakings or cancels agreements in economic activities] is as heinous as he who worships idols."[15] These need not be flagrant abrogations of contractual obligations but may be subtle subterfuges or insidious behavior. This can be seen in the comment of Rashi to the above talmudic statement as referring to one who alters his voice in order to defraud.

Following the accepted pattern in Judaism, this philosophical disapproval of unfulfilled contracts becomes translated into legal decisions, even in those cases where no financial loss was incurred.

> If the owner hired workers and they wish to cancel their agreement [each may do so and] they have no [financial] claims against each other, except *taromet* (resentment). [This applies where the work was not commenced since labor contracts become valid halakhically only upon commencement of work or allied actions such as traveling to the place of work.] In those cases where the workers would have been able to find alternative employment, and now as a result of his retraction they are unemployed, he has to pay them the wages as a *po'el batel* [that which one would pay to enjoy a day of leisure].[16] [The same source rules that where the workers renege and cause a financial loss, monetary compensation has to be paid by them.]

Mere legal protection against the avoidance of one's contractual obligations is often not sufficient to prevent a behavioral pattern. So, as in many other instances, Judaism provides here a vehicle for the expression of public disapproval through the ritual of *Misheparah*. The

Shulchan Aruch, the monumental codification of Jewish Law by Yosef Caro in sixteenth-century Safed, which became the authoritative code for all Jews as a result of the gloss of the Rama (Rabbi Moshe Isserles), rules:

> Where one paid money for an article but did not take possession [essential in Jewish law for a transfer of ownership], any party who reneges on the agreed transaction does an act not befitting a Jew. This applies both to the buyer and to the seller. Whoever reneges on an agreement, even if he only paid part of the purchase price [and therefore the deal may be considered not to have been completed], becomes liable to the rebuke. *Misheparah*–He who demanded payment . . . [shall demand payment from you].

How is the *Misheparah* ritual performed? The guilty party is arraigned in the rabbinical court. The Rabbis publicly rebuke him by saying, "*Misheparah*–He who demanded payment [for their sins] from the Generation of the Flood, and from the Generation of the Tower of Babel, and from the people of Sodom and Gomorrah [all considered to be role models of evil deserving of total destruction] and from the Egyptians who were drowned in the Red Sea, He will demand payment from whosoever does not keep his word."[17]

This halakhic emphasis on refraining from unethical business practices as distinct from the rabbinic involvement in settling cases arising out of them is clearly shown in the rabbinic treatment of false weights and measures. The biblical injunction "Thou shall not have diverse weights and measures" (Deuteronomy 25:13) is understood by the *Sefer HaChinukh* to refer to an injunction against possessing the deficient weights as distinct from their use. The purpose of this injunction it to train the Jew to achieve the role of holiness allotted to him. The *Shulchan Arukh* codifies this as law and then continues:

> The punishment for false weights and measures is greater than that of sexual immorality. The latter is only a sin against God whereas the former is a sin against man [as well]. [Furthermore] it is possible to do *teshuvah* for the latter whereas how shall one repent for the injuries caused by false weights and measures [such penitence halakhically presupposes the return of the theft or payment for its value. Since the user of false weights] has defrauded so many people [cannot possibly remember the amount of loss caused to each one] he cannot return that which he has stolen. So let him do good

deeds and charitable acts [in this way possibly achieving some form of repentance].[18]

These two strands of halakhic injunctions, both those against dishonest actions and the provision for rectifying them, constitute legal forms. Over and above them there are spiritual requirements that extend the moral obligations beyond the fabric of mere legalisms. In this respect there would seem to be three primary concepts that expand the very concept of dishonesty: *kiddush HaShem*, sanctification of God's name; *lifnim mishurat hadin, chayav biyedei Shamayim*, guilty before God; and *lifnei iver*, a stumbling block in the path of the blind; all actions beyond the demand of the Law.

KIDDUSH HASHEM–SANCTIFICATION OF GOD'S NAME

It is common wisdom to understand *kiddush HaShem* as referring to the acts of martyrdom with which Jewish history is so replete. Over and above this, however, Judaism has a concept of such sanctification through the commercial intercourse of the Jew. After all, each Jew is a standard bearer of the dignity of the Jewish people and their God, so that morality in the marketplace leads to the sanctification of His Name, and dishonesty, to *chillul HaShem*, the desecration of His Name. The religious status, the degree of Jewish identification, and the communal position of the perpetrator all influence the degree of *chillul HaShem*. The greater the personality, the greater the disgrace.

The story concerning Shimon ben Shotach, the foremost rabbinic scholar of the Hasmonean kingdom (c. fourth century B.C.E.), exemplifies this *kiddush HaShem*. He sent his disciples to buy a donkey from an idolator in Ashkelon. When they returned they found a jewel attached to the halter bag of the donkey. They rejoiced, seeing this as an act of Divine Providence rewarding their teacher. He, however, insisted that they return the jewel. When they did so, the idolator exclaimed, "Blessed be the God of Shimon ben Shotach."[19]

Here one must bear in mind the codification of Maimonides that *kiddush HaShem* in all its forms is a *mitzvat asei*, a positive commandment incumbent on all Jews, men and women, and applicable in all times. This places a constant obligation to consider each economic act, whether at the corporate or individual level, as buyer or seller, employer or employee, and its implications for sanctifying or desecrating God's Name. Naturally, this obligation exists even in those cases where there is no legislation enforcing moral acts or where the courts are powerless to exact compensation for damages arising out of such acts.

LIFNIM MISHURAT HADIN–BEYOND THE LETTER OF THE LAW

In every act of business immorality, the two strands, the halakhic injunction against such behavior and the halakhic correction of the act, intermingle and merge so that theft in its widest sense is forbidden by Divine decree even in those cases where no human correction is legally justified or possible.

All the codes rule that a thief or robber only becomes liable to make restitution for objects that are of some minimal value–defined halakhically as *shaveh prutah*, literally, worth a penny. This however does not condone theft or robbery even of less-valuable goods, but simply sets the parameters for legal action. Rabbi Joel Sirkes (Poland, 1561-1640) in his classic commentary *Bayit Chadash*, to the codex *Arbaah Turim*, explains the reason for setting such parameters. The *Arbaah Turim*, like the *Mishneh Torah* and *Shulchan Arukh*, forbids stealing irrespective of the value involved.

"Jews are prepared to waive their rights of ownership over items of little value and it is this waiver which led the codes not to penalize theft or robbery of lesser items. At the same time, however, one who steals such items remains a thief and therefore they are careful to state 'it is forbidden to steal even less than *shaveh prutah*.'"[20]

This concept of the moral imperative even where no legal responsibility exists is repeated in many other halakhic decisions. So Baal HaTanya of Lubavich [Shneur Zalman, founder of *Chabad*] rules that stealing back one's own goods or money from a thief is theft, and so is forbidden. Rather one is obliged to go through the *bet din* for redress.[21] So, too, "one is not allowed to take fruit from the orchard of a friend without his permission, even when one knows that he would be happy and pleased when he finds out that you have benefited from his property."[22]

The Sages of the Talmud found the cause of the destruction of the Generation of the Flood in the overlooking of such forbidden yet legal acts.

"Since one is not liable for the theft of less than a *shaveh prutah*, each man, woman, and child in the town picked one olive out of the silo of a farmer till none were left."[23]

Such theft of marginal items is defined as *chamas*, for which, the Bible tells us, that generation was destroyed.[24]

Further, there are many cases in which human courts are not able to prosecute or even to enforce a pattern of behavior, but in which the person is liable before the Heavenly Court. In such cases, people are supposed to act in such a way as to clear themselves before God.

The Sages in the *Mishnah* discussed a case where an adult gave a child or an irresponsible adult hot coals, which the individual fanned and thereby caused a fire. Here they ruled that since there was no real agency, the sender was not liable for the damage caused, since it is normal for such coals to cool. The sender could not be obligated, therefore, to have foreseen that the individual would fan the dying coals. However, the sender was liable before the Heavenly Court.[25]

Such moral obligations, rather than legal ones, are clearly shown in the biblical discussion in Leviticus (5:20-26) concerning a thief who swears a false oath denying his theft. If he subsequently regrets and voluntarily restores or repays the debt, he is obligated to bring a sin offering and repay the debt, plus an additional 20 percent, to the real owner. However, in the case where witnesses appear and the court finds the thief guilty, there is no fine or sacrifice. All that he is able to do is to repair the physical loss caused. His spiritual loss, however, cannot be rectified simply by the fine or sacrifice, since here the thief does not regret or repent.

In addition to this concept of guilty before Heaven, the Sages introduced a further spiritual dimension into their halakhic view of dishonesty, that of "*lifnim mishurat hadin*," beyond the requirements of the Law. Pious and scholarly people, the Jewish role models, are expected to act not only in accordance with the positive and negative injunction of the *Halakhah*, but to conduct their commerce in righteousness. This involves the voluntary relinquishment of legal rights in favor of others. For example, *onaah*, protection against price fraud, is possible only for something that is *shaveh prutah* and for an overcharge of one-sixth or more of the market price. Yet the Rosh, Rabbenu Asher ben Yechiel, the post-Maimonidean authority, writes that God-fearing men should abstain from overcharging even when the goods are not *shaveh prutah* or when the overcharge is less than one-sixth. Furthermore, they should not overcharge even for those goods for which the halakhic rules of *onaah* do not apply, such as real estate.[26]

It is sometimes suggested that such actions are not halakhically obligatory but merely acts of righteousness. Indeed some authorities hold that the rabbinic courts cannot force people to actions beyond those required of them by law, yet disapproval is expressed at such acts as not befitting a Jew. Nevertheless, there is widespread support for the halakhic opinion that "we may force one to refrain from the acts of the people of Sodom."

MICHSHOL LIFNEI IVER—A STUMBLING BLOCK IN THE PATH OF THE BLIND

There are acts in commerce and business that although there is neither theft nor fraud either of price or quality, nevertheless present moral problems. It may well be that there is no financial damage, but the action may not be permissible. In the main they are directed at the effect on the spiritual and moral well-being of one the parties.

The Jewish frame of reference for dealing with these issues is the biblical injunction "You shall not put a stumbling block in the path of the blind" (Leviticus 19:14). In interpreting this verse the Rabbis did not see it as referring to the prevention of placing physical objects in the path of a blind man. That was understood as part of the natural morality common to all mankind. The Torah comes to add dimensions, divinely revealed, to this natural morality, and so *lifnei iver* has to be understood as having wider ramifications. Indeed the Sages understood *lifnei iver* as referring to the giving of unwise business advice to someone or the supply, through perfectly legal transactions, of goods that are to the buyer's moral detriment.

The emphasis is on the moral detriment of the recipient. It is true that one may not sell or give another goods that are physically harmful to him nor may one, it may be assumed, advertise or encourage him to buy them from somebody else. This would include the production and sale of cigarettes or drugs. However it is not necessary to apply *lifnei iver* here. Halakhically a man may not cause damage to his own or another's body, or to his property either through the body or through the misuse of property. Such injunction comes under the category of *nezek*, damages, and the injured party has recourse to the rabbinic court. *Lifnei iver*, it would seem, refers to a different category of actions primarily affecting the moral well-being of both parties.

Maimonides codifies *lifnei iver* as follows:

> Everyone who causes the blind to stumble in anything [in which he is not knowledgeable] and knowingly tenders him advice that is to his detriment, or those who strengthen the hands of evildoers who are [figuratively] blind and who because of their lusts do not see the true way [of the Torah and the Divine Commandments] transgress a negative commandment even as it is written: You shall not put a stumbling block in the path of the blind.[27]

Broadly speaking, therefore, *lifnei iver* in the marketplace may be considered in two different forms: assisting a person to perform actions that are detrimental to himself–*mesayeh ledavar aveirah*; and the giving of bad advice, as distinct from incorrect advice. In both cases, the blind person is considered to be the one who is blind or willfully blinds himself to the consequences of what he is doing. Most of the rabbinic responsa and legal codes refer to the first form of *lifnei iver*, so it will be considered first.

Mesayeh LeDavar Aveirah–Assisting the Perpetrator of an Evil Deed

One of the common commercial examples of this is the trade in stolen goods. Here the buyer, by creating a market, is providing the rationale for the thief's actions, which are forbidden ones. The *Mishnah*, and subsequent codes, rules that "one may not buy sheep or wool from the shepherds [in those days guardians of other people's flocks, meaning that these goods probably did not belong to them] . . . nor may one buy saplings or fruit from the watchmen of the orchards . . . nor may one buy anything which the seller asks to be hidden."[28]

By the same logic, one is not permitted by Jewish law to sell articles that are forbidden, so one may not sell nonkosher meat to a Jew who is not allowed to eat it, nor may one sell clothes that are immodest since Jews are required to dress modestly. In all these cases, the sale causes the person to do something forbidden to him, and therefore the seller is putting a spiritual stumbling block before him. The concept extends beyond ritual and encompasses spiritual issues basic to Judaism's concept of the world and mankind. One of the seven Noachide laws that Judaism consider to be binding on all men forbids idolatry. In terms of the market this means that one may not sell to a non-Jew items that can be used or that are commonly used for idolatry. The non-Jew would thereby be encouraged or enabled to do that which the Torah forbade him, and the Jew, an accessory to a forbidden act, is guilty of *lifnei iver*. It would seem logical therefore that items that were spiritually bad for one like pornography would also fall into the forbidden category of *lifnei iver*, since both Jew and non-Jew are commanded to observe laws of sexual morality.

In present-day Israel, this injunction of *lifnei iver* has very serious macroeconomic implications. Israel is a major trader in arms and that trade is an important component of its balance of payments. Maimonides codifies as law the *mishnah* in *Avodah Zarah* that "it is forbidden to sell to gentiles weapons of war nor may [one] sharpen swords and spears; [in modern times repair] weapons; nor . . . chains [to be put on the necks or feet of captives,] nor lions nor bears nor anything that may be used to harm the public."[29] The rationale is that the primary use of all these arms is not self-defense but rather murder, suppression, or war. In the Israeli case, the arms trade has to be examined in the light of *lifnei iver* to determine whether it is permissible within a Jewish framework. The arms trade not only affects the government as a supplier, but also includes a large number of people who are engaged as agents, as middle men, or even as experts needed to train the buyers in the correct use of the weapons systems. Furthermore, many people employed in the high-tech industries are also involved, since the military establishment, as in all countries, is a major purchaser of their products.

As long as the armaments are meant for self-defense, there is no halakhic problem, since a man is obligated to take steps to protect his own life. The armaments industry is an important part of that obligation both at the macro- and the microlevels. In Israel, the creation of a military industrial complex is an acceptable and essential part of that self-defense in view of the constant state of war imposed by her Arab neighbors and the repeated armament embargoes that have been placed upon her in the past. Part of the export trade is essential to this independent armament industry, because it lowers the per unit cost of each item and therefore makes the self-defense more easily realizable.

The problem however arises when the trade in armaments becomes a business just like any other. Then despite its highly profitable nature, it becomes morally questionable. This moral problem is heightened even more by the fact that the regimes buying the weapons are not always those of Western Europe or the United States. Often they are regimes that are either immoral or that violate the basic rights of people. As often as not the weapons are used against their own citizens or in aggression. The aspect of *lifnei iver* in the armaments and allied industries, is obviously not limited to Israel except that the independent Jewish state, would seem to provide greater scope for implementing this Jewish moral injunction.

Lifnei Iver—Providing Misleading Advice

An alternative view of the *lifnei iver* concept refers to the injunction of giving misleading advice. This is not the same as providing business consultancy that results in a loss, but refers to the kind of information in which the recipient is blind either to the final effects of the advice or to the special interest that the consultant has in such advice. Consultants and advisers such as accountants, lawyers, insurance agents, investment advisers, and stockbrokers would seem to be obligated to review the advice given to their clients in order to obviate the possibility of putting a stumbling block in the path of the blind.

The *Midrash* relates to *lifnei iver* by enjoining us, "Do not offer another advice that is detrimental to him. Do not tell him to leave a town early in the morning, knowing full well that there is a danger of him being attacked by robbers, nor [tell him] to leave in the afternoon, knowing that this will cause him to lose his way. Do not tell him, sell your field and buy a donkey and when you intend to buy a field [and Rashi adds, to sell a donkey]."[30]

Underlying the simple example provided by the *Midrash* and the commentators is an important and primary injunction, relevant to the whole gamut of financial and advisory services. In view of the modern explosion of these industries, *lifnei iver* becomes more important perhaps than ever before in economic history. A number of examples of its present-day relevance should be considered here.

In many countries, commercial bankers serve as investment advisers to their depositors, yet at the same time buy and sell stock on their own account, issue their own stock to be traded on the stock exchange, and underwrite the issue of corporate stock to the public. They are also related through various devices to insurance corporations, mortgage banks, and even industrial or commercial enterprises. It may very well be that a conflict of interest exists between those functions and the advice given to their depositors, which if not revealed, would seem to be a case of *lifnei iver*. One of the reasons for the regulation of the financial institutions after the Depression in the United States was to prevent such conflict of interest by restricting the activities of the commercial banks.

Banks, credit institutions, and large retailers maintain a sophisticated and intensive advertising campaign to encourage people to buy goods or services on credit, while concurrently consumer credit is made relatively easy to obtain. People, unable to withstand the temptation of instantly gratifying their wishes, use such credit without any knowledge of their future resources or even the feasibility of repayment. Social welfare studies have shown that such ill-considered use of consumer credit in all its forms can be a major cause of poverty despite a relatively high income. Perhaps it is stretching the concept of *lifnei iver* beyond its halakhic framework, but it would seem to the author that the implications of such advertising for those blind to the consequences of debt necessitate further halakhic examination. This examination is, however, complicated by the problem of interest. One way in which consumers may be protected against the ill effects of credit is by making mandatory, full disclosure of the real cost of delayed payment. This enables the consumer to evaluate more correctly the burden he is assuming. However, credit sales for a known interest rate are usually not allowed in Jewish law because they may constitute *avak ribit*—interest through commercial transactions that is rabbinically forbidden (in contrast to interest charged on a straight loan, which is forbidden in the Torah).

An insurance broker recently described to the author how he had handled the problem of *lifnei iver* in regard to advice given to his clients. Since his commission varied among the different policies and different corporations, he became concerned that perhaps the policies he was offering were more a reflection of his own potetial earnings than the needs or benefits of the specific client. By programming all the data regarding the client and his family, he was able to let the computer choose the best policy and conditions, so saving himself from *lifnei iver*.

It is important to stress that irrespective of whether *lifnei iver* is understood as giving misleading advice or as helping someone do acts harmful to himself or forbidden by *Halakhah*, a common element of secrecy exists. The Bible closes the verse in Leviticus 19:14 forbidding placing a stumbling block in the path of the blind by adding, "and you shall fear the Lord." Wherever this phrase appears in the Bible, it is understood by the Rabbis to refer to actions hidden from the human eye and operating in the recesses of the human heart. Since white-collar crime, economic oppression, and misplaced trust operate primarily in secret, this affirmation of the fear of God is Judaism's major defense against them.

All the spiritual underpinnings of Judaism's moral business and economic framework, as distinct from its halakhic legislation, are strengthened by the concept of *pattur aval assur*–not liable to punishment but forbidden. As often as not, many immoral acts in business are carried out within the letter of the law; fear of judicial punishment being the primary restraint. Jewish sources, however, based on all the aspects discussed in this chapter, ruled that in order to be clean before God and man, there are acts that although perfectly legal are nevertheless not permitted. Our sources understood that there are legal actions in regard to wealth and business that can easily create a moral laxity that, in turn, leads to acts that are illegal. A simple example is the following discussion between Beit Hillel and Beit Shammai, the two classical schools of halakhic teaching during the last days of the Second Temple.

During the *Shmittah* year, the Torah permits everybody to go into orchards and fields and eat of the fruit or of the grain that grew on its own (Exodus 23:11). Beit Hillel and Beit Shammai were divided over whether it was necessary to obtain permission or to thank the owner, despite the fact that the Torah permitted the free entry and the eating. The Rabbis ruled in accordance with Beit Hillel that in order to educate people to respect private property, it was necessary to get permission from the owner during *Shmittah*. In this way, the legal right of free entry during the Sabbatical year would not become a habit that would then continue into the other six years, leading to actions that are forbidden.[31]

3

Justice and Righteousness in the Marketplace

INTRODUCTION

Not withstanding the importance of the moral perspectives of business practices and the injunctions against unethical behavior in the marketplace, Judaism's insistence on the communal aspect of religion and on formalized legally enforceable acts applies in this respect as it does in prayer, sex, and food. Without this insistence, the spiritual dimension of unethical behavior and the injunctions to develop more honest business practices would remain ineffectual moralizing, resulting in a welter of good intentions rather than an effective social and legal framework for the marketplace. It is necessary therefore to describe the halakhic forms determining the parameters of permitted and forbidden economic acts within the Jewish community, both in its limited sense in countries of the Diaspora, and in Israel, the independent Jewish state that is the natural habitat for their implementation.

The forbidden and permitted acts of *Halakhah* in the marketplace extend the concepts of justice and righteousness far beyond the parameters of dishonesty or fraud. Competition, prices, profits, and physical damages create social, ethical, and spiritual dilemmas, in addition to their relationship to questions of efficiency, material standards of living, and individual choice. It is in regard to these dilemmas that Judaism as a value system provides the specific parameters discussed in the previous chapters.

This is intrinsic to the very nature of the contribution of Jewish sources to the whole gamut of economic activities, which is concerned primarily and one may even argue, exclusively, with the moral parameters of such activities rather than the economic theories determining them.

Such an emphasis does not detract from the economic knowledge that the rabbinic Sages possessed or from its relevance to the halakhic decisions. Rather it emphasizes that such knowledge is not specifically Jewish or intrinsically different from other knowledge.

THEFT AND ROBBERY

Halakhah distinguishes between these two forms of immorality both as regards their character and the legal methods of punishment, suiting the latter to the former.

Theft

"Who is a thief? One who stealthily takes money [or assets] that belongs to another without the knowledge [or consent] of the owner; for example, he who puts his hand into the pocket of another and takes out his money, without the owner being aware of it. However, one who publicly takes [another's property] by force, and against the owner's will, is not a thief but a *gazlan*, a robber."[1] In accordance with this definition, Maimonides includes within the laws of theft also fraud through weights and measures, as well as forbidding the buying of stolen goods.

In almost all countries today legislation exists to prosecute thieves and to prevent theft. Similarly, weights and measures are regulated in many countries by public authorities, and infractions carry penalties, thus protecting society against abuse. The halakhic rules, therefore, might seem superfluous were it not for the insistence that theft refers to stealthy and secret acts. Most economic crimes are conducted in exactly this atmosphere. A whole area of accepted business practices exists within which the distinction between moral and immoral acts is blurred. Gray areas develop within which the individual operates without being able to discuss openly what forms of behavior are permissible. In this secretive atmosphere, a pattern of underground antiethical actions is easily developed. Here the rabbinic discussion of theft, stealth, and secretive crimes is a pertinent one as it creates a moral climate within which people are able to operate ethically.

Perhaps two examples will suffice to make clear the halakhic distinction between permissible and nonpermissible actions that may be considered to be theft.

1. An employee receives a per diem for work done away from his home base. If he is willing and able to manage on less, using cheaper transport, board, and lodging, does keeping the excess constitute theft?

Perhaps a relevant halakhic attitude may be seen in the talmudic discussion concerning the housekeeping money given to a woman by her husband. "If the husband gave her a sum of money with which to conduct the affairs of the home, and she is thrifty and careful she may keep the difference [between her actual costs and the sum given]. If, however, she is to be reimbursed for money spent on the home, she may obtain only that which she actually spent."[2]

2. Reuven, the buying agent for Shimon, is offered a 10 percent commission by Levi if he will purchase goods from him. Whether acceptance of this commission should be considered theft or not will depend on the effect that the actions of Reuven have on the business of Shimon. In those cases where Reuven is buying inferior goods or paying above market prices, then it definitely constitutes theft. However, it may well be that Shimon suffers no loss since the goods and prices are the same as those offered by other suppliers. In this case, Reuven would have to pay half of the commission to Shimon, since one may not have a benefit from someone else's money. After all it is Reuven's position as buying agent for Shimon, with all the financial and commercial power that flows from it, that enables him to receive the commission.

Levi's role in this case should not be overlooked. The commission he is offering is an elegant euphemism for bribery, and is a simple variation of an important moral problem in the international trade of the developed countries with states in South America, Asia, and Africa. The United States of America has passed legislation prohibiting American corporations from giving such bribes in order to make sales or obtain contracts in foreign countries, despite the fact that no such legislation exists in most other Western countries. Naturally, this places the American corporation at a distinct disadvantage, the price for a moral decision. Israel has no such legislation, but a survey by the author of exporters there showed the overwhelming majority to be in favor of enacting it.

Bribery for judges is forbidden in the Bible since "it blinds the eyes of wise." It would seem that the purchasing agent or his equivalent actually has the status of a judge, since he adjudicates between the rival claims of various competing corporations. If this is correct, then it would be halakhically forbidden to offer such commissions. Such moral blindness affects not only the receiver but also the giver.

The legal principles involved in these and similar cases may compensate the injured party for a loss suffered from the theft, yet one wonders just how effective such principles can be in preventing such secret and hidden actions. It would seem that the spiritual dimension seen by the Rabbis in the laws of weights and measures may provide such protection.

The biblical verse in Leviticus (19:36) containing the injunction "Just weights and measures shall you have" continues, saying, "I am the Lord your God who brought you out of the Land of Egypt."

This linkage seemed strange to the Rabbis of the *Midrash*, since the Exodus does not seem to be related to weights and measures, any more than any other *mitzvot*. They explained, "The God who distinguished between the first seed of the Egyptians [the First Born] and other Egyptian sons who were not killed in the plague [a distinction based on the most intimate and secret knowedge known only to God] shall surely punish he who soaks his weights in salt in order to cheat [in secret]."[3]

It is this awareness of the pervading Divine knowledge that constitutes Judaism's ultimate protection against stealth and secret theft.

When Israel Baal Shem Tov, the founder of Chasidism, the spiritual movement that swept eastern European Jewry from the eighteenth century on, was once riding in a coach, the driver said to him, "I am going to stop now and go and cut some oats in that field, for the horses. Please watch out and when you see somebody watching, warn me." The Baal Shem Tov agreed, and the coachman reined in the horses and got down from his seat. He had barely reached the field at the side of the road when the Baal Shem Tov called out, "They see, they see." Needless to say the coachman ran back, got in his seat, and started to drive away. He turned his head and seeing no one, rebuked the Baal Shem Tov saying, "Nobody sees, why did you call out?" The latter, pointed to heaven and said, "Indeed, One does see, One does see."

Robbery

In addition to armed robbery, included within the halakhic definition of *gezel* are acts of exploitation and coercion. So, one who borrows money and then refuses to repay it or fraudently claims to have done so, one who holds trust money and uses it for his own purpose, and tax authorities who exceed the tax levels approved by law or who have discriminatory or arbitrary policies are considered to be robbers.

However, the concept of *gezel* is widened even further to include coveting. The biblical injunction expressed in the Ten Commandments is understood halakhically to include one who covets the property of another and then prepares ways to buy it. Even though this is a mental framework without action, nevertheless Maimonides sees it as having repercussions in the marketplace. "One who lusts after another's property [the version in the Ten Commandments in Deuteronomy] becomes involved in coveting [as in the Ten Commandments in the Book of Exodus] and this brings one to robbery. Coveting the goods, he offers high prices and uses his acquaintances to pressure the owner to sell them. When all this fails, he will have recourse to robbery even as foretold by the prophet Micah, 'They covet houses and rob.' This shows that he who covets transgresses one negative *mitzvah*, while he who buys the object he covets through pressure and coercion transgresses twice." [This would seem to have serious moral implications for corporations or financial institutions engaged in hostile takeovers where the shareholders are pressured through the media or by tantalizing price offers to sell shares they would not like to sell].[4]

The distinction made by Maimonides between theft and robbery is not merely one of semantics but represents a basic spiritual dimension that is expressed in the punishment prescribed in Jewish law for these two types of immoral actions.

A thief is obligated by the Torah (Exodus 23:3) to pay back the value of the stolen goods, in addition to a fine equal to its value.

"The punishment for one who sins against his fellow is that he shall suffer that which he intended to cause to the other . . . he [the thief] shall pay twice the value of [the stolen goods] to the owner. Namely monetary restitution of what he stole, but [he] shall also lose that which the owner stood to lose."[5]

Should he have slaughtered or sold the livestock he stole, the thief is obliged to pay back five times the value for a stolen ox and four times the value for a sheep.

The robber, on the other hand, is liable only for returning the stolen goods (as distinct from paying their monetary value) and a fine to the owner of 20 percent of their value.

This disparity between the punishment of the thief and of the robber of goods of equal value is explained by the Rabbis solely as befitting the difference in the spiritual basis of the two acts. The robber, openly defying man and God, is treated more leniently than the thief, who, by the stealth and secrecy accompanying his immorality, shows a fear only for man, thus denying God as the source of justice and morality. It is this understanding that underscores Judaism's view of theft and robbery not merely as acts against other individuals, serious as that is, but also as a rejection of the Divine injunctions against them. They become transformed, therefore, from rational social demands, necessary for the smooth operation of the market, into acts that destroy the spiritual well-being of mankind. So the Sages of the Talmud taught that the Generation of the Flood was destroyed because of theft and robbery.[6] Finding difficult the connection between the laws of weights and measures in Deuteronomy and the commandment to destroy Israel's archenemy, Amalek, Rashi comments, "When you are lax in regard to weights and measures, I will send the enemy upon you."[7] This spiritual dimension to business dishonesty becomes even more pronounced when one considers Jewish provisions for truth in trading, which include forms of fraud, and its treatment of all the aspects of competition.

TRUTH IN TRADING

All the Codes, *Mishneh Torah*, *Arbaah Turim*, and the *Shulchan Arukh*, provide Jewish laws regulating commerce. Maimonides codifies these as five separate *mitzvot* of the 613 obligatory on every Jew, one a positive one and the other four negative *mitzvot* prohibiting fraudulent actions between buyer and seller.[8]

Din Mekach U'Memkar—The Law of Buying and Selling

This does not refer to a specific action or set of actions, but it is in general a reference to laws concerning commercial transactions and the legal status of the various parties to these transactions. This would concern such issues as when a transaction is complete, how ownership may be acquired, and other legal matters regulating the transfer of assets from one party to another. For example, the Rabbis decreed that unlike real estate, movable property is not acquired by the mere transfer of money but requires some physical or symbolic act of ownership.[9] This distinction, not mentioned in the Bible, does not seem to have any moral implications but merely to represent a technical ruling. However, bearing in mind the Divine nature of the Law, it is not surprising to find in it an important moral consideration. As long as the buyer has not taken physical possession, in one form or another, of the movable asset, there would be a great temptation for the seller not to handle the property of his fellow carefully and scrupulously. After all, Reuven has already received the money for the cow that Shimon bought from him, even though it is still standing in his stall. So naturally he will be inclined not to give that cow the careful attention needed. Perhaps this may cause the cow to die, and he would have caused Shimon a loss, which the Torah forbids. So mere transfer of money is not enough to cause changes in ownership and therefore of responsibility for movable property. This halakhic distinction refers not only to the buying and selling of cows but has to do with the whole wide range of consumer or movable goods, making their sale a matter of moral consequence.

Fraud

Unlike theft and robbery, which are blatant and obvious, preventing fraud is complicated by the fact that it is so often interwoven with normal commerce and trade that it is sometimes difficult to distinguish between legitimate business practice and fraud. The four negative *mitzvot* cited by Maimonides stress, therefore, the moral consideration as a discerning feature for Jewish commercial behavior. All concern *onaah*, which refers to the verse "When you sell to your neighbor or buy from your neighbor's hand, you shall not oppress one another" (Leviticus 25:14). The Hebrew word *onaah* in this verse has been variously translated, according to its legal implications, as fraud, oppression, and overcharging. All three involve different aspects of the marketplace and so have to be considered separately.

The word *onaah* is also used in different biblical verses to refer to the oppression of strangers, widows, and orphans (Exodus 22:20 and Leviticus 19:33). Here the implication is not a question of financial immorality but an exploitation of their legal or emotional weaknesses through one's own status or power. So in the same way, this element of oppression with regard to *onaah* in commerce has to be constantly borne in mind.

Onaat Devarim

Onaat Devarim literally means verbal oppression or verbal fraud. It refers to criticisms of converts or of repentant sinners, in which they are reminded of their former lives. It does, however, also have relevance to trading, as the talmudic definition of this fraud includes the case when one asks a trader or a seller the price or other particulars regarding goods that he has no intention of buying. The seller suffers psychologically through the loss of an expected sale and the loss of time or money involved in providing this information. He had hoped to make a sale, so he was willing to invest in this customer. Since the buyer never had any real intention of buying the goods, however, he is guilty of verbal fraud.

Does this mean today that comparison shopping or random browsing would constitute a violation of the *onaat devarim* principle? It would seem here that considerations of business practices, primarily flowing from the effect of size, would have to be considered. In large firms, department stores, or chain stores, modern merchandising methods may minimize the importance of this issue. Here merchandising methods are actually aimed at encouraging purchases through open display, by a free supply of information or samples, and of floor space devoted simply to the purpose of allowing the consumer to browse. These methods assume that a calculation of costs has been made, in which the seller analyzes his own past experience or that prevalent in the particular industry. On the basis of this data, the investment in time, space, and money of such marketing methods would have been compared to the possibilities of increased sales. In these cases, the *onaat devarim* principle would seem not to apply. However, in the case (and there are many such examples) of a small trader, the *onaat devarim* principle would apply to the consumer who only uses the store for the purpose of discovering styles, prices, and so forth. Such practices are considered a form of business dishonesty. It may well be that there is no recourse to a *bet din*. Nevertheless all the codes express their moral disapproval as expressed by the *Shulchan Arukh*, "Verbal oppression is more serious [morally] than monetary fraud, since the latter may be compensated for, unlike the former. The former affects man's whole being whereas the latter only his money. The prayers of one against the verbal oppression done to him are answered immediately."[10]

Rabbi Yehoshua Falk (eastern Europe, late sixteenth century), in his commentary on the *Shulchan Arukh*, *Meirot Einayim*, points out that the repetition of *onaah* in verse 17 of Leviticus, chapter 25, includes the phrase "thou shall fear the Lord your God." He explains that because the motive behind the speech involved in *onaat devarim* is a secret one, only the fear of the All-Knowing Deity can prevent it, whereas verse 14, dealing with price fraud, does not mention fear of God.

Jewish business ethics consider two further types of fraud, namely that regarding prices and that pertaining to fraudulent practices related to the quality and quantity of goods or services. The term *onaah* is used in halakhic literature based on Leviticus 25:14 primarily to denote cases of price fraud, and it is these that will be considered here first.

Onaat Mamon—Price Fraud

In almost all economic systems and in most societies, the question of fair profit or a fair price (which in economic terms tend to mean the same thing) is a commonly voiced concern. Moralists and social philosophers as well as ordinary laymen are concerned about overcharging, excessive profits, and unfair pricing. It is not surprising therefore that the Jewish sources also devote attention to this issue.

Profit margins and prices can be determined by the reaction and interaction of market forces of supply and demand. These would establish the quantity and type of goods produced, as well as their price and the profit—the return of investment to the supplier of those goods or services. Alternatively, prices and, by definition, the type of goods and the quantities of goods produced can be determined within a planned economy. Here, some centralized agency will allocate production quotas, administer their distribution, and decide what the price will be. Between these two theoretical extremes most economies in the modern world operate within a variety of combinations of the free market with administrative controls.

Judaism itself is not an economic system in a way that either the free market or the planned economy are. So it would be an error to view the Jewish treatment of this question of a fair price, or any other economic issue for that matter, primarily as constituting a theoretical economic framework. Rather it must be seen as a moral framework within which the ethical issues in economics have to be handled just as moral issues flowing from sex, social organization, food, clothing, and so forth, are. Furthermore, Jews have lived in a variety of economic systems and therefore have had to relate the changing economic philosophies or the adoption of new techniques, which bring new moral issues, to their own specific ethical framework. What is of concern here, however, is primarily the price abuse by one party to a market transaction, as well as the ignorance of the other parties, their inability to protect their rights, or their economic strength to withstand exploitation. This is the moral issue regarding price fraud, and it is this aspect that Judaism addresses.

Free marketers would argue that the market mechanism on its own, without any public intervention and without any regulation, will adjust itself in order to minimize or obviate these problems. For example, a shortage of particular goods will lead to a short-term rapid rise in price and perhaps put them beyond the reach of certain members of the society. Market forces, however, will in the long run adjust supply to a new price level, which will restore equilibrium to the market. Alternatively, the demand for labor will lead to a rise in wages, thus enabling weaker and poorer sections of a society to obtain the basket of goods that they desire.

Basically this approach is based on the idea of having one buyer and one seller, both with a free flow of information regarding price and availability, and both unable to determine the price or quantity sold. Unfortunately, in real life this scenario does not always operate. Usually buyers have less information than do sellers as to the conditions of the market and the availability of goods. There are also members of society who because of a lack of education or sophistication are unable to use market information, even where it is available, which places them at a marked disadvantage. Furthermore, the free competition between suppliers does not always exist, since they can cooperate through cartels, trusts, and monopolies to control the market and thereby earn extraordinary profits for themselves. Certain sections of society can lack the economic resources to wait out the time required for the changes in the supply and demand curves that will lead to a new equilibrium price. Alternatively, the goods may be so essential to human existence that a lack means extreme poverty or even death. It is not the theory of the free market that is called into question but rather the ability of this mechanism to answer the market needs of the weak, the poor, and the inefficient.

It would seem that Judaism, on the basis of what we are able to deduce from the halakhic sources, would tend to understand the efficiency of the free-market system. So the Rabbis of the Talmud insisted that the merchant who bought and sold without making a profit was not engaged in any real activity. Rabbi Akivah, one of the Sages of the *Mishnah*, described equilibrium price in a simple variation of the rules of supply and demand, saying, "The market price is the stable one [an equilibrium price], since the buyer would not pay more and the seller would not take less."[11] Nevertheless, these and other indications of an understanding of the efficiency of the free market did not blind the Rabbis to the moral issues involved in questions of profits and pricing. The law of *onaah* (price fraud) is one of their ways of handling these issues. Perhaps the moral turmoil of the former Soviet Union, resulting from the unregulated move to free markets, can serve as a modern-day illustration of the necessity for solving such issues.

The Jewish concept of the "just price" has two aspects, one related to overcharging, that is a price above market price, and the other relating to a profit margin over and above all the expenses involved. The objection against excessive profits measured as one-sixth (*shetut*) above costs appears in the halakhic Codes from the *Mishneh Torah* through the *Arbaah Turim* and the *Shulchan Arukh*. Nevertheless, the responsa reflecting the actual cases brought before rabbinic courts deal, throughout the centuries and in all the countries of the Jewish Exile, primarily with price fraud above market price.

The halakhic concept of *onaah* presupposes the existence of an equilibrium market price. Any excess price, within the limits of one-sixth of that price, is considered to be of no consequence, and the sale or transaction is considered a valid one.

At exactly one-sixth, the injured party can claim *onaah*, and so reclaim the difference between the market price and the price charged. At a price above that, the injured party could cancel the sale, despite the rabbinic condemnation of violating contracts already referred to.

The moral justification for the cutoff point of *shetut* flows from the concept that people are prepared to waive their property rights up to a certain point. So, slight overcharging may be considered to be waived by the average person and therefore should not serve as grounds for litigation. At one-sixth and above, however, people are not prepared to waive their rights and therefore the protection of *onaah* applies. It is true that there are authorities who argue in addition that the markets cannot operate unless some leeway in price variation, the one-sixth cutoff point used, exists. However this seems to be an additional explanation that does not explain many of the halakhic rulings. In contrast, the understanding of the law of *onaah* as consisting of a waiving of a legal economic right and the element of exploitation discussed previously do help to explain all the rulings with regard to *onaah*.

Maimonides and the later authorities following him held that where the disclosure was made of the extent of overcharge, the injured party could not claim the protection of *onaah*. Since he had been told of the overcharge by the seller, acceptance of the transaction showed his waiving of that which was legally his, so that even something over one-sixth of the market price cannot be held as a case for canceling the transaction.[12]

By the same standards, a person who claimed that he had been coerced into the transaction and therefore, even though he had agreed, had not really been prepared to waive his rights, has been upheld in the halakhic rulings as having the right of *onaah* and of canceling a sale to which he had previously agreed. This is based on the classic story in the Talmud of the man who was being chased by bandits, came to a ferryboat, and agreed to pay the boat owner an excessive sum to be transported across the river. Upon arriving to the other side, he claimed "excess above the market price." The boat owner naturally argued that since the man had agreed knowingly to the transaction, he had no legal rights of *onaah*. The passenger's claim that he had had no alternative and was therefore coerced into agreeing was upheld by the Rabbis.[13]

Rabbi Joel Sirkes (1561-1640), one of the important commentators on the codex of *Arbaah Turim*, in his responsa *Bayit Chadash*, has the following ruling. In this case, Reuven had agreed to buy goods even thouh he knew that he was being overcharged. Since he needed the material in order to make up a large order for a customer, he really had no alternative. Now he claims protection of *onaah*. Answer: "Reuven has to pay only the market price, and can claim the excess. It is true that he had agreed to the higher price. However, the seller, understanding that the buyer would pay any sum in view of his large contract, had coerced him and therefore the right of *onaah* is upheld."[14]

The protection of *onaah* against overcharging extends both to the buyer and the seller. Since Torah justice is symmetrical, the same protection is extended to buyer or seller, both having the right to reclaim the overcharge at one-sixth of market price or to cancel the sale for anything in excess of that.[15] It may well be that at first glance, the seller seems to have no need of such protection. After all he is an expert and therefore knows all the forces at play in the market. In real life, however, sellers are not always large conglomerates, nor are buyers always small storekeepers or ignorant consumers. For example, small firms are as often as not suppliers of large corporations and do not always have the same expertise or data available to them concerning market forces as do their customers. Furthermore, in many industries the large corporation is the sole customer of such small firms, making the latter more susceptible to exploitation.

Both moral aspects of *onaah*, the element of coercion and the willingness of people to waive marginal discrepancies in prices, require the free flow of information as to market conditions. It would seem in effect that we are dealing not with price fraud but with the wider issue of exploiting ignorance. So Maimonides rules, and this became normative, that "If the seller says to the purchaser, 'This article that I am selling at 200 is sold in the market at 100,' this is not a case of *onaah*."[16]

At the same time, there exists an obligation on all parties to a transaction to make the other party aware of any discrepancy between the price asked for a good and that prevailing in the market. Failure to make such full disclosure not only entitles the injured party to redress under the law of *onaah* but makes the other party to the transaction guilty of transgressing a negative *mitzvah*, the religious precept of "Thou shall not defraud." This is a spiritual dimension over and above any legal action that may or may not result, reflected in the rabbinic discussions regarding both the minimum monetary value of the transaction for purposes of *onaah* and the question of whether one may *a priori* overcharge.

We have already mentioned that anything less than a *shaveh prutah*, the lowest demonimation of currency, is not the basis for rulings of the *bet din* in cases of theft or robbery. However, there is no minimum value required to make a man guilty of religious transgression before God. Jews are prepared to waive their property rights for such marginal sums so the courts do not have to deal with them. However, it is forbidden to steal even something that is not *shaveh prutah*. The law of *onaah* in regard to legal action remedying overcharging is also limited by this value of *shaveh prutah*. The Rabbis, however, were concerned as to whether it was permissible to overcharge consciously even less than that amount. While people may not pay much attention to such trivial sums and therefore may not require the protection of the law, Judaism concerns itself primarily with the effect on the morality of the person doing the overcharging and, in the larger view, with the spiritual life of society in general. Here the financial value of the crime is irrelevant, since the spiritual damage is in no way determined by the size of the economic fraud.

The Rosh, Rabbi Asher ben Yechiel, in thirteenth-century Spain, whose decisions form the basis for the *Arbaah Turim*, the post-Maimonidean halakhic code, writes, "Men of spiritual integrity who wish to be clean before God should take care that they do not overcharge even something that is not *shaveh prutah*. In the end, one is guity [even if not punishable] of *onaah* and therefore of *gezel* even for sums that are smaller."[17]

Another indication of the concern for spiritual and moral damage seems to lie behind the rulings that extended the protection of the law of *onaah* to those categories of property initially excluded from it by the *Mishnah*: "The law of *onaah* does not apply with regard to real estate, to slaves and to promissory notes" (*Baba Metzia* 4:9).

It must be stressed that this exemption refers only to the obligation to return the *onaah*. It in no way should be understood to permit overcharging. The exemption from paying the one-sixth overcharge flows halakhically from understanding the text of the Bible that says, "When you come to sell or buy from each other, you shall not defraud each other," to apply only to things that could be sold. Since this land was not something that could be sold in perpetuity, it was automatically excluded. So, too, was property belonging to the Temple, because this public property did not have an owner so to speak, and therefore could not be bought and sold. Slaves were regarded in this legal framework to be similar to real estate and were also excluded.

Promissory notes in Jewish law were regarded as mere admissions of debt, not real assets and therefore could not be bought and sold. It was only in the eleventh century that the Rif (Yitzchak Alfasi, Fez, North Africa) wrote that as the merchants view a promissory note as an asset to be bought and sold, it represents a real economic asset rather than merely a recognition of debt. This meant that there was no justification for forbidding the buying and selling thereof.

Nevertheless, the exclusion of real estate from the protection of *onaah* was seen to apply only to the one-sixth level above market price. The rulings of most of the authorities were that where excessive overcharging was concerned, real estate too was protected.

> Concerning the house which Reuven bought from Shimon at twice the market price, you should know that the law of *onaah* does not exist in the sale of land. The Rif, has claimed, in accordance with the ruling of the Rambam, that a sale of land cannot be voided even if there is great overcharging. However Rabbenu Tam [the *Tosafist*—grandson of Rashi in twelfth-century Franco-Germany] stated that in the case of twice the market rate, *onaah* exists even in real estate. This is the correct decision [other authorities have agreed with the Rosh only if the overcharge was more than 100 percent].[18]

It is important to note that all the authorities, whether they agree or not with the Rosh that in excess overcharging there is *onaah* even in transactions of real estate, hold that it is not permissible to a priori overcharge.

In view of the difficulty in gauging market price, it may seem that this protection against price fraud through *onaah* is irrelevant in the modern economy. However even the most superficial survey of modern merchandising will show that this is not so, and even today, there are many transactions that have to be referred to rabbinic authorities for a halakhic ruling. Some such cases are presented here in order to demonstrate the scope of the problem.

In many outlying areas or even in the suburbs of a large town, one will find that the price of goods is usually higher than items of the same quality or quantity in the center of town. Shall we say that the merchants in these areas lay themselves open to the law of *onaah* by overcharging? This is not only a question of the costs of moving the goods or the service from one area to another, but often flows simply from the monopoly status enjoyed by the merchant in these areas. Free marketeers would probably argue that, after all, if it is worth the consumer's while, he will make his way to the center of the town and buy the cheaper goods there. Since he does not do so, this shows that he is willing to pay the price or, in halakhic terms, to waive the overcharge. Bearing in mind the question of coercion, lack of information, and inequality between the two parties, which underpins the whole concept of *onaah*, it seems that despite this view there is a moral problem involved. Therefore we find authorities who rule that the local merchants can be made to conform to the law of *onaah*.

Even within a town, the same goods are often sold in different stores at different prices. It is true that the large, elegant firm has additional costs, such as advertising, higher labor costs, extra floor space, fixture, fittings, and so on. This alone does not seem to entitle such firms to fix their prices above those of the market. There are however many different factors comprising pricing policy, and so we find various opinions expressed by the Rabbis. Some were not sure that the law of *onaah* applied. After all, the consumer knows that in these stores the price is much higher for the same article, and therefore by doing business there, he has waived his rights. The common knowledge that there exists a price differentiation between the stores provides the information needed in *onaah*. Possession of this knowledge gives the consumer the ability to judge and therefore to decide for himself, so there is no *onaah*. Other authorities have argued that in many of the larger firms, the consumer receives extra information regarding the goods, guidance on how the articles are to be used, and perhaps even better repair service. In actual fact, therefore, the goods here are not identical, and since one is not buying the same article, *onaah* does not apply.[19]

A particularly interesting example is that of transactions conducted through public auction. Very often the customs, police, and other public authorities sell goods that they have accumulated or confiscated. These sales are usually conducted through public auctions. In many countries, a common form of selling real estate is through public auction. Antiques, art, and many other specialized articles are also sold in this way. The halakhic question in such sales arises when a person who bought an article at an auction paid more than the market price for it. Is there a claim of *onaah* if the overcharge was over one-sixth? This is dealt with in the responsa of the Sho'el U'Meishiv (Rabbi Shaulshon, eastern Europe, nineteenth century). In this discussion two important facts are considered basic to the law of *onaah*: the existence of a market price and the knowledge of all the parties to the terms of sale. He writes:

> Everybody knows that in sales of this type, one sometimes pays less than the market price and sometimes more. The same applies to the people who put their goods on auction. Sometimes they receive less than the market price and other times more. The whole concept of the auction is based on this knowledge and on the assumption that on one article or one type of good, a person will lose something but will gain on another article, relative to the market price. Therefore, anybody entering this kind of transaction cannot claim protection of *onaah* if he paid more than or received less than the market price.[20]

Many educational institutions and charitable organizations conduct economic activities that also involve questions of fair pricing. The issue is clouded by the charitable nature of the seller. Nevertheless it is necessary to consider even here the halakhic question of *onaah*. It is possible to argue that because the *onaah* law does not apply to *hekdesh* (Temple property), charitable institutions should be exempt from the same law. Furthermore, one could argue that people do not object to paying more than the market price if the proceeds go to charity, thus waiving their right to the overcharge.

The question was raised with Rabbi Menashe Klein (New York, twentieth century) as to whether books sold by the library of a *yeshivah* were protected by the law of *onaah*. The librarian wrote that he often sold excess copies of books at a price above the market price. The rabbi, in answering the question, ruled:

> The laws of *onaah* do apply. The customers of this library are *yeshivah* students and they assumed that the books being sold were being sold through the yeshivah library at below market prices. This is not the same as those charitable auctions where people go prepared to pay much more simply because of the cause behind it [in that case one may assume that their purchases are acts of charity rather than business transactions as the price factor is irrelevant]. Since in this case, the consumer's assumption was that the books would be at least market price and even below it, *onaah* applies and the charitable status of the *yeshivah* does not give it the same protection enjoyed by *hekdesh*.[21]

Most authorities do not hold that charitable funds today have the same legal status as that enjoyed by the Temple property. For example, the former do not have the right to transfer funds from one purpose to another without the agreement of the donors, except in those cases where the donor has made a general gift.

Nonprice Fraud

Over and above the question of price fraud, there is a whole spectrum of transactions in the market in which the quality and quantity of the goods sold are not as specified by the contract or as advertised. In the Jewish framework these forms of fraud are dealt with as categories of *geneivat daat* (literally, stealing another's mind), *mekach ta'ut* (fraudulent sale), and *lifnei iver* (a stumbling block in the path of the blind). As in the case of *onaah*, here too the issue revolves primarily around the question of full disclosure; to what extent is the buyer or seller obligated to reveal flaws in the nature of the goods to be bought or sold. The Romans formulated a concept that became incorporated into most of the legal systems of the world, *caveat emptor*—Let the buyer beware. This puts the onus of all inquiries regarding the quality of the goods sold fully on the buyer. This idea of "let the buyer beware" has also been incorporated into much of free-market thinking. Buyer and seller are considered to be equal. Both are obligated to do the necessary research in order to see what they are buying or selling. The assumption is that those engaged in the market have already studied all the trends and made themselves cognizant of all the features concerning the transaction. If somebody cannot be bothered to do so, is unwilling to pay the price thereof, or even unable to get that information, then that person should not be involved in the transaction at all or should have others do it for him. The popular phrase "if you can't stand the heat, keep out of the kitchen" is applied to many transactions, especially in the financial markets. Halakhic rulings, however, place the onus of revealing defects and shortcomings squarely on the shoulders of the seller. It is always a case of "let the seller beware" that he is not defrauding the other party in any way in the transaction.

Geneivat Daat

The marketplace relies on certain ways and means to convey information regarding prices, quality, and type of the goods or services offered. These may be very simple and primitive methods, such as word of mouth or crying one's wares in the street or squares of a city, or they may be the highly sophisticated means of modern mass-media advertising, or other intermediate forms. Nevertheless, they all share the same moral issue. Obviously, there is no ethical issue involved in publishing data regarding the availability of goods and services, nor is there any objection to advertising or packaging that presents the goods favorably and attracts buyers. However, there is always the danger that in the advertising process, the true nature of the goods, their relative price, and any defects they may have are withheld from the buyer, or presented in a distorted form so as to deprecate alternative goods and services unfairly, thus defrauding the consumer. The buyer, too, is not always free of this moral problem. He may reverse the process by denigrating the quality of the goods sold or by quoting low prices supposedly available elsewhere.

It is precisely because advertising, in its widest connotation, is so intrinsic to the whole merchandising process that the element of fraud is all too often lost. The difficulty of making a clear demarcation between legitimate marketing practices and those that defraud contributes to the blurring of the border between permissible and nonpermissible acts. This helps often to legitimize in the mind of the defrauder actions against other religions or social or ethnic groups that would be unthinkable within his own social unit. This immoral taxation then becomes a way of life, permitting unethical acts against all.

Moshe Chaim Luzzatto (Italy, early eighteenth century) saw the insidiousness of this type of fraud when he wrote in *Mesillat Yesharim*, one of the classical moralistic works in Judaism:

> Most people are not outright thieves simply taking their neighbor's property and putting it into their own premises. However, in their daily business dealings, most of them have a taste of stealing, whenever they permit themselves to make an unfair profit at the expense of another, claiming that such profit has nothing to do with theft. It is both good and honest to do everything possible to show the buyer the real value and beauty of the article. However for one to cover and hide a defect is nothing less than deceit and is forbidden.[22]

Halakhically these nonpermissible acts are *geneivat daat* and constitute a form of theft. As in the more easily recognized acts of theft and robbery, here, too, the sources devote themselves both to the educational or spiritual injunction against such actions, and the provision of legal compensation for them in the form of *mekach ta'ut*—the fraudulent sale—whereby the injured party may cancel the sale.

Judah the Pious, one of the leaders of the medieval Jewish moralistic movement, in his book *Sefer Chasidim* writes that "the buyer [negotiating a purchase] should not say, 'These goods are inferior, these goods are worthless.'"[23]

Later authorities advised that, in order to shield oneself from *geneivat daat*, one should train oneself spiritually. One rabbi wrote that a person should conduct his business affairs in such a way that all who deal with him will know that his original price offer is also his last one, so as to prevent both sides from arguing the price down or up.[24] Another ruled halakhically that it is permissible to praise one's goods or services slightly, but that exaggerated or misleading advertising is an act of theft.[25]

Since Judaism does not rely merely on education and moralizing, it is not surprising to find these ideas translated into practical legal rulings.

These rulings that appear in all the codes make quite clear both the moral imperatives determining Jewish behavior in this ill-defined area and the legal consequences to be imposed by the rabbinical courts for infringement of these rules. In this regard it should be noted that *geneivat daat* does not presuppose or require intent to defraud in order to make restitution necessary.

Yosef Caro's *Shulchan Arukh*, codifying the discussion of the Talmud, which flows through all the other codes and is included in the responsa, both earlier and later, writes as follows:

> It is forbidden to defraud people [this explicitly including idolators often considered to have put themselves beyond the pale of civilized behavior] in buying and selling or to steal their minds [*geneivat daat*]. For example, if there is a defect in the article being sold, one is obligated to reveal this to the buyer. [This obligation exists over and above forbidding concealment of defects.]
>
> So one may not sell [because of *geneivat daat*] the skin of an animal which dies of natural causes and present it as being that of one ritually slaughtered [the latter being of superior quality]. Nor may one sell a cask of wine with oil floating on top [this in view of the incident of one who bought such a cask for a party, thinking that he had oil which was more significant, with which to pleasure his guests. When he found that there was only a layer of oil, his shame was so great that he hung himself]. One may not mix a small quantity of inferior fruit with a large one of quality fruit in order to sell it all as first grade. This applies even to the mixture of newly ripened fruit with older fruit [considered to be better quality] even if the latter are more expensive, since the buyer wishes to age [or dry] them himself [and the mixture defrauds him].

> It is forbidden to beautify neither the man, nor the animal nor the utensils. For example, to dye the beard of an old slave in order to make him look younger at the sale or to feed the animals special bran which bloats them and makes their hides gloss and firm . . . not to paint old utensils to make them appear new.[26]

The examples provided by the *Shulchan Arukh* should not mislead us as to the importance of their implications for modern merchandising. The *Shulchan Arukh* is categorically prohibiting any form of advertising or display that makes unsubstantiated claims for goods or that exaggerates the quality of the goods or conceals any defects.

This is something over and above defrauding through defective weights and measures, which is simple theft. In the present case, the emphasis is on the efforts of the seller to create a false image in the mind of the buyer that will lead him to purchase the goods. It should not be difficult for us to make the mental transaction from the simple examples given here to the false packaging that makes something look better or bigger than it really is, or to the many moral problems created by modern advertising.

The issue of *geneivat daat*, however, goes beyond advertising in marketing. The explosion of the service industries and information, and the increased sophistication of the financial and money markets all over the world make the question of *geneivat daat* a paramount one in modern business morality.

It is well known, both in the accounting and consultancy professions, that financial reports can be presented so as to give a desired picture that may nor may not always be absolutely true. The window dressing of financial data would therefore seem to be a clear case of *geneivat daat*. The current Hebrew accounting phrase, *leyapot*—to make beautiful—makes this clearer than the polite English window dressing. The techniques are many and varied but all of them have the same purpose in mind, which is to present a picture favorable to the seller, underwriter, or entrepreneur and to hide any flaws, defects, or liabilities from the potential investor. For example, changes in the way inventory is calculated, the shifting of income or expense from one period to another, and alternative methods of calculating the depreciation of fixed assets all change the profits of the firm without any relationship to the results of its operations. So, too, hiding the true personality of the major investors through straw corporations or offshore corporations, together with a lack of disclosure concerning future earnings and past performance or other weaknesses and strengths, creates a different price for the shares of the corporation, thus leading to a different behavior. The institution of the Securities and Exchange Commission in the United States was part of the Roosevelt administration's reaction to the widespread fraud in the American Stock Exchanges prior to the Great Depression. Many other countries have not followed the American pattern, and thus leave the individual shareholder with less access to protection and to parties involved in it, with great opportunities for *geneivat daat*. The Jewish insistence on the responsibilities of the seller to make clear the true position of the corporation would seem to make public supervision and a disclosure in corporate reports part of a financial market regulated by *Halakhah* in order to prevent *geneivat daat*.

In all cases of *geneivat daat*, where one party can show that he suffered a loss, the sale may be canceled as a *mekach ta'ut*.

> If one sells his fellow by weight or by measure or by number and errs even slightly [differentiated from stealing or robbery which require a value, *shaveh prutah*, for litigation], the transaction may be canceled without any limitation of time. [It is interesting to note that violations of the laws of *kasrut*, food ritually pure for Jews to eat, require some minimum quantity, whereas the eating or possession of leavened bread on Passover is transgressed by any amount.] This is different from *onaah* since that applies only to price fraud [and requires *shaveh prutah* and within the time required to get expert valuation of the article].
>
> One who sells ground, slaves, cattle, or movable goods and [the buyer] finds a defect in them which he was not aware of at the time of the sale, the buyer may return it even after many years since this is a *mekach ta'ut*.

These decisions of the *Shulchan Arukh* are part of the remedy available to one who suffers from *geneivat daat*.[27]

COMPETITION

In the main, the free competition between seller or producers of goods and services on the one hand and limitations on it through government or communal regulation on the other are seen as questions of economic efficiency. Indeed the experience of the past decades in very different countries–ranging from China to the USSR and Eastern

Europe, to the socialist economies of the United Kingdom, France, and Israel, to the underdeveloped economies of Africa and Asia—has shown that competitive markets are most efficient in providing the quantity and quality of goods that the market desires, at prices it is prepared to pay.

Limiting the analysis of competition solely to its economic aspects may, however, lead us to ignore the moral and ethical effects of the lack of the free market and of the alternative methods of restraining such competition. Some employees and some entrepreneurs may suffer a loss or even the complete destruction of their livelihood, both from the competition between existing producers and from that presented by new technologies or the entry of new firms. Restraints on competition, while perhaps preventing such losses, will impose an unfair burden on the general public in the form of higher prices and inferior goods.

While generally speaking, Jewish legal sources are prepared to let society choose whichever type of economic system it desires, the concern has always been that of morality. Unfortunately much recent research on the halakhic perspective of competition, such as that of Levine and Lieberman, has focused on examining the economic effects of these perspectives.[28] I have found that in my own work *With All Your Possessions: Jewish Ethics and Economic Life*, published some years ago, the macroeconomic implications of competition led me to make a similar analysis.[29] Further consideration both of the halakhic sources and the questions raised during the course of many lectures has, however, made it clear that all that concerned the rabbis throughout the centuries was the degree to which competition constitutes dishonesty. Competition can take the shape of price cutting, nonprice competition, advertising, or the entry of new firms or techniques. Irrespective of which type of competition is examined, it is this element of potential theft, understood in its widest form, that is the basis of rabbinic considerations. This makes their rulings even more substantive and relevant, since this moral issue of theft applies to whatever economic system society chooses.

Maimonides included the discussion of free entry both of new local firms and of "foreign ones" in the laws of neighbors, since the issue is basically whether or not the veteran entrepreneurs have acquired a property right for a monopoly for the pursuit of their business. In this way competition is viewed as a question of *nezek* or damage to the property of others. Yosef Caro, in the *Shulchan Arukh*, does not include the question of price or nonprice competition in *hilkhot mekach u'memkar*—laws of buying and selling—as does Maimonides, but rather in the separate category of price fraud and the fraudulent sale, once again demonstrating the halakhic concern with the moral as opposed to the purely economic questions involved.

Basically the problem is twofold: namely, the morality of an entrepreneur depriving another of his livelihood through competition contrasted with the morality of depriving society of the benefits of lower prices, new products, or improved ones through restraints on competition, protecting entrepreneurs or workers.

Since the tension between these two is difficult to define clearly and consistently, the real dishonesty is not always easy to determine, so it is not surprising to find a wide spectrum of halakhic decisions in this area.

> Rabbi Yehudah says the merchant may not distribute roasted ears of corn or nuts, to the children [or in another variant to the servants] since he accustoms them to buy from him [thereby harming the business of the other merchants. However] the sages permit the practice. [Furthermore Rabbi Yehudah says] nor may he lower prices. [But] the sages say, The memory of the shopkeeper who lowers prices shall be blessed [since he benefits the community by lowering prices].[30]

This *mishnah* is the basis for the rabbinic discussion of price competition and of the halakhic rulings in the Codes and the responsa. Actually two types of competition are considered here. Before considering the issue of price cutting, Rabbi Yehudah presents the additional problem of attracting customers through the giving of gifts of nuts and cereals. While this seems to be a problem of petty trading or primitive economies, even a casual glance at modern merchandising will show how it is reflected in many forms of interfirm competition. Banks, with an excess of liquidity, offer new depositors gifts such as vacuum cleaners, toasters, and so forth, while retail chain stores offer participation in lotteries, foreign trips, or cash and other prizes for those purchasing above a certain level or within a certain period. The variations of this form of what is commonly known as nonprice competition are almost endless. Actually this is, in economic terms, tantamount to price cutting, since the consumers, or some of them, are getting goods or services below the usual or advertised price.

The basis of the difference of opinion between Rabbi Yehudah and the Rabbis has been seen by some to reflect two opposing schools of mishnaic economic thought, with the former representing protectionism and the latter free marketers.[31] Unfortunately this view, while interesting and convenient, is somewhat dimmed by the subsequent discussion in the Talmud and the responsa. It is also rendered irrelevant when reading the prior and subsequent *mishnayot* in the same chapter, all of which deal with fraud, theft, and false advertising. Rabbi Yehudah is seen as being concerned with the possible theft of the livelihood of others. The Rabbis permitted the nonprice competition since Reuven can say to Shimon, "I distribute nuts, you can distribute corn." It is this possibility of the competitor emulating the gifts of his competitor that makes the action morally acceptable. In all those cases where the act cannot be duplicated, the Rabbis agree with Rabbi Yehudah that it is not permissible.

The same moral reasoning is to be found in the discussion about the price cutting opposed by Rabbi Yehudah but encouraged and praised by the Rabbis. Rabbi Menachem HaMeiri (Provence, thirteenth century) in his Talmud commentary, *Beit HaBechirah*, holds that for Reuven to reduce his prices with the intent to raise them again once he had attracted new customers, was not, as may be thought, a priori a case of *geneivat daat* and was permissible.[32]

Rashi comments that the Rabbis in the *Mishnah* maintain that such individual price cutting will lead all the other merchants to similar actions. Some authorities indeed limit the ability to cut prices only to such cases where the action leads to others following and so reducing the general price level. In this way the law is offsetting the public welfare against the loss suffered by the other merchant.[33]

In modern merchandising, a firm will often reduce the price of some articles even below cost, defined as "loss leaders," in order to attract customers who will then purchase other goods. Other firms will specialize in selling discounted goods. One would like to argue that this would be in accordance with the opinion of the Sages in the above *mishnah*, which became the halakhic norm. Rashi's stipulation would seem to be met by the empirical evidence that both these actions do in fact lead to a decline in the general price level, thus benefiting the consumer.

It would seem, however, that where the sale is at such low prices that nobody else can compete, the *Meiri* quoted above holds, and so do many other authorities, that the price cutting is forbidden. This would be analogous not to price competition, but to "dumping" in order to drive others out of business.

Previously the *onaah* concept of overcharging was discussed in relation to the market price, but this question of price competition is closely linked to the other aspect of *onaah* relating to pricing policy of the firm. The same acceptance of one-sixth as being the cutoff point for price fraud is also used as a limitation to profit over and above costs. This may be seen from the ruling of the *Shulchan Arukh*, repeating the talmudic discussion in *Baba Metzia* and those of the *Mishneh Torah* and the Tur:

> He who deals in truth does not have [the protection of] the law of *onaah*. For example [a merchant says to the buyer] this article costs me so much and so much and my profit margin is so much [here the profit is a function of costs, not of market price, so] if he bought goods of varying quality, he does not have to sell each article at a different price but may fix their price as a whole. If he bought ten lengths of cloth at ten dinarim, but some are worth more than a dinar and others less he does not have to calculate the value of each piece separately [and then add his profit margin] but may consider them as a whole [even though some are being overpriced]. He may add to his cost, price transport, porterage and his lodging. He may not add his own profit to his cost but must declare [to the customer], "I earn such and such a profit margin [over the total cost]," so that there is no claim of *onaah*.[34]

Maimonides limits this disclosure and the one-sixth limit to cost-related profits to basic commodities, and so do most authorities, except that the definition of essential articles varies among them.

Free Entry

Competition through the entry of new firms or new techniques is tantamount, in economic terms, to price cutting, since the new firms lower the general level of prices or prevent them from rising. Alternatively, they introduce new or better products, thus in effect lowering prices of the old ones. In the halakhic framework, however, they seem to introduce a new concept of *nezek*–damage to the property rights of other, as distinct from the fraud, involved in price distortion or overcharging. The basic issue seems to be, therefore, to what extent the old firms acquired a property right, which the newcomers are, so to speak, stealing from them.

Those authorities who objected to free entry based themselves on a moral objection voiced by the talmudical authorities. This was summarized by the comment of Rabbi Acha the son of Rabbi Chanina, on Ezekiel 18:15, "hath not defiled his neighbor's wife." This verse, depicting one of the merits of a just man, was understood by Rabbi Acha to refer to one who did not infringe on his neighbor's livelihood. This is bolstered by the rabbinic treatment of the biblical comment (Deuteronomy 19:14) against removing a neighbor's landmark (the stones that served as the boundary markers between fields)–*hasagat gevul.* Since the Torah had already forbidden theft, which *hasagat gevul* is, the Sages taught that whoever annexed his neighbor's domain in the Land of Israel was guilty of both transgressions, theft and *hasagat gevul.* Since land was the primary source of people's livelihood, this ruling was easily applied by some authorities to infringement on the source of another's wealth through competition of entry. Furthermore, forestalling or preempting the negotiations of another firm or individual for goods or for supplying services was similarly frowned upon. This may be seen in the talmudic dictum "a poor man was negotiating for the sale of a cake and he who forestalls him is called an evil person."[35]

On the basis of these three ideas, *nezek*, *hasagat gevul*, and forestalling, there are authorities who upheld the right of the veteran entrepreneurs against encroachment either by new competitors or by price cuts, seen by them as forms of fraud. Conversely, there are authorities who, while accepting these moral injunctions, ruled that the veterans did not possess such a property right protecting their trade, or where they did so, it was overshadowed by the welfare of the community served by the competition.

It seems natural to distinguish between the free entry into the market of local factors and the competition offered by outside firms. After all, the local corporations are members of the same community and share the same rights as those of the veteran firms. Outsiders, firms from foreign communities or different states or communities, may seem to be in a different category, since their rights differ from the local veteran firms. Indeed, the halakhic sources discuss these two types of competition separately.

Local Competition

Regarding the local firms, we read in the Talmud, "It is permitted for a man to set up shop alongside shop, grain mill alongside grain mill, bath house alongside bath house, and the existing firms cannot prevent it. The new entrepreneurs can argue that you conduct your business on your property and I do the same."[36]

It should be noted that the rationale behind this free-entry principle is the right of the people to pursue their livelihood on their own property. Therefore, the veterans do not have the right to limit this. Actually the discussion on free entry is a corollary to the limitation of economic activity so as not to cause ecological damage, or to limit such activities to special industrial zones, so as not to cause such damage.

Maimonides, and all the other codes, rule in accordance with this opinion of the Talmud: "If there already exists in this courtyard [or in this town] an artisan, or a bath house, or a mill, and one of the inhabitants opens a similar business, the veteran cannot prevent him saying, 'you destroy my livelihood.'"[37]

Throughout the Far East, the Middle East, and North Africa, one can see similar marketing arrangements, which, apart from being exotic, produce a far more competive market than the shopping centers common to modern town planning, with their emphasis on one firm for each type of business.

This free-entry ruling seems to contradict another talmudic decision that a fisherman can force others to withdraw a distance equal to that of a fish's swim from his nets.[38] Rashi, however, demonstrates the difference between the two cases when he comments:

> The fishermen [devoted time and skill—a form of investment], knows the hole where the fish wait, and puts his bait there since he knows that the fish are used to swimming to this place for food. When he spreads his nets therefore he is confident that he has captured them. [Another fisherman spreading his nets nearby is therefore stealing the property of the first one and this is forbidden.] In the case of the new firm, however, the owner can say to the veteran "whichever customer comes to me will do so and whoever comes to you will do so."

An attempt to use the fisherman argument in the case of a village with a single store is rejected. The argument was that just as once the fisherman has cast his net he is assured of the fish, so too the owner of the store is assured of the patronage of the villagers. With respect to this, the Avnei Nezer (Avraham of Sochochow), explains that whereas the original fisherman has a sort of property right, no such right exists here, since the money of the customer belongs to him completely and the shop owner has no share therein.

This aspect of competition and the halakhic views thereof as an issue of damage to a property right or to the theft of someone's wealth are well illustrated by the responsum of Rabbi Zalman Margolis (Poland, early nineteenth century):

> It would seem that the problem of one who opens a store next to [the existing one] of his neighbor, has to be seen in relation to the discussion between Rabbi Jossi and the Sages in the *Mishnah*, covering the obligation of the planter of a tree to distance it from the existing water cistern of his neighbor. There, Rabbi Jossi holds [and that is the halakhic rule] that each person has the right to do in his domain whatever he wants to, even though he causes delayed damage [the time it takes for the roots of the tree to reach the walls of the cistern]. The Rabbis, however, maintain that since his money [the tree], is causing the damage, even if it is delayed, he has to move. The fact that in the case of the tree, the argument concerns monetary damage whereas here it concerns only the prevention of earning a profit, [either a reduced future profit or by the newcomer preventing him from earning a profit by opening his store], is irrelevant. In our case, there is not even delayed damage [only a reduction in earning], so that it is obvious that the veteran cannot prevent the newcomer from opening a store alongside him.[39]

Infringing on another's livelihood through competition may take the form of taking away his workers, and this raises questions of morality as we learn from the following answer given by Rabbi Avraham, the chasidic *Admor* of Sochochow, to Rabbi Shlomo the head of the rabbinic courts in Neustad, eastern Europe, at the turn of the century.

> Question. Reuven has a factory for producing buttons and uses an agent to hire workers. Now Shimon has established a similar factory and wishes to hire away Reuven's workers, even though it is possible to hire others; however, these are experienced people, so that new workers will be more costly. I would argue that Shimon may not do so on the basis of the ruling in the *Shulchan Arukh* that where a poor man was negotiating a cake for sale, one who forestalls him is called an evil man. This applies both to cases of hiring and to the buyer as we learn from the discussion by the Mordechai (Rabbi Mordechai ben Hillel, Franco-Germany, late thirteenth century) that

when a seller rejects the price offered to him by a potential buyer and another buyer enters and buys the goods, he is not considered evil, since no loss devolved on the seller; this indicating that where such a loss does occur one must desist from entering ongoing negotiation.

Answer. In truth, we have to say that such forestalling is forbidden only when the original parties would otherwise have completed their transaction. However as long as the seller does not want to sell to the original buyer, or a buyer does not want to buy from the seller, there is no law of forestalling. After all, there is nothing wrong with people selling their goods to whom they wish. It is also wrong to view the seller as lacking in faith in Divine Providence for his rejecting the original offer in favor of another higher offer [as would be the case where one party broke an agreement]. After all, the workers had never agreed to work for him forever, nor had he agreed to retain them forever. Rather the hiring was on a contingency basis, so that if either of them wishes to either employ others or go to work for another firm, they are not among those who lack faith.

There is nothing to prevent the new factory owner from hiring workers already employed by Reuven. This is just as in the case in *Baba Batra*, where a new storekeeper can say to the veterans, "whichever customer comes to you will do so and whosoever comes to me will do so." So too, all employers are free to hire these workers. This is not similar to the case where both parties to a transaction have already agreed to a price. Then a third party cannot intervene, because without his intervention the original transaction would have definitely been fulfilled.

The complaint of Reuven that new workers which he may have to hire are less efficient and more costly is also not tenable. We know that [the *Shulchan Arukh* and other authorities have ruled that] a parent may hire a better and more accomplished teacher for his children [this makes it permissible for Shimon to compete for the more qualified workers.] Furthermore the Rama [Rabbi Moshe Isserles, the authoritative Ashkenazic gloss on Yosef Caro's *Shulchan Arukh*], has ruled that cheaper goods [offered in the course of negotiations] is like finding a lost article and therefore the law of forestalling does not apply.[40]

Halakhic support for free entry disappears, however, either when no benefit accrues to the public or where the veteran firm is faced with the total loss of its source of income, as opposed to diminished profits or the prevention of earning increased profits. So a modern Israeli discussion prevented a competitor from hiring the blockman from another butcher, when it was shown that the whole business would fail were he to leave.[41]

The right of a worker to leave his employment whenever he wishes to do so is entrenched in Jewish thought, since Jews are slaves to no one except to God. Halakhically, what has to be adjudicated is the damage done to the employer. On the other hand, such a restraining decision could sometimes mean that a skilled worker might never be able to leave in order to set up his own business or to better himself with a different employer. Dayan Weiss of Manchester, later of the *Eidah Hachareidit* in Jerusalem (the court of the separatist Orthodox groups), limited such restrictions to a certain time period depending on the circumstance in those cases where the worker competed through the customers of his previous employer.[42]

The definition of diminished profits, so often crucial to the halakhic decision regarding competition, is a very generous one, not restricted to subsistence earnings. It seems to depend on the socioeconomic status of the plaintiff. So, Rashi considers that even a reduction in the standard of living as a result of competition would not be permitted. The Chatam Sofer ruled to prevent the entry of a new firm if it would reduce the established firm's earnings below the average earnings of its peer group. This, it must be stressed, is not based on economic considerations, but rather is an implementation of "You shall love your neighbor" and the resultant Jewish principle of charity. While poor people are to be helped only to maintain a certain minimum standard, as was explained in the previous chapter, a prosperous person who becomes impoverished or the poor descendants of a wealthy family have to be assisted to maintain some semblance of their former status, and charity has to include "even a horse to ride on." There would seem to be a communal obligation, therefore, to provide for the displaced businessman or the worker made redundant as a result of competition, not only concerning that which is needed to keep body and soul together, but also the assistance to offset the mental and psychological damage suffered as a result of "becoming redundant."

All rabbinic authorities, including those who were most lenient with regard to competition that reduced profits, have ruled against free entry or price cutting, whether local or from "foreign firms," which resulted in the destruction of the veteran's livelihood. The simplest example of this is seen in the case of a cul de sac in which the customers have to pass the new store before they can come to that of the veteran. The Chatam Sofer maintained, however, that the mere physical obstacle, namely, that the new firm was situated at the open end of the street, was not sufficient to prevent the competition.

> It was necessary, in addition, that it be the kind of business where the owner or his agent stands in front of the store and by shouting or other means entices the customers. In this case, the site of the new business is important since it prevents the customer from continuing to the old store. However in tailor shops, for example, where no such enticement exists, we cannot apply the ruling of *avi'asaf* [preventing new firms at the entrance to a cul de sac].[43]

It is interesting to speculate whether modern advertisement would constitute such enticement in the opinion of the Chatam Sofer.

Free Entry of "Foreign Firms"

The moral question of foreign competition seems to be more complicated than that of the business activities of local entrepreneurs. After all, the latter are all members of the same community and tend to view the competition of outsiders with far more resentment and anger. The Chatam Sofer (Hungary, late eighteenth century) writes that "all the people of a town have the right to be able to earn their livelihood there."[44]

While they are prepared to waive their rights in favor of local entrepreneurs and permit new firms to enter the market, it may be argued that they are not prepared to do so with regard to strangers. This objection to the free entry of foreigners is an old-new one. Most nations even today limit the freedom of nonnationals to work or engage in business primarily as a means to protect the local workers or entrepreneurs. On the other hand, the outsiders are, as often as not, prepared to offer their goods and services at a lower rate, and it is really this price or wage competition to which the local residents object. In the past such resentment has led, in most economies, to racial persecution of the foreigners and to legislation banning their entry. Tariff walls and customs levies are simply other forms of preventing such competition. Many countries use technical requirements and quality control to prevent foreign imports, which are no different really from the free entry of the foreigners themselves. While such protective measures keep local jobs and enable local firms to continue despite their inefficiency, the general population suffers from higher prices and or inferior goods. It requires, therefore, achieving a balance between the welfare of the general society and that of those workers and firms who profit from the protection. The ethical questions, therefore, are, do there exist special property rights providing such protection, and is it moral to allow the attack on these rights posed by the competition?

Rabbi Huna, the son of Yehoshua, argued successfully in the talmudic discussion that a foreigner has full rights of residence, including the right to compete, provided he pays the local taxes. (To allow freedom of entry without a corresponding participation in the tax burden would be immoral and unfair.)

Payment of the taxes, however, does not solve the problem of the foreign price-wage competition, so that an additional decision is needed, as we find in the landmark responsum of Rabbi Yosef Ibn Migash of eleventh-century Spain, which became the basis for those opinions permitting free entry.

> The local businessmen can prevent outsiders from operating similar business [even if they pay the local taxes], provided there is no loss caused to the consumers—for example if the outsiders sell their goods for the same price as the locals [in this case these suffer a loss with no corresponding benefit, which makes little sense. Jewish law does not require one to beggar himself in order to give charity to another, which would simply be exchanging one poor man for another]. If however they offer the same goods more cheaply or provide goods or services of better quality, then they cannot be prevented from operating. The reason for this is that we cannot make a ruling that will benefit a small minority [the local businessman] at the expense of the community.[45]

The opinion of Ibn Migash highlights the clash of interests represented by competition. If we consider the loss caused to the veteran firms by new firms or by price cutting as a form of theft, then we would similarly have to consider as theft the imposition of higher prices, inferior goods, or a more narrow choice on to the general public by restraints on competition. Since Judaism is a community-oriented religion, intent on creating a "nation of priests and a holy people," rather than merely pious or saintly individuals, the community acquires, as it were, property rights, which have to be maintained just as do those of the individual.

This aspect of public good or communal welfare is highlighted in many different responsa. For example:

> In a certain town where there was no *mikveh* [ritual bath for women], an individual built one at his own expense. He charged high entrance fees thus bringing many to err. So the community built itself a *mikveh* and reduced the prices. The individual then claimed that they were destroying his livelihood and therefore the competition should be forbidden. We cannot uphold this restriction, because it concerns a *mikveh* [which is obligatory on all] and furthermore we cannot allow a whole community to have to be dependent on the welfare of one individual.[46]

The Bach (Rabbi Joel Sirkes) maintains that even the arunda (a monopoly right discussed below), which the community has given to an individual or a group of individuals, can be rescinded, if it is to the public good or for the welfare of the poor.[47]

The arunda referred to in the responsum was a restrictive right recognized in many Ashkenazic communities of central and eastern Europe, from the Middle Ages down to the nineteenth century. It existed also in the Sephardic communities of North Africa and the Middle East, where it was known as *marufiyah*, literally Arabic for "friend." In essence, these were restrictive arrangements whereby an entrepreneur obtained a monopoly or near monopoly to trade or manufacture certain goods or to supply services. Such arrangements were not specific to the Jewish world. Until the modern period, most commerce and manufacture were conducted under license from the king, religious or lay lords, or the community, and such licenses prevented others from competing. Generally speaking the arunda and the *marufiyah* described the relationship between a Jewish entrepreneur and the gentile authority, not on a racial or religious basis, but simply on the basis of possession of an economic good. Halakhically, the holder acquired a property right for which he had paid in money or in services, and therefore any competitor was, in fact, guilty of theft, so that he could be halakhically restrained from competing. This applied not only to actual price or entry competition but also to attempting to acquire the monopoly right itself.

There exists in the halakhic framework another source of restrictive practice that flows from the ability of the traders or artisans to legislate prices, terms of trade, entry, and quality control. Such power stems from the rights of neighbors or citizens of a town to force each other to participate in all the tasks necessary for the welfare of the town. These trade associations were already permitted in talmudic times. "The people of the city are permitted to regulate weights, prices, and wages of workers. They also have the right to punish those who do not carry out their regulations."[48] This communal right was recognized by the codifiers and commentators as expressed by the Rashba (Shlomo ben Aderet, Spain, thirteenth century). "This would apply to every association organized for one purpose which is to be considered as a 'city,' even if the other members of the community are not party to their decision. Even if only members of one occupation, like the merchants, butchers or sailors, make regulations and articles of association their decisions are binding."[49]

The arunda and the communal right of members of a trade or profession to institute restrictive practices maintain their importance today, in view of the many different forms in which they appear in our society. The trade unions are only the most obvious examples. There are many others. Licensing arrangements and zoning laws, which restrict free entry to noncompeting firms, medallions for taxicab ownership, or permitting the practice of a certain profession only to recognized members of professional associations, as in the case of doctors, accountants, lawyers, and so on, are examples of community-sanctioned monopolies or restraints on competition. In many countries, electricity, water, public transport, sewage, postal and telephone services, and higher education are supplied either by the state and its various local authorities, or by publicly regulated utilities and institutions.

Theoretically, such restrictive arrangements are meant to protect the public interest by enforcing quality control, regulated pricing, and an investment policy that will contribute to the general welfare. Such associations are all seen as having social aims in addition to merely that of profit. In reality, they also serve to protect the livelihood of the members, holders of the license, or concessionaire, and to prevent others from competing. They usually lead to higher prices, restraints on entry that prevent others from enjoying the profits earned, and to inferior goods and services. Therefore such monopolies yield abnormal profits over and above those that would be determined by market forces, and such abnormal profits make them attractive both to their possessors and to potential competitors.

Society has to balance the advantages and benefits accruing from such restrictive organizations or monopoly rights against the harmful effects of monopoly and cartelization. In recent decades, this became even more imperative, since both the power of unions and trade associations and the regulatory authority of the state to grant monopoly status or to operate in the market with social-political aims have increased tremendously. The breakdown of communism and the weakening of the Socialist parties during the 1980s were caused by their inability to maintain this moral balance. There is, however, a grave danger of a backlash in all countries, Western and Eastern, against any form of public intervention or regulation. This backlash could lead to an ignoring of the social and moral needs of society in favor of an unbridled selfish materialism, so the halakhic treatment of these restrictive arrangements would seem to have great importance.

The power of these restrictive arrangements lies in the ability to prevent others from entering the profession or trade in which the monopoly occurs. While the state apparatus obviously has such power, which it can impose on public utilities, and so forth, the power of trade unions is not so obvious. Halakhically, most authorities permit both the forming of trade unions and their right to strike. The former is in the spirit of the ruling of the Rashba and the latter in accordance with the talmudic ruling mentioned previously that workers, unlike other parties to a contract, can withdraw from an undertaking. Naturally any damage flowing from the withdrawal has to be paid, the right being only a moral one. Whether they can prevent the employment of other workers, however, is not so clear. Rabbi Moshe Feinstein upheld the right of ritual slaughterers (*shochetim*) in New York to form a union and to make all the *shochetim* adhere to whatever the union decides. "Where the union represents a majority it can prevent the others [workers who refused to join the union] from working on the grounds of *marufiyah* and the endangering of their livelihood. This right is bolstered by the general public disapproval of strikebreaking."[50]

Rabbi Avraham Yitzchak HaKohen Kook, the first chief rabbi of modern Israel, saw the issue of unionization as follows:

> In the organization of workers for the purpose of protecting their working conditions, there is an element of justice and *tikkun olam* [literally, repairing the world]. Unorganized labor works for lower wages and for longer hours and this is to the detriment of the working conditions of the organized worker and causes him economic loss. Such losses can be claimed through a law suit. . . . Should neither of the parties [employers and the unorganized worker] agree to arbitration . . . before the *bet din*, the organized workers can use other methods approved by the courts to force them to appear. [However], irrespective of whether a strike is aimed at preserv-

> ing working conditions [contracted conditions, which not being fulfilled are being renegotiated] or improving wages . . . it is not permissible. . . . [In claiming their rights] the union workers are no different from the parties to any form of monetary conflict. It is possible, however, to use the strike as a weapon to force the employer to appear before a rabbinical court.[51]

Recognition of the right of the associations to the limiting of compeition did not blind the rabbis to the problem of protecting the public from the excesses of such restraints.

At the outset, it is clear that the granting of monopoly rights and the legality of the trade associations require democratic decision. While this is obvious in the case of state-given monopoly rights, it applies equally to the restraints on competition created by unions, trade or professional associations, and licensing arrangements. The Maharam of Rothenburg, the foremost halakhic authority of his time (Franco-Germany, thirteenth century), held that the regulations of such associations required the unanimous approval of their members.[52] On the other hand, the Rashba ruled that a majority vote was sufficient.[53] Both of these opinions would seem to prevent the minority rule so prevalent in many modern trade unions or professional associations that become hostages to well-organized minority groups. A recent research paper at the Bank of Israel showed that the veterans of the Israel Medical Association used their status in order to create an almost feudal system resulting in a great discrepancy between their wages and those of the new and younger doctors.

The democratic process alone is not sufficient to prevent the monopolist or cartel from acting against the public interest. The main halakhic protection is to be found in the concept of an *adam chashuv*—important personage. This is a person (according to some a rabbinical specialist, but according to others a publicly accepted lay person was also acceptable) whose function it is to mediate between the public interest and that of the holders of monopoly rights. Almost all the codes and the responsa make their restrictive policies dependent on the approval of the *adam chashuv* or operative only in those cases where no such person exists.

Already in talmudic times, Rabba annulled the arrangements of the butchers whereby they allocated specific days for each to have the sole right to sell meat. This was done because they had not obtained his approval.[54]

This concept of the *adam chashuv*, codified as law by the *Shulchan Arukh*,[55] places Jewish law firmly behind the concept of obligatory arbitration between unions and employers as well as between the professional or trade association and the public. The widespread governmental intervention in the economy that exists in almost all countries would seem to indicate the necessity of such a independent arbitrator, perhaps along the line of the Scandinavian ombudsman, to oversee the monopoly rights enjoyed by state-owned corporations or regulated public utilities and industries. These monopoly rights and all government decisions are, as often as not, the result not only of unfettered public interest but also of the special personal or party interests of the legislators, which makes such independent arbitration even more crucial. Additional support for such a rabbinic role is provided by the fact that, while fiscal policy is by and large relegated by *Halakhah* to the lay authorities, nevertheless the *bet din* serves as a court of appeal.[56]

Perhaps of greater importance than any of the defense mechanisms provided by Jewish law against the abuse of monopoly rights and restraint of trade agreements are the moral strictures aimed at their holders or participants. After all, without these, legislation alone is not very effective in preventing evasion and abuse.

The source of these moral strictures lies in the *Mishnah* describing the monopolies of certain priestly families in the Temple in Jerusalem:

> These shall be remembered for rebuke: the House [clan or family] of Garmu, who refused to teach others how the shewbread for the Temple service was baked; the house of Avtinas who refused to teach the manner of making the incense; Hugrass ben Levi, who was in charge of the singing of the Levites in the Temple, but who refused to teach his special art of singing [he would put his thumb and index finger into his mouth thereby creating different tones and notes, which astonished his fellow Levites with their beauty]; and Ben Kamtza, who refused to teach others his special art of writing [placing four pens between his five fingers and writing four syllables simultaneously]. Of the former [cases of performers of charitable acts reported in the previous *Mishnah*] the verse of Proverbs applies (10:7), "May the memory of the righteous be blessed." For those [mentioned in our *Mishnah*], the verse promises, "But the name [memory] of the wicked shall rot [be blotted out]."[57]

The subsequent discussion in the Talmud tells of a strike by the House of Garmu and by the House of Avtinas. This would parallel strikes by workers in modern essential services, since the Temple could not operate without the shewbread or the incense. When the Sages, in an attempt to break the strike, brought experts from the Jewish temple in Leontonus, Egypt, the quality of their products was not satisfactory. So the two priestly houses were reinstated at a 100 percent rise in wages. This brought upon them the public criticism of the Sages, who, after agreeing to the wage rise, demanded an explanation. Both the answer of the priests and the reaction of the Rabbis show that the primary problem was not merely a financial one, but a moral one.

The priests of the House of Garmu vindicated themselves by saying, "We have a tradition from our fathers that this house [the Second Temple] will be destroyed, and we were concerned that our knowledge [of making the shewbread] should not be used for mundane or profane purpose." This of itself is a repetition of the claims of all professional associations that their sole purpose is the public welfare [in this case a ritualistic one, but nevertheless one of public benefit]. The *Gemara* tells us, however, that the sons of the House of Garmu never ate refined bread in order that people should not gossip that they used the holy shewbread for their own purposes. In the same way, the wives and daughters of the House of Avtinas never left their homes perfumed and scented, so that they should not be suspect of using their status for selfish reasons.

It is this moral imperative that is essential to the preservation of the public welfare in all restraints on competition that flow either from government regulatory powers or from the existence of trade unions, professional associations, and licensing arrangements. Otherwise they will function in a way that encourages abuse of these restraints for the financial benefits of the holders of the anitcompetitive rights. For this reason, the Rabbis forgave the priestly families.

There is a further spiritual element involved in the formalized or legalized restraints on competition and the granting of monopoly powers. By their very nature, they prevent outsiders from gaining knowledge or skill, since, when these are obtained, they make competition by new entrants possible. Skills and knowledge are as much gifts from God as are material assets, and just as one is required to do charity with the latter, so, it would seem, one would be obligated to share these gifts with others. Maimonides rules that the highest form of charity is to support a fellow Jew who has become poor by giving him a gift or a loan [to establish his own business], or by forming a partnership with him, or by providing him with a job "till he is no longer dependent on the generosity of others." We have discussed this at great length in the previous chapter and will return to this subject in the following one. Here it suffices to support the concept of sharing knowledge as a form of charity, even if this leads to increased competition and therefore a loss of income. After all, such sharing of professional knowledge has the same economic effect as helping to establish the poor in business.

It is instructive to note that many authorities consider the prevention of competition by veteran firms as a form of negating the biblical precepts of "you shall love your neighbor" and "you shall do that which is good and be righteous in the eyes of the Lord," and something that pious people should refrain from doing.

> It is permissible for a person to open a store alongside an existing one . . . and a storekeeper may distribute nuts and corn . . . and reduce prices in order that they should come and buy from him [since in both cases they do so within their own property and can emulate each other while the customers are able to do business wherever they wish]. Nevertheless it is a meritorious act not to interfere with the livelihood of one's neighbors.[58]

This concept of legal acts that, nevertheless, should be avoided by God-fearing and righteous people, is codified by Maimonides as being the mark of the commerce of the *talmid chakham* (the Jewish role model) when he writes "he does not compete with the livelihood of his neighbor [and infringe his boundary]."[59]

It is the opinion of Rabbi Bachrach (author of *Chavat Ya'ir*) that when King David reduced the 613 Divine Commandments to 11 basic principles, all of them referred to refraining from doing those things that are legal and for which the infringement involves no punishment. They are acts of *lifnei mishurat hadin*, acts beyond the requirement of the law, and are the basis for molding the moral and ethical character that is the aim of the righteous and the pious.[60]

THEFT OF INTANGIBLE ASSETS

The revolution in the high-tech industries and in the field of information that has characterized the world economy recently has led to what appear to be new issues in business morality. Much of the assets of individuals and corporations in these industries are no longer physical ones, but rather intangible. Instead of the plant, machinery, and inventory of the classical manufacturing and commercial firms, there are heavy investments in research and development. This change has created legal vagueness as regards the proprietary rights enjoyed by the investor and the ability of others to use the results of such research and development without the permission of and without payment to the investor. It would seem, however, that basically the moral issue remains the same. There still exists the necessity for balancing the public welfare, served by the wide use of the knowledge, expertise, and experience of the veteran, against the economic loss suffered by him through the free use by others of those same assets.

Within the scope of this book, it is only relevant to suggest possible patterns of Jewish thought, flowing from the preceding discussions, to the moral issues raised by the entry into the computer age and the allied scientific development. Many practical questions that arise, however, all have to be referred to a competent and authoritative rabbi.

Such questions range from the right to copy or use computer programs to the degree to which the public right to know permits a "hacker" to gain entry into a data base, to the protection offered to authors, publishers, musicians, artists, and scientists to the fruits of their talents or research. If no protection is afforded to the intangible assets of the mind and the diligence of the individual, nobody will invest in them, and society will be deprived of their fruits. On the other hand, if they are completely protected, the holder of such proprietary rights will enjoy a monopoly, and society will pay an exorbitant price for the benefits.

The existence of copyright legislation, both national and international, would seem to make irrelevant any study of the Jewish perspective, since in monetary matters, the law of the land, *dina demalkhuta*, has halakhic status. Further consideration, however, would seem to indicate otherwise. There are many countries, especially in Asia, Africa, and South America, where such legislation either does not exist or is more breached than honored. Not all intangible assets are easily patented nor is it always easy to prove infringement. Above all, for Judaism to be viable and meaningful, its moral and ethical guidelines in all concepts of life have to be studied, irrespective of whether or not they are supported by non-Jewish legislation or general public opinion. Only in this way can these guidelines shape the individual's Jewish conduct of his business affairs. This is especially true in the State of Israel, which presents in addition an independent vehicle for the implementation of specific Jewish ideas and values at the communal level.

In their restricted legal sense, the laws of theft and robbery apply only to tangible goods. This is derived from the verse in the Book of Samuel, "And he [David] stole the spear from the hand of the Egyptian [Goliath]."[61] Such theft or robbery then creates a liability to return the actual stolen object plus a fine in the latter case, or to pay its monetary value plus a 100 percent fine in the former case. In both cases, these acts are forbidden.

However, in their wider sense of dishonesty, theft and robbery apply to a much wider spectrum of actions, each bearing their legal punishment and each similarly forbidden. So the theft of intangible assets has to be seen in this wider sense. The discussion of competition as a possible form of theft may be used as a guideline to the treatment of the theft of the intangible asset. Perhaps this may be summarized as follows:

1. The ruling requiring other fishermen to remove their nets from one already spread was based on an "investment" by the owner that made the capture of the fish a certainty. This could apply to the research and development invested in the intangible asset. For example, copying a computer program could be forbidden over and above the issue of the disk itself. The disk is a tangible asset and is protected by the laws of theft, but the investment by the programmer is an intangible that creates the real value, and this would be protected by the fisherman ruling. Some authorities have suggested protection through the lease, rather than sale of the disk, which would retain the programmer's right to sue for any use of the disk other than the purpose for which it is leased.

2. Since people engaged in the specific industry or occupation agree that one may not infringe on goodwill, patent, or other intangible rights, it becomes incumbent on all to behave accordingly. This would follow from the status accorded in *Halakhah* to the enactments of trade associations.

3. The infringement of intangible assets is a form of competition, and there is halakhic protection against any form of competition that destroys another's livelihood or that cannot be emulated. So such in-

fringements would have to be examined as to whether they are not cases of *hasagut gevul* (removing a landmark) or *hayoreid le'omanut shel chavero* (he who descends to the livelihood of his neighbor).

While these halakhic considerations would seem to protect the owner of the intangible asset in the form of know-how and research, the public good has to be considered, as in the case of any other monopoly or restraint of competition.

Rent control and the copyright enjoyed by publishers form the basis of much halakhic discussion and many responsa. The public welfare issue at stake is different in each case, so they will be presented separately.

Rent Control

During much of their history in the various countries of their Diaspora, Jews were tenants of gentile landlords. For over a thousand years, the areas available to them to live in were curtailed and limited, even if the degree of limitation varied from country to country and century to century. These limitations meant that severe constraints were placed on the supply of housing and stores. Any influx of Jews from other cities, states, or countries and any natural increase in the local population meant increased pressure of demand on the limited supply and therefore had to lead to increased rentals. The veteran tenants were faced with competition for living space; naturally this particularly affected the poorer ones.

Though, under normal conditions, there is no difference between competition for housing and any other form of competition, the monopoly of the gentile landlords created a special case in which competition between the Jewish consumers for a scarce commodity could only mean social misery. Public welfare therefore demanded some equitable solution that would provide protection at least for some part of society. This concern for public welfare created an intangible asset, the right of residence, in favor of the veteran tenant, who was thus assumed to have a greater right to be protected. This is reflected by the communal enactments and the responsa.

Already in Crusader Europe, the enactments of Rabbenu Tam (grandson of Rashi, perhaps the leading of the Tosafists) included such a restriction against competition for housing:

> We have further received [accepted] a *cherem* (a ban of excommunication) of the Ancients [reference to Rabbenu Gershon MeOr HaGolah; pre-Crusader Franco-Germany, issuer of the ban against polygamy] that if a Jew lives in a house of a gentile, whether for rent or as loan, no other Jew may rent the house for a whole year after the first removed from the house. This ordinance applies only to the house owned by a gentile, but not to that owned by a Jew [who would not use the great demand for housing to demand exorbitant rents].[62]

As late as nineteenth-century Europe, scarce and cramped housing remained a severe problem for the Jewish communities of eastern Europe, as can be learned from the following responsum of Rabbi Avraham of Sochochow:

> In the case of Reuven, who had rented a house from a gentile and after a few years the house was destroyed by fire. Now the landlord has rebuilt it and the honoured rabbi wishes to know whether another Jew may try and rent it. We have already seen in the responsa of Maharam Mintz, that the *cherem* of Rabbenu Gershon applies, so that no Jew may negotiate the rental for three years after the previous Jewish tenant left the house. The further question is whether we can force somebody to vacate the house, if he rented it despite the *cherem*. Normally we would rule that since the enactments [of the community] do not specifically mandate this he does not have to vacate the house. However, because of the *cherem* of Rabbenu Gershom, the Jew who negotiated the hire is to be forced to vacate it in favor of the original tenant.[63]

Even though the special status of scarce housing created a monopoly right, it was nevertheless limited by further halakhic decisions. The Maharam of Rothenburg exempted from the monopoly on housing any case where the present tenant no longer intended to remain or where he tried to have his rent reduced. This ruling of the Maharam prevented part of the abuse of rent control since it forbade the sale of the monopoly right, a practice that perpetuates the lack of competition between tenants to the detriment of the landlord. Furthermore, restricting the free-market mechanism for renting houses, a negation of the halakhic ruling that one may do with one's property what one wants, applied only to the house in which the Jewish tenant lived. All other property rented by the same Jew was considered to be a subject of free competition by other Jews. Interestingly, the heads of the community were obligated, in a number of communal enactments, to take steps to increase the number of housing units available in order to solve the shortage.[64] This corrects a negative aspect of rent control that usually operates to restrict the supply of housing, since it reduces the profitability of the landlords. By making increased housing a communal priority, the Jewish councils were able to preserve both aspects of the public welfare, protecting the existing tenants, but also preventing a black market in housing or deteriorated housing, as a result of decreasing profitability.

Copyright

The advent of printing created a new Jewish industry, the writing and publishing of books for a mass market. With increased standards of living, this has become even more pronounced in our present society, together with the proliferation of radio and video cassettes. In all its forms, the publishing industry means an increased supply of knowledge that is to the public benefit. Judaism's insistence on Torah study, not merely as something desirable or important, but as a perpetual religious obligation on every Jew, irrespective of his age, education, or economic status, makes the use of this increased supply of knowledge an essential ingredient of Jewish life. Unlimited competition would increase this supply and lower its costs, thus making extensive Jewish education possible and so contributing to the public welfare. On the other hand, authors would be fearful of writing. Entrepreneurs, moreover, would be wary of investing in publishing or marketing of books and cassettes, in fear of not being able to recoup their investment, including their profits, owing to fierce competition. So the custom of *haskamot*, rabbinical decrees forbidding competitors from republishing books without the consent of the author and the publisher, became common. This has been extended by present-day authorities to include tapes and cassettes. In addition, communal enactments also limiting competition were legislated by the various Jewish councils. At the same time, however, by and large, care was taken to limit the monopoly status of the possessor of the intangible asset so as to prevent the community suffering from restricted supply or higher prices as the result of this status. One example of the conflict between these two principles of public welfare may be seen in the two opinions quoted in one of the commentators of the *Shulchan Arukh*, the Pit'chei

Teshuvah (Rabbi Tzvi Hirsch Eisenstadt, central Europe, nineteenth century).

> Rabbi Mordechai Bennet [Moravia, early nineteenth century], rules that "the *haskamah* (approval) given by the great scholars to publishers, preventing others from reprinting their books is definitely binding, even though it is not verbal [the usual prerequisite for a valid oath]. However [although the *haskamah* was given for a limited period] when the publisher has already sold the entire edition [and recouped his investment and his profit] he may not prevent others from reprinting the book and thus hinder their work of Heaven [by preventing the spread of Torah learning]. This is true, even if the period for which the original ban was given has not yet ended, since he is not losing anything [to prevent this would have resulted in abnormal monopoly profit].
>
> Rabbi Zalman Margolis (Poland, early nineteenth century), however, opposes this. He holds that even if the publisher has sold his entire original edition, the ban is valid until the period for which it was given expires [thus giving him the extra profits from a second or perhaps even a third edition]."[65]

4

Corporate Ethical Issues

CORPORATE OR PERSONAL MORALITY?

At a first glance, many of the ethical and moral issues discussed in the previous chapters do not seem to have the same relevance in the modern corporate world that they do to the activities of the individual in the marketplace. Sometimes this is presented as a consequence of size, as in the criticisms of the multinational corporation or even the giant national corporations, whose turnover is larger than that of many national states. The effect of size, however, only aggravates the consequences of immoral actions; it does not create the moral issues that are common to all corporations, irrespective of their size. Rather, many of the ethical issues regarding corporate business activities and social responsibility flow from the separation of identity, recognized by almost all legal systems, between the corporation and the individual shareholders of that corporation. Primarily, this is reflected in the nature of the liability of the shareholders, which in contrast to partnerships or single ownership, is limited only to the equity of the corporation. Creditors, in those cases where the corporate assets are insufficient to meet their claims, have no recourse to the private wealth of the shareholders.

At the same time, however, this separate legal identity also creates moral issues, for the following reasons:

1. The shareholders, directors, and employees view the corporation as a depersonalized economic force, devoid of any mutual noncontractual rights or obligations. This permits the individual, director, and manager to relax the ethical standards and avoid the social obligations to which he would adhere in his private life. The same duality affects the morality of the employees of the corporation. They all too often develop habits or practices in regard to the impersonal corporate employer that they themselves would consider as being highly immoral in relation to an individual employer. The shareholders are able to view the corporation as a simple capital investment made in order to yield maximum profits, the ethical issues involved in earning them being no concern of theirs.

2. By introducing varying degrees of separation of ownership from control and management, the corporation enables shareholders and directors alike to evade responsibility for the ethical issues facing its operations. The directors maintain that they have no way of ascertaining the moral preferences of their shareholders or that these vary widely or often contradict one another. Therefore their sole yardstick is the earning of maximum profits within the limits imposed by the law; to do otherwise would mean being derelict in fulfilling their obligations and even liable to dismissal. Shareholders argue that they have no control over the daily operation of the corporation, and often not over general policy either.

Naturally, the greater the dispersion of the stock ownership and the greater the degree of reliance on hired, nonowner management, the greater will be the effect of these arguments on the moral behavior of the corporation.

Jewish law can recognize a business form as the corporation in which claims of the creditors are limited to the share capital of that corporation, with no recourse to the private assets of the individual stockholders. After all, the fact of such a limitation is public knowledge and therefore the bank, the suppliers, and other creditors are all aware of it at the time obligations are created. They make their business decisions in light of this knowledge and so claims or counterclaims can be judged accordingly.

Judaism, however, does not seem to accept the separation between the corporation and the individual when it comes to abrogating the responsibilities of the latter as seen in Jewish business law. This may be seen from the following halakhic decisions.

1. Interest, halakhically, needs to be directly between two individuals. Since the corporation is not a human being, the biblical injunction against taking interest may seem to be inapplicable to loans between two corporations or between an individual and a corporation. This, however, has been rejected by most rabbinic authorities, so that a corporation whose shareholders are Jewish would suffer the same restrictions on lending money at interest as do individual Jews.[1] Similarly, individuals may sue a corporation in a rabbinic court in order to obtain repayment of sums seen as *ribit mide'oraita*–biblically forbidden interest–just as they can sue other individuals.[2]

2. The laws of Pesach teach a similar rejection of the corporation as a separate legal entity in regard to halakhically mandated behavior. Individuals or partnerships are not permitted to own *chametz*–leavened bread–during Passover, but are required to follow a specific rabbinic procedure. Corporations with a majority of Jewish stockholders have been obligated to follow the same procedure.[3] Therefore, one could not buy *chametz*, for example, from a chain store whose shares were either completely or primarily owned by Jews that did not adhere to halakhic procedures prior to Pesach.

3. Man is considered always to be liable for damage caused directly by his own efforts or those of his assets. This is true also when he operates through an agent. So conceivably, the private assets of shareholders could be subject to claims in lieu of damages suffered through pollution or neglect, where the corporate equity is insufficient.[4]

This halakhic restriction on the limited liability and making the shareholders individually responsible for the actions of the corporation can be viewed, for example, in relation to the recent case in the United States pharmaceutical industry, where the development of drugs was carried out by wholly owned, daughter corporations. This legal arrangement protected the parent company from being sued when the drugs proved to be harmful. The limited-liability nature of the daughter corporation restricted claims to its equity, which was limited to a minimum, thus leaving the injured parties without recourse. Would the halakhic treatment prevent this by making the individual shareholders responsible for the damage?

It may be argued that, if so, then in effect the corporation would disappear as an economic form, since nobody would be prepared to invest equity and make himself liable for claims on his personal wealth. Firms would be funded only by loan capital or credit whose liability is by nature limited.

It seems, however, in view of empirical studies in leverage that there is little likelihood of this really happening. In all countries, in nonlisted, small and medium corporations, or closely held corporations, the major shareholders are usually required to supply the creditors with personal guarantees that enable the debts of the corporation to be covered, if necessary, by the sale of their private assets. Nevertheless, this has not led to the disappearance of the limited-liability corporation. Furthermore, it has been shown that in many countries, the equity investment is not the product of profitability or risk of the individual corporation, but rather is determined to a large degree by the socioeconomic framework prevailing in a particular economy.[5] This means that the shareholders are not able to decide what leverage ratios they wish to operate with, but rather there exists an accepted range of ratios within which the firm is obligated to function. Be that as it may, it is still necessary to formulate a Jewish answer to the responsibility of the shareholder for damage caused by the corporation.

Assuming that the damage was such as to make the firm halakhically liable, the treatment of the personal assets of the shareholders would depend on the structure of the equity.

a) The first distinction would be between those corporations listed on a stock exchange and those closed corporations with a limited number of shareholders. Many countries treat the two types of corporations differently regarding taxation, financial reporting, and so forth. This flows from the fact that participation of the shareholders in the decision-making process and their knowledge of the firm's policies differ. In the closed corporation, the small number of shareholders and their role in the day-to-day management make them active participants in the policies of the firm. Halakhically therefore the limited-liability provisions would seem to have to be reviewed, perhaps making the individual stockholder personally liable for the firm's actions.

b) The listed corporation, too, would have to be viewed according to the degree of shareholder participation, as this varies even in this type of corporation. Since holders of preference shares and nonvoting ones are in effect mere creditors, they cannot be saddled with the cost of the firm's decisions. Even those holding only a limited number of voting shares would also be considered nonactive, nonresponsible owners. Nevertheless, it may well be, however, that it would be considered preferable for both of these groups to sell their stock in a corporation guilty of unhalakhic behavior, since one is not allowed to have a benefit from forbidden acts. For example, the Jewish shareholders of a corporation that involved non-Jews working on *Shabbat*, even as independent agents, were advised to sell the corporation, since their ownership was common knowledge and they would be seen as earning a profit from the *Shabbat* work.[6] On the other hand, large listed corporations or multinational ones in which Jews are majority shareholders or active managers would seem to have to be run according to Jewish moral concepts. They in effect control the activities of the corporation and therefore cannot escape their responsibilities to pay for any damage caused by the corporation by use of the separate identity of limited liability.

4. A Jew is not permitted to allow his assets to work for him on *Shabbat*, even indirectly, and therefore, this would apply to corporations with Jewish stockholders. The following responsum (Hungary, eighteenth century) regarding the use of a gentile to operate a plant on *Shabbat* would help to clarify this.

> Concerning those Jews who hold a contract from the prince, giving them permission to dig in the mountains and to bring out the ore. Iron is made from the ore, by burning and refining in fire day and night. So also is the work of the glass makers. How shall they conduct their business since if they do not work on the *Shabbat*, they will lose money?
>
> Basically, the contract for the smelting operation is prohibited since the Jew has a benefit from the work on *Shabbat* and is interested in its continuation. The digging of the ore from the ground is different. This would be permitted if the contract is made for the job and not for the day so that the gentile worker is paid for a certain number of wagon loads. Smelting and refining, however, are continuous processes, in which the gentile has no choice or alternative as to his work schedule. If the Jew would sell all the large ingots of iron before the *Shabbat* for a specified sum, then the gentile works for himself and his own profit in turning them into small ingots, and this is permissible. In this case there is no need to be concerned with *marat ayin*—appearances that the Jew is benefiting from labor on the *Shabbat*—since he is selling part of the contract he obtained from the prince.[7]

The above responsum and the more modern ones that followed it clearly show that the Jew may not use the gentile to earn profits from work forbidden to the Jew on the *Shabbat* unless the non-Jew were working for himself without the Jew sharing in the *Shabbat* profits. At the same time, it would seem that if the work entailed something that the non-Jew himself would be forbidden to do in Jewish law—theft, murder, and so on—then even if the gentile were "self-employed," the partnership with him would not be permissible.

The following quotation from a modern responsum of Rabbi Menashe Klein of New York sums up quite clearly this restricted role *Halakhah* gives to the limited liability nature of the modern corporation.

> According to my opinion, the corporation is simply a partnership like all the other partnerships [or joint ventures] in the world, excepting that this partnership, called a corporation or limited, is one in which the partners have pronounced two conditions.
>
> In this project [for which the corporation has been created], irrespective of what happens, they do not accept on themselves any bodily lien (*shiabud haguf*), only a lien on the assets [of the corporation]. This means that at the time of their forming the partnership, each one invests a certain sum of his own money, as do each of the partners [these sums then constitute the corporate equity]. Each participates according to their agreement, on condition that all the activities and the projects which they [i.e., this corporation] will conduct from this day on, will be conditional on the lien existing on its assets only. From this it follows that if there should be losses and insufficient assets to cover them, then the parties will not have to meet any further obligations [from their private assets] . . . since halakhically, all conditions expressed on monetary matters are binding and therefore [in the limited liability corporation] there is no *shiabud haguf*.[8]

These rulings, dealing with different halakhic aspects of the nature of the corporation, restrict its separate legal or operative entity solely to the limitation of the rights of the creditor to the equity of the corporation without recourse to the financial assets of the shareholders. It would seem to follow that other limitations on business activities imposed by Jewish moral teachings and by rabbinic law, together with the social obligations flowing from the possession of wealth that apply to the individual, are therefore binding on the corporation as well.

Jewish executive officers of Jewish-owned or dominated corporations cannot therefore claim that their sole responsibility is to maximize shareholder profits, even in those cases where this violates ethical and moral principles. This claim is invalid in the case of the individual businessman, and the corporation status of the enterprise does not validate it. *Halakhah* does not accept the argument of a *shaliach ledavar aveirah*–an agent for performing forbidden acts[9]–and therefore executive officers cannot hide behind the "instructions" of their shareholders or assume that thereby they are free not to observe the ethical limitations imposed on them by the Torah.

Jewish executive officers of large or multinational corporations in which no individual holds a large bloc of shares would similarly, it would seem, be liable to follow halakhic rules since there is no effective shareholder control or direction. Such a separation of ownership from control means that the executive officers are in effect the operators of the wealth of the corporation and are therefore obligated to maintain Jewish ethical principles in those operations regarding their investments in such large corporations. In the same way, the shareholders would seem to be required to dismiss their corporate officers if these would perform, on their behalf, policies that would be considered halakhically to be immoral or nonpermissible; otherwise the responsibility, moral and legal, devolves on them as it would in the case of the partnership or single-owner firms. This would apply, even to a greater extent, to institutional investors, like mutual funds or pension funds in Israel where the investors too are Jewish.

ETHICAL ISSUES IN FINANCIAL MANAGEMENT

Over and above the moral issues flowing from the legal separation between the corporation and the shareholders in regard to the limitation of liability, there are others that flow primarily from the disclosure of financial information regarding the operations of the corporation. Such information is essential for equitable relations between the shareholders vis-à-vis each other, between the shareholders and the executive officers, and between both the groups and the public-sector regulatory agencies. In essence, the ethical issue concerns the degree of disclosure, the veracity of that disclosure, and the ease with which it is available. Such disclosure of information enables all concerned to conduct their relations with the corporation in a manner most beneficial to them. The lack of sufficient information prevents this, and therefore raises moral questions of injustice, fraud, or exploitation. Some of the recent developments in corporate affairs, such as insider trading and the leveraged buyout, may be seen as examples of these questions, while the nonlisted closely held corporation raises issues of its own that have been in existence for many years.

Closely Held Corporations

In all countries, most corporations are not listed on a stock exchange but are owned by a relatively small number of shareholders. However, it is incorrect to equate the moral problems of such corporations with size alone, thus assuming that they exist only in small firms. There are many large, even listed, corporations that share these problems, since they flow not from size but from the degree of control and active involvement enjoyed by the major shareholders.[10]

In these corporations effective control is vested in a small number of stockholders or members of their families, who often serve in active managerial positions. As a result, it is often difficult to distinguish between the affairs of the corporation and the interests of the major stockholders. Over and above problems of management, such as nepotism in hiring, especially in executive positions, this lack of distinction leads to moral problems in distribution of profits.

Empirical research has shown that such firms distribute their profits either completely or at least predominantly in the form of personal expenses, salaries, and perks rather than in the form of dividends.[11] The major reason for this is the double taxation practiced in many countries, whereby the corporation pays income tax on its predistribution profits, and the stockholder pays personal income tax on dividends received from the same profits. The nondividend forms of profit distribution are usually considered as deductible expenses for tax purposes, the recipient sometimes being liable to personal tax; however, this tax has been shown to be extremely difficult to collect. This tax problem does not concern us here, as it is not a particular corporate one. However, since not all the stockholders are active in management and so are unable to enjoy these nondividend forms of profit distribution, moral problems arise regarding the obligation of the major stockholders to divulge the nature of such distribution to them.

Since only part of the salaries, perks, expenses, and so forth, are in fact actually connected with the functioning of a firm, some are actually distributed profits, so the share of the nonactive shareholders is affected. They, in addition to the tax authorities, are paying for the profits distributed in these forms to the active stockholders.

Expanding the concept of dishonesty beyond theft or robbery, Judaism included therein acts of *geneivat daat*, those acts that in effect steal the minds of others. As discussed in chapter 2, these include nondisclosure of defects or shortcomings in the quality of goods, false packaging or advertising, and in any way presenting the goods to be other than they are. Presenting the financial statements to the shareholders without revealing to them the element of profits distributed only to the active stockholders would seem to be a similar distortion, this time of the financial affairs of the corportion. They disguise the actual asset value of the stock, which is affected by the profit stream of the corporation. Since the shareholders are actually buyers of the corporation, such distortion would seem to be a transgression, similar to the one forbidden halakhically by *geneivat daat*.

So the owner-managers would seem to be obligated to set their salaries at the market rate for corporations of similar sizes and financial achievements; this makes them regular expenses rather than profit sharing. They would be permitted only to use corporate funds to buy motorcars essential for the functioning of the corporation and to travel, entertain, and so on, also solely for that purpose. This will increase the amount of profits to be distributed to the nonactive stockholders. If not, they are at least obligated to disclose to the other minority shareholders what proportion of the benefits are in fact legitimate business expenses and what are a withdrawal of profits.

There is another halakhic concept of dishonesty that would seem to be applicable to the same system of financial management. This is the concept of *onaah*, literally, oppression, or in classical English, to vex, and is the basis of preventing price fraud or overcharging relative to the market price. Maimonides rules, as shown in chapter 2, that where there is full disclosure of the market price, the law of *onaah*, which allows for cancellation of the sale or for compensation for the overcharge, does not apply.[12] At the same time, undue influence or oppressive use of another's need has been seen by the halakhic sources to reinstate the protection of *onaah*, even where there was full disclosure, but the injured party nevertheless agreed.[13]

Seen in this light, *onaah* would seem to obligate the active stockholders to distinguish clearly the distributed profit element from the legitimate salaries, expenses, and perks they have paid to themselves. This would allow the other shareholders to ascertain more correctly the profit earned and therefore the price of their shares. Furthermore, it would seem that the active stockholders would not be allowed to use the fact that they usually have a greater number of shares than the others and that they are in daily control of the corporation to "exploit" as it were, the other stockholders, as described through the *onaah* principle.

These two principles of *geneivat daat* and *onaah* obviously apply to executive affairs of listed corporations, too; the emphasis here on the closely held corporation was made only because the problem is less well known.

Listed Corporations

There are two characteristics of corporations listed on a stock exchange that create an area of ethical issues. While they exist in varying degrees in different countries and vary substantially even within a specific economy, these characteristics are (1) a widely dispersed share ownership and (2) a separation of management or ownership through the chief executive officers who are not major shareholders. The individual shareholder is almost captive in the hands of the CEOs, having little control over their actions. At the same time, the interests of the shareholder and those of the CEOs are often not identical. The former are primarily interested in maximizing their profits at an acceptable level of risk. The latter, however, having no share in the profits, are more interested in achieving growth of sales and assets that give them status, power, and continuity of employment. The common practice of providing hired executives with stock options, and so on, which effectively transforms them into owners, is one of doubtful morality, since it is aimed at getting them to adopt policies to the benefit of the owners, which is actually what their salaries were supposed to do.

Insider Trading

What is commonly known as insider trading is in effect the use of information regarding the present or future prospects of activities of a corporation. Business information falls, broadly speaking, into two groups. One is perfectly legitimate, but legislation prevents the use of the other. There is no argument, legal or moral, against entrepreneurs gathering information regarding economic trends in the market or in regard to a specific corporation and then operating in accordance with such information. All business activity requires the collection of data, and all decisions will be made in the light of such data. The problem arises only when such information is gathered from sources only available to some, either on the basis of their positions or as a result of their special relationships with the source of the information. This insider information places all the other participants in the market at a disadvantage, which they cannot overcome by their own efficiency or efforts. In order to provide protection against such unfair practices, some countries have legislated against the use of insider trading. Others, in view of the difficulties involved in distinguishing between insider information and legitimate forms of information, have ignored the issue. Implied in such a policy is the assumption that anyone engaged in the stock market should be able to discern the use of such information and protect himself against its misuse. "If you cannot stand the heat, keep out of the kitchen" or "let the buyer beware" would seem to be the basis for this assumption.

In those countries where legislation exists forbidding the use of insider trading, its use becomes halakhically illegal. This flows from the rule of *dina demalkhuta dina*—literally, the law of the land is the law—through which halakhic sanction is given to legislation in economic and financial matters, provided it does not contradict Jewish law. Such legislation becomes binding and can be used in litigation before a rabbinic court. The injured party can claim that he assumed that the law of the land was observed and therefore is entitled to restitution for any loss suffered as a result of an act made illegal by the secular or non-Jewish legislator.

The Jewish issue of the use of privileged information only becomes acute in those countries in which preventative legislation does not exist or in the case of Israel, if one wanted to conduct a stock exchange on the basis of *Halakhah*. Halakhically, insider trading has to be viewed from a number of perspectives. It is important in all of these to remember that the share being bought or sold represents, after all, ownership of part of the assets of the corporation. All the concepts discussed in chapter 2 regarding truth in trading apply therefore to the share, just as they would if all the assets were being sold.

1. Halakhic sources do not recognize the Roman concept of "let the buyer beware" and place the onus, both legal and moral, on the seller to make sure that the buyer has full information regarding the nature and quality of the goods sold. If this is not done, he is guilty of *geneivat daat*; the transaction is a *mekach ta'ut*—an erroneous sale and may be canceled. On these grounds it may be argued that the sale or purchase of stock that is not what it appears to be, in view of the information available to all the participants in the market, would be *geneivat daat* and a *mekach ta'ut*.

2. Alternatively, since the price of the stock with public knowledge of the information held by the insider trader would be higher than that of the market price prevailing, the seller could claim protection of *onaah*, the Jewish just-price concept. Since full disclosure is an integral part of the concept of *onaah*, it seems that the use of insider trading, which prevents the market from access to the real value of the stock, would not be permitted in *Halakhah* even if there were no external legislation.

3. An important principle in Jewish law is the notion of custom, determining the rights and the obligations of the parties to market transactions. For example, if it is the local custom for the employer to provide workers with certain benefits, then all workers in that area are automatically entitled to these benefits even if their contracts do not specify them. It is assumed that both parties understood this obligation and accepted it unless there exists proof of the contrary.[14] In those countries in which legislation prevents the use of insider trading, one who suffered a financial loss from such use could claim compensation in a rabbinic court on the grounds that he assumed the law or even the customary rules of trading were being observed. Since it became clear that this was not so, he could have redress in the *bet din*, over and above any action initiated by the regulatory authorities, for breach of the stock-exchange regulations.

4. There are cases where insider information is bought from somebody else who had access to data as part of his employment. For example, a lawyer working for a firm of brokers, a bank official involved in the financing of a takeover through the issuing of bonds, or a government official privy to decisions regarding future zoning regulations, instead of using the information himself, sells it to somebody else. This sale introduces a new element into the use of insider trading, namely the receiving of stolen goods. The halakhic codes forbid the buying of

stolen goods, seeing the buyer, in the words of Maimonides, "strengthening the hand of evildoers since if he wouldn't be able to sell the goods, the thief would not steal."[15] In other words, the buyer is creating a market, thus making the theft profitable and so shares in the immoral act. A user of insider information obtained in this manner is therefore not only faced with problems of *geneivat daat* or *onaah* but also of being a *mesayeh ledavar aveirah*—an accomplice to a forbidden act—theft.

Leveraged Buyouts (LBOs)

The 1980s were characterized in the United States, and to a lesser extent in the United Kingdom and western Europe, by a wave of buyouts of corporations through the use of borrowed funds, leading to a high degree of leverage. These funds were usually raised through the issuing of "junk" bonds, bearing prospects of high profits but also of high risks if the buyout did not materialize or the transaction proved to be less secure than originally anticipated. Do such buyouts represent moral or ethical issues, and if so what is a Jewish answer to them? Although much scorn and even abuse have been poured onto the initiators of such buyouts, leading them to be called raiders and predators, one needs to examine carefully the phenomenon before we decide whether their actions are immoral or in conflict with Jewish principles.

Leveraged buyouts can be divided into two separate types of business activity. One concerns the buyout of all or of the controlling stock of a corporation, while the other relates to the management buyout. It seems that while the former poses few problems, the latter is replete with ethical issues, so they will have to be dealt with separately.

General Leveraged Buyouts

The leveraged buyout has to be carefully reviewed in order to ascertain whether there are aspects that differentiate it from any normal purchase or takeover of one corporation by another, or from the purchase of control by one group of stockholders from another. Basically, it would seem that halakhically there is no objection to such normal purchases or takeovers per se, since in effect they are no different from any purchase or sale. The same rules that apply to the latter would apply to the former; any deviation from these rules is invalid irrespective of the method. It seems however that in the LBO two special conditions exist that make infringement on business morality easier or more frequent.

1. The role of the investment bankers or financial advisors who guide the buyers, provide the estimates of the strengths and weaknesses of the corporation, and who construct the financing of the buyout has been seen as one of possible moral infringement. Their fees have no relationship to the outcome of the transaction, to the future performance of the bought corporation, or to the status of the bonds used to finance it. Halakhically, it would seem to be no different, in this respect, from any agent hired to make an investment for his principal. The talmudical Sages held that the principal could, in the case of a loss, say to his agent, "I hired you to improve my situation, not to aggravate it."[16] This could make the bankers and the advisors liable to claims for any losses incurred as a result of the buyout. At the same time in order to become so liable in a *bet din*, the principal has to prove that the investment banker provided him with information that was incorrect, which would be *geneivat daat*, or withheld details of a conflict of interest, which would be *lifnei iver*.

2. In some leveraged buyouts, the existing stockholders are pressured to sell their stock or to agree to a takeover by a new management.

Such pressure is exerted in the form of direct meetings, proxy fights, and media advertising, and may be considered to be a form of coercion that constitutes a moral issue. Maimonides classifies coercion, in any form, of a person to sell his goods a form of robbery, *oshek*, forbidden by the Mosaic Code. He maintains that this is so, even if the price paid to the owner is above its market value.[17] Yosef Caro, the author of the *Shulchan Arukh*, however, deletes this phrase, leading to the assumption that the coercion is permissible if the seller receives an above-market price.[18]

3. In some cases the leveraged buyout or the change of management is beneficial to the stockholders, since the old management was inefficient, leading to losses, or lethargic, preventing them from earning a better return on their investment. Here, attempts by management to prevent the takeover, buyout, or change in stockholding would seem to be a negation of their function as agents acting on behalf of the stockholders and so advice against them would be a case of *lifnei iver* (a stumbling block in the path of the blind), understood in halakhic terms to refer to hidden conflicts of interest.

4. The increased leverage resulting from the funding of the buyout does not need to constitute a moral problem nor does it seem to clash with any halakhic principle. There was indeed concern expressed that, since such increased leverage means a greater degree of risk to the economy, it required government invention to prevent or restrict the LBOs.[19] It would seem, however, that the market is able to rectify this increased risk through the price of the bonds used to fund the buyout or through that of the stock of the corporation concerned. Furthermore, there is no empirical evidence that there exists a certain macroeconomic level of leverage that causes recession, even while it is true that during recession, firms with high leverage are more likely to fail. The international differences in leverage, of themselves, do not make the Japanese or Germany economies more liable to recession than those of the United States or United Kingdom. At the same time, the increased leverage does pose a problem for institutional investors, such as pension funds. By investing in the LBOs, they change the risk element of their portfolios and therefore of their stockholders. Since the latter are not consulted in regard to the risk change nor for that matter are they, as individuals, able to move their pensions to another more conservative fund, it would seem that public-sector action is called for to protect the pension holders. Halakhically, this would seem comparable to the guardians of orphan's funds. While they are allowed to invest these funds even at interest, normally forbidden by Judaism, in order to increase the orphan's wealth, they are restrained from doing so in high-risk ventures.[20] This would necessitate both full disclosure of the increased risk through the LBO (*geneivat daat* or *onaah*) and a communal restriction on changes in the investment portfolio of the pension fund.

Management Leveraged Buyouts (MLBOs)

The entry of current management into the LBOs is a major area of halakhic concern, raising issues ranging from *geneivat daat*, through *lifnei iver*, down to the negation of the rules regarding bailees' *din shomrim*, literally, the laws of the watchmen.

The moral issues arise even before the MLBO occurs. The price that will be paid to the existing stockholders will, inter alia, be affected by the economic performance of the corporation prior to the sale. It is obviously to the interest of the management during this period to operate the corporation as badly as possible; low profits, low sales, and inefficient performance all contribute to a lower price that they will ultimately have to pay. This is simple *geneivah*, theft, defined by Maimonides as "removing another's wealth without him [the existing stockholders] being aware of it."[21] Since the executive officers are the agents of the stockholders, they are halakhically bound to operate so as to maximize their benefits. Any dereliction on their part, therefore, lays them open to legal action before a rabbinic court.

In both the authoritative codes, the *Mishneh Torah* of Maimonides and the *Shulchan Arukh* of Yosef Caro, it is written, "A paid bailee (*shomer sachir*) is not liable to pay for losses resulting from theft or adverse business conditions but is required to take an oath that he was not negligent nor used the property for his own use. If he wishes to free himself of the oath he may pay for any damage."[22]

During the negotiations regarding the MLBO, the management is in the potentially immoral situation of being simultaneously both the buyer and agent of the sellers. In order to be clear of transgressing *lifnei iver*, they have to make sure that this conflict of interest is clearly defined and publicized, even if the stockholders understand it by themselves. So too the rules of *geneivat daat* require that full disclosure of the past performance of the corporation and an undertaking that management was not negligent or abusive of the trust would be required. Even the increased risk accruing to the remaining stockholders as a result of the MLBO has to be made clear to them, and their consent obtained, if the management is to be innocent of *geneivat daat* or *onaah*.

ETHICAL ISSUES IN CORPORATE LABOR POLICIES

The moral issues raised by the activities of the modern corporation are not restricted to the internal relationships of management and shareholders. They are also reflected, perhaps even to a greater extent, both in the employer-employee relation and in the effect that corporate activity has on the environment. Since the environment is the subject of a separate chapter in this book, the discussion here is limited to the field of labor relations and policies. While this area is important even in the noncorporate firm, it becomes even more important within the corporation, due to the depersonalized nature of labor relations in this form of economic organization.

Basically the halakhic nature of the employer-employee relationship is simply a hiring or leasing transaction. Indeed, both the relevant talmudic discussion and the codified laws are placed in those sections dealing with the hiring of work animals and the leasing of houses, equipment, or farmland. Therefore, all the rabbinic rulings regarding the implementation and cancellation of contracts, claims for damages, prices, coercion, and so on, that apply to these transactions apply equally to this relationship.

The employer is obligated only to the terms of the contract or to the conditions laid down by local custom, which usually provides the worker with extra benefits, even if these are not explicit in the particular contract. Additional factors found in much modern labor thought, whereby the employer has to consider such aspects as job satisfaction, on-the-job training, professional counseling, and so on, have to be seen in this light. Where they are part of the contract or of the "custom," they become obligatory. In all other cases, they remain in the realm of charity or have to be considered by the employer purely in terms of economic benefits, such as increased productivity or industrial peace.

Since all that is involved halakhically is the buying and selling of services, the employer has no political, social, or personal claims on his workers. In the same way, the only obligation that the worker has is to fulfill in good faith all that he has contracted to do or that is required by custom. He is not required to have any extra loyalty or to be servile to his employers. In the same way, the employer is not an evil person interested in the exploitation of the worker, or a thief whose whole economic function is to steal the fruit of labor, the sole cause of economic wealth. To view labor relations in any other way would validate class division and ultimately foster friction or struggle between "haves and have nots." Such a division is diametrically opposed to the concept of communal unity and national identification, which is so basic to Judaism. It would seem that the Jewish attraction to socialism in all its various forms is primarily an attempt to achieve social justice in a non-Jewish form, even though this leads more to class loyalty than to the concept of *klal Yisrael*, the community of Israel. Jewish trade unionists in South Africa protested against Jewish immigration in the 1920s since it constituted competition to their predominantly non-Jewish rank and file. This was merely following precedents in the United Kingdom and the United States. Far more destructive was the identification with communism that allied Jewish leaders with Stalin in the USSR even though this meant organized discrimination and persecutions.

The halakhic detached view of the employer-employee relationship may not always be seen as being to the worker's benefit. Indeed, in their search for job security, employees are often willing to forgo the benefits of freedom given by Jewish law. The Japanese model with its lifelong employment, group vacations, meditation and exercise, and almost feudal loyalty to the corporation is only one example of this trend of thought. Judaism, however is quite emphatic in distinguishing between servitude and the halakhic form of hiring a service.

It is true that this halakhic form has a price. Not only does it preclude the Japanese model, but it also places the worker at a disadvantage.

Maimonides writes:

> It is not permitted to make the Hebrew bondsman perform degrading work . . . such as carrying his personal belongings to the bathhouse or to remove his shoes . . . nor may he make him a bathhouse keeper for the public [but he may only perform private tasks that do not entail any shame]. . . . This refers however only to a bondsman since his soul is humbled by the sale [servitude]. However a Jewish free man may be used even as a slave [to perform all manner of work, excepting that which is harmful to his health] since he only works of his own free will and with his full consent.[23]

All that can be offered in return for these disadvantages is freedom. So the *Shulchan Arukh* rules:

> An employee who commenced his work [which constitutes the implementation of his contract] and wishes to negate it at midday, may do so [naturally any damage suffered by the employer has to be paid for]. Even if he already received advance payment for the complete job, and he does not have any money to repay that part of his unearned wage, he may leave and the money will be a debt owing the owner [provided he has a source to repay it since the Torah permitted him to stop working but not to steal]. This right to stop work flows from the verse "for unto Me are the Children of Israel slaves and not slaves to other slaves" [the Jewish employer].[24]

The Rama in his gloss added, "Therefore a worker, even a teacher or a Torah scribe, may not hire themselves out to be in the householder's house permanently for three years [actually as pointed out by the Shach it has to be over three years according to the source in the Talmud]." The three-year period is the dividing line between the bondsman and the free worker. It should be noted that the agreement by the worker does not affect the ruling of the Rama, since what is at stake is not merely the economic welfare of the worker but his spiritual freedom.

The employer, on his part, may offer lifelong employment or special benefits, which in effect are meant to make it economically disadvantageous for the worker to move to alternative employers. These contracts obligate the employer, yet the worker, halakhically, may go elsewhere. Even in those cases where the employee indicates, either contractually or by implication, that he wishes to remain for a long period, the Rabbis stressed his ability to do so only for a limited period. So the Chatam Sofer (Austria-Hungary, eighteenth century) rules that Rabbis may sign a contract only for three or for five years, in accordance with the Rama.[25]

In large public institutions or corporations, the tenure and security of permanent employment carry with them a real danger of limitations on personal freedom. All too often the price for this security is pressure for social conformity, in-house publications molding the individual's political and cultural views, and a managerial hierarchy that makes individual initiative and deviance unprofitable and unacceptable. There are countries or circumstances where pension benefits are nontransferable or where corporate perks cannot be exchanged for money, so that the real ability of the worker to move freely from one employer to another is severely curtailed. The halakhic concept of employment as simply an agreement of hiring or leasing together with the Rama's ruling would seem to be of great spiritual significance, militating against the blurring of the boundary between bondsmen and freemen.

Since workers are not simply factors of production, Judaism provides special protection over and above those laws regarding contracts of hiring and leasing. Such protection is essential due to the direct dependence of the worker on his wages, often his only means of livelihood. Contrary to some free-market theory, workers and employers are not equal economically. The former lack the accumulated equity that serves the latter as a cushion against losses and provides a breathing space for existence until conditions improve or investments can be transferred to other more profitable areas. The worker, therefore, is more vulnerable to sudden changes in the marketplace, changes that are beyond his control. Furthermore, as often as not the legal system is tilted against him, since he often lacks the expertise and the funds to obtain that which is legally his.

Nevertheless, since in Judaism justice is symmetrical, employees and employers, corporate and single businesses, alike have both rights and obligations.

Wages

There are five biblical injunctions, including both negative and positive actions, regarding the employer's obligation to pay his employees on time. Originally framed in the language of the daily worker, they apply also to those receiving weekly or monthly wages. The phrase in Deuteronomy 24:15 that explains the moral justification for such Divine concern, "for he is poor and unto it [the wages] he turns his soul," is usually considered to refer to the worker. With insight into the realities of the market, some authorities see it as a reference to the lusts of the employer for the interest-free loan resulting from the withheld wages. For this very reason Maimonides classifies the delayed payment of wages as an example of *oshek*—extortion.

Withholding of payment of wages is very prevalent in many sectors, even in today's sophisticated economies. In single proprietary firms and small closely held corporations, attempts are constantly made by the owners to delay payments. Hard-pressed local councils and state-owned corporations in many countries find such delayed payment of wages a means of alleviating temporary illiquidity caused by cuts in the public-sector budgets. Illegal immigrants, workers in sweatshops, and transients in the capitals of the industrialized countries are often the targets of such delays. In all these cases the withholding of wages causes severe suffering. Sometimes, the strained family budget is insufficient to cover basic necessities. At other times, workers are forced to use expensive consumer credit, to have recourse to the excessive use of credit cards, or to become entrapped in an unbreakable cycle of usurious loans. Indeed the "soul" of the worker is harmed by the delayed payment of his wages.

Are we then to view the increasingly prevalent withholding of wages in the form of participation in mutual funds, pension funds, profit sharing, or annual bonuses as being a transgression of "in his day you shall give him his hire"? The answer to this would seem to depend on whether the delayed payment is to the benefit of the worker and done with his consent. If both of these conditions are met, there would seem to be no halakhic problem. Furthermore, as mentioned in the previous chapter, collective contracts providing for such deferred wages cannot be negated by individual workers for whom the collective contract is binding.

Nevertheless even where such deferral is to the benefit of the employees and made with their consent, there remains a major moral issue. All too often, wages withheld for social benefits, for saving schemes, or insurance and compulsory state loans are actually never distributed to the beneficiaries. Sometimes they are ignorant of their rights, lose the required evidence, or have moved. It would seem therefore that the halakhic injunction of prompt payment would place an obligation on the withholding corporations, fund, or public-sector agency to seek out the beneficiaries and pay them their due.

While workers are preferred creditors during their wage period—in his day will you give him his hire—once the period has passed, the debt now becomes merely one of the debtor's obligations. In cases of bankruptcy, the workers would have to take their turn among the other creditors. It would be plausible, however, that if the workers were poor and their wages constituted their "soul," they would be preferred creditors. This may be inferred from the special status accorded to the worker relative to regular creditors in two instances.

1. "[In the case of] a hired worker who claims his wages when they are due [at the end of the period for which he was hired], but the employer maintains that he has already been paid, the worker takes an oath [that he has not received payment] and is entitled to his wages."[26] This ruling of the *Mishnah*, reproduced in the codes, stands in contrast to the legal principle in *Halakhah* that "whosoever claims money from his fellow, he has to provide the proof."

2. One who claims an unsecured debt from another cannot force him to sell his goods in order to pay the claim, yet a worker who is poor can force his employer to do so.[27]

There is a further difference in the legal status of wage earners that has important implications for wage policy: While a normal creditor can be paid either in money or in near money, a worker has to be paid in money.[28] The moral reason for this is clear. The worker suffers a loss that he, unlike the normal creditor, is not able to bear, since his "soul" is related to his wages. When the worker is paid in kind, the goods may not be according to his preferences or needs, while if he has to sell them, there may be a loss in time, effort, or money. In many Socialist systems, in order to maintain the facade of an egalitarian wage structure, the wage gap is kept to a minimum, but perks or benefits are paid to some workers in the form of motorcar allowances, telephones, vacations, and so on. It may well be that the worker's preferences, if he were free to choose, would be for an actual monetary wage that he could use according to his own judgment, rather than a pattern of consumption forced on him either by collective-bargaining agreements or by the corporate policy in favor of certain benefits. Since this is to the detriment of the worker, it would seem to be questionable in a Jewish framework just as the payment of wages in near money is rejected. Obviously, where these nonmonetary wages are to the worker's benefit, and with his consent, the halakhic objection would be withdrawn.

There is, however, a nonfinancial benefit provided by Jewish law based on Deuteronomy (23:25). There the Bible gives a worker the right to eat the grapes or other agricultural produce with which he is working, in addition to his usual wages. Halakhically this still applies to all workers engaged in the production of food, both in agriculture and in the food industries, provided the process has not been completed, for example, grapes before turned into wine or dough into bread. Even though this would seem to be only of limited application in the modern, sophisticated world, nevertheless, there are rabbinic limitations and insights that have great implications for workers and employers in all industries and walks of life. These are aimed at stressing the moral obligations of workers, all too often ignored in the discussion of labor relations, which seem to revolve only around the obligation of the employer. The limitations deny the existence of any gray area in our day of corporate expense accounts, fringe benefits, and so forth.

The Tur, basing himself on Maimonides, rules:

> The worker in the vineyard may not eat bread or other food together with the grapes, in order to be able to eat more grapes . . . and may not crush

> the grapes on a rock even if this is done by his wife and children, so that he does not stop work to do it . . . may not eat as a glutton . . . and the Rambam wrote that one who stops working in order to eat during the working hours or ate before the completion of the work day, transgresses a negative *mitzvah* [and is guilty of theft].[29]

So the worker is not allowed to abuse the right given to him by the Torah. He may not take the food home or give it to other people, as this is considered to be theft. So too, in nonfood related industries where this biblical right does not apply, any benefits granted by the employer by contract or according to custom may not be abused in any way. This applies to prolonging rest periods, using cafeteria facilities for nonworkers, or wasting expenses paid by the firm.

The Tur then goes on to limit the activities of the employee outside the place of work, where these may detract from his ability to do the job he had undertaken to the best of his ability.

> He may not work [elsewhere] at night and then hire himself out in the daytime, he may not fast or mortify his flesh as these weaken him and then he is unable to do the work of the employer properly. In the same way as the employee is not allowed to steal the wage of his employees [the poor] nor to delay their payment [or not to fulfill his contractual obligations or those imposed by custom], so too the worker is not allowed to idle away his time, a little here and a little there, until his whole day is fraudulent. After all, the sages freed him from the collective grace after meals, and the fourth blessing of that grace [in order to protect the interest of the employer. A shortened form of eighteen benedictions and the ability to recite the *Shema* without descending from the tree or the scaffolding are other examples of rabbinic concern for preventing theft through piety].

Nonfinancial benefits, however, that are part of local custom or of the labor contracts are obligatory for the employer, but the employees can agree to monetary payments instead of these benefits. Furthermore, it seems that a corporation may save itself the costs of providing these services and pay the value of the services instead. For example, a corporation could close its cafeteria and pay the workers a sum, in addition to their wages, equal to the cost of the cafeteria. This may be seen in the responsum of the Maharsham, "We see that in the case of an employer who hired workers and agreed to feed them, there is a dispute between the Rabbis and Rabbi Meir in the Jerusalem Talmud

. . . as to whether the preparation of the food is an obligation of the workers and the rule is according to the rabbis that this is so. Therefore the employer is obliged to pay only for the value of the food."[30]

The Rama and the majority of the halakhic authorities rule that an employer is not liable to pay a worker for absence due to illness unless, for example, there is a contractual obligation in the form of specific sick leave. Rabbi Chaim Palachi (Izmir, nineteenth century) concludes from that "if he is liable to pay only for the work done [but not also for the period of the sickness], it is clear that he has no obligation to pay medical costs involved."[31]

This is true even where the illness is work-related, incurred under normal working conditions, but not where it results from the negligence of the employer or his failure to provide reasonable protection. In such cases the full costs apply, including loss of income, loss of limb, medical expenses, pain, and the shame resulting from the injury. As we shall see in Part II, there is a concept of reasonable risk in Judaism that limits the responsibility for damages, and this concept applies to workers as well. So the Tzemach Tzedek (Rabbi Krochmal, Moravia, sixteenth century) writes in his responsa:

> Ramban [Nachmanides, Spain-*Eretz Yisrael*, fourteenth century] writes, "In accordance with the biblical verse *It is on this* [*the wage*] *that the worker sets his heart*, the worker is prepared to climb a scaffold or ascend a tree even though he knows that sometimes people fall and are killed." So we can understand that it is common knowledge and a reasonable risk that there exist risks in all work, even fatal ones. The worker therefore, at the outset, understood and accepted that perhaps he may be killed during the job. If this is so, why should the employer be obligated to pay for his illness?[32]

Nevertheless both custom and the enactments of the Jewish communities in many countries obligated the employer to share in the medical costs of work-related illness, as can be seen from the following examples:

The responsum of Rabbi Chaim Palachi mentioned above contends that, "even if the worker becomes ill, it is the custom to pay him the full salary agreed upon and the full medical costs involved. The reasoning behind the custom is that the probability of the worker becoming ill is increased by the job, which required him to travel away from his city and wander from place to place."

Maimonides, describing the officials appointed by the Temple authorities in Jerusalem, includes the following: "The priests who stand barefoot on the paved floor and who eat large quantities of meat [in order to prevent it becoming ritually impure] and wear only one shift [and in his commentary on the *Mishnah* he adds the text of the Jerusalem Talmud 'and they drink water'] suffer from intestinal diseases. Therefore an overseer has to be appointed who will supervise them and cure their ailments."[33]

A communal enactment of the Jewish community in Cracow,[34] in the late sixteenth century, placed on the employer the full financial responsibility for the first two weeks of a maid servant's hospitalization. If a further two weeks were required, the costs were divided equally between the worker and the employer. The costs of a longer period were to be covered by the charitable funds.

It should be clear, however, that both the halakhic exemption of the employer from paying health costs and the custom of obligating him to do so are not relevant to industries that cannot be operated without constant or widespread physical damage. Here the risk is not a normal one or something that occurs once in a while, but rather an inescapable consequence as in the case of coal mining, asbestos production, and perhaps nuclear radiation in various industries. There is a biblical dictum, "And thou shall surely guard yourselves very much" (Deuteronomy 4:15). This has been understood halakhically as requiring people not to place themselves in a situation that could cause them any physical or spiritual danger. This general principle, as codified by Maimonides, applies also to workers who are thereby proscribed from accepting employment entailing more than reasonable risk, even if the employer is willing to pay for the exposure to real danger.

"It is a positive *mitzvah* [on all people, not only the owner] to remove anything that is liable to cause fatal injuries and to be extremely careful to avoid and guard against them exceedingly, as it is written, 'And thou shall surely guard yourself.'"

Many things were forbidden by the Sages because they are dangerous or fatal (as shall be shown in Part II). Anyone, therefore, who does not guard himself, but says, "I am prepared to endanger myself," "This has nothing to do with anybody else but me," or "I do not pay attention to such dangers," is liable to corporal punishment by the courts.[35]

In view of this *mitzvah*, "Thou shall surely guard yourself," as described by Maimonides, it may well be that, given our present stage of technology, certain industries that are hazardous to health may not be viable in a halakhic system.

Job Security, Severance Pay, and Pensions

In recent decades, corporations have assumed a greater degree of responsibility for the social welfare of their employees. Corporate job-security measures, severance pay, and pension plans, together with public-sector policies aimed at full employment, have become a common characteristic of many economies. The corporate responsibility adds to the costs of doing business, while the public-sector full-employment policies place fiscal burdens on the state budgets, often leading to inflation or to the economic waste involved in such work projects, which are not economically viable.

It would seem that there exists in Judaism a separation between corporate obligations and those of the general society as expressed in government policies and public-sector spending. In both cases, the responsibility is a function of charity, except of course where there exist contractual obligations or those imposed by custom. Yet it should be borne in mind that the individual's charitable obligations are limited to a greater extent than those of society. When, for instance, the *Shulchan Arukh* rules that there exists an obligation to provide the poor with all their needs if it is within the budget of the individual, the Rama adds, that for this kind of charity, the individual only has an obligation to draw the attention of the communal leaders to the needs of the poor. Naturally he has to pay his share as a member of the community, but it is not his sole responsibility. So too, the charitable obligations of the corporation regarding job security and welfare are limited, even though the corporation is required to shoulder its share through the tax mechanism.

Retrenchment

Changes in the business cycle or even in the specific market in which the corporation operates may create a change in the employment policy of the firm, leading to redundancy and retrenchment in order to protect the profitability and sometimes even the existence of the corporation.

The workers who are now unemployed suffer a dual loss, that of income but also the social cost of being considered redundant, with all its consequent peer and family disdain. As such they are surely entitled to the support and protection of others, yet the prime question in the present discussion is, to what extent does the employer have to provide that support simply because of the relationship between him and the worker?

It would seem that within the halakhic framework no such obligation exists, beyond honoring any labor contracts, so that the employer per se would not have to retain the workers when this is to his detriment. Naturally, it would be a fine act of charity if he did so, as providing employment is the highest form of charity. Perhaps this would be feasible when the number of workers is marginal, so that the loss involved would be marginal. Beyond this point, even the charitable obligation no longer exists, since one is not required to beggar oneself in order to give charity.

There are, however, forms of assistance other than continued employment that the corporation, even more than the small one-owner firm, can give to cushion the effects of unemployment. These would be in accordance with the halakhic dictum of providing assistance in order to prevent another from becoming dependent on the charitable funds. The corporation could allocate part of its profits to fund interest-free loans to redundant workers for establishing themselves in business. It could use its plant and machinery to provide technical retraining, to enable these workers to reenter the labor market, and it could use its data-gathering facilities to provide knowledge of alternative job opportunities. Similar actions have shown themselves to be very effective in Holland, the United Kingdom, and the United States in enabling unemployed workers to establish themselves as independent entrepreneurs during periods of high unemployment. They also have radically increased the annual number of new small firms, which in turn have provided more jobs than the large corporations.[36]

Even after the necessity to fire workers has been established, there still exists a management decision as to the sequence according to which workers will be laid off. In most societies there is a principle of "last in–first out," according to which those workers hired most recently are the first to lose their jobs. This presupposes that the veteran workers have, as it were, acquired a real property in the workplace. A modern responsum by Rabbi Moshe Feinstein (New York, twentieth century) has many parallels in modern labor negotiations and reflects a mixture of mutual help and legal rights:

> If there is a contract stipulating the order, of dismissal or if there is a local custom [an important halakhic principle that offers protection in the absence of a specific contract], these have to be followed. Lacking such arrangements, the workers are in a situation similar to that of two partners who wish to divide up their common property; in our case, the work. The workers can each do half a day's work, thus dividing the wages between them [a practice often followed by workers when they decide to accept a cut in wages in exchange for the retention of every worker's job]. Alternatively, one can say to the other, "Buy my share or sell me yours." [In effect, thus denying the veteran workers a property right in the place of employment.][37]

Such a policy would leave decisions as to the sequence of dismissal to the workers themselves, rather than to management.

Over and above the issue of retrenchment, workers may be released for a variety of reasons, such as the termination of a contract, age, or illness. In these cases, too, the obligation of the corporation regarding the welfare of these workers has to be examined. Naturally, if a labor contract provides for pensions or severance payments, or if these are required by the law of the land and custom, the Jewish corporation is halakhically obliged to fulfill them. Nevertheless, it is important to consider whether such benefits are an intrinsic part of Jewish labor legislation and enforceable by a *bet din*, irrespective of other considerations. The course of Jewish economic history until the previous century was such that most of the disputes regarding the treatment of dismissed workers or those who were unable to continue at their previous levels of productivity, either through old age or illness, were concentrated in the public sector. They covered rabbis, teachers, cantors, ritual slaughterers, and other similar employees. Even today, in a Jewish economy like that of the State of Israel, this public sector is a major employer, accounting for almost half of the total labor force, so that the halakhic decisions have relevance and importance. Nevertheless, the moral obligation of the private corporations toward its employees is not substantially different from that of the public sector, since the economic cost is very similar whether it is in the form of direct welfare payments or as employee benefits. Recent decisions of the Israeli rabbinate have, moreover, extended the moral obligations to the private firm. Further, the halakhic literature reveals basic and distinct Jewish ideas in this field, and therefore it is relevant to the modern corporation.

Severance Payments

Severance pay has been a form of compensation for the loss of income long practiced by the Jewish communities in many countries in regard to their public servants. It must be stressed that this is viewed even by those authorities, like the Bach (Rabbi Joel Sirkes) and Rabbi Mordechai ben Hillel (Franco-Germany, fourteenth century), who held that the rabbinic courts have the right to force wealthy people to do righteous deeds even beyond their legal obligations[38] only as an act of righteousness and not a legal right of the workers.

There are two main concepts that lie behind these acts of righteousness, the law of the Hebrew bondsman and the verse in Proverbs 2:20, "In order that you . . . go in just ways and follow the paths of the righteous."

1. The Hebrew Bondsman

The Bible obligates the buyer of a Hebrew slave to give him a grant at the end of his period of servitude. Although the text refers to a Hebrew slave, in fact what existed was a form of indenture for a limited period, at the end of which the man could go free. On his release, the Bible instructed the owner, "And you shall surely grant him from your flocks, and your granary and your wine press, with which the Lord your God has blessed you" (Deuteronomy 15:14). On this verse, the *Sefer HaChinukh* writes as follows:

> Even though this law [of the grant] applies only to a Hebrew bondsman during the period [when the Jubilee Year applies, as when the Land of Israel is divided between the Twelve Tribes] nevertheless, even in our own times, the wise man will observe and derive knowledge therefrom, so that if he hires a fellow Jew for a long period of time or even for a short term, will, upon termination of the work grant him some of the wealth, which the Lord has blessed him with; the basis of this *mitzvah* is that we should inculcate in our souls good and elevating habits . . . if we should deserve and the good Lord find pleasure in us and deal graciously with us [granting us wealth], it is to our credit and to our prestige, that we should have mercy on those who laboured for us and give them of our wealth as a righteous act, over and above that which we have obligated to give as his wages.[39]

The codifiers, too, saw this grant to the Hebrew bondsman and, subsequently, severance pay to the modern worker, as an act of *chesed*, loving-kindness. So Rabbi Shabbtai HaKohen (Shach, eastern Europe, seventh century], one of the classical commentators to the *Shulchan Arukh*, dealing with the collection of debts, writes, "It is well known that the grant flows from the law of *tzedakah*, while the Panim Meirot [Rabbi Eisenstadt, Hungary, nineteenth century] follows saying, the grant to the Hebrew bondsman does not flow from a legal obligation but rather from a waiving of rights and the giving of a gift as acts of forgiveness."[40] Modern rabbinical courts in Israel have translated this discussion into rulings in favor of granting severance payments to long-tenured workers.

The principal of the school of the Belzer *chasidim* in Haifa was dismissed after years of service and claimed severance pay. The *bet din* held that "the *Sefer HaChinukh* has obligated every employer to make such a grant on the basis of ethical and moral principles, so that the employee should not go empty handed. . . . They may otherwise find themselves penniless and impoverished at the end of their tenure."[41]

It is extremely difficult to judge to what extent the widespread practice of severance payments in modern Israel is a consequence of Jewish roots or an application of secular Socialist ideologies. So too, there may be a sliver of suspicion that the rabbis of the court were in effect tailoring Jewish principles to common practices in the Israeli economy. However, it seems that these principles, which predate Israel's welfare state, have indeed become so deeply rooted in the national subconscious that they have maintained this Jewish idea of acts of righteousness, despite the secular garb. For example, in a survey conducted by the author of the major Israeli corporations, it was found that the overwhelming majority of them paid their redundant workers over and above the severance payments regulated by law and even by their specific labor contracts.

2. "In order that you should go in good ways and follow the path of the righteous" (Proverbs 2:20)

Rabbi Chaim HaKohen Rappaport (eastern Europe, eighteenth century) replies in this vein to the question of a redundant ritual slaughterer:

> The community had hired a *shochet*—ritual slaughterer—for an undetermined period of time [which represents in Jewish law an agreement for long-term employment] whose wages were to be paid on a per capita basis. Recently the community has had to transfer the *abbatoir* to another city. He claims that they should continue to pay his hire. According to the law, justice is with the community, which is not liable to pay. However, it is fitting and correct that they should deal with him *lifnim mishurat hadin*, since he is poor and his children depend on him.[42]

Perhaps the best expression of this element of charity and righteousness in the severance pay and the ability of the rabbinical courts to enforce such acts is the ruling of the late chief rabbi of Israel, Rabbi Ben Zion Uziel:

> The courts have the power to take money, within their discretion, from the employer in favour of the workers, in all these cases where this element of the "paths of the righteousness" applies. Consideration has to be made of the financial situation of both the worker and the employer and the reasons for the dismissal [in order to permit justified dismissal in case of negligence or fraud without any severance pay]. . . . Therefore in every case where the *bet din* is convinced that the worker is harmed, they are obligated to rule in his favour, which is actually also a favour to the employer since this enables him to personally fulfill "and you shall walk in the path of the righteousness."[43]

Pensions

This is a form of support for aged and infirm long-term employees, of which there are many examples both in the responsa literature showing rabbinic legal discussion in real situations and in the enactments of the autonomous communities representing legislation.

The pension includes both those workers who because of old age are unable to work at all and those who are still partially able to continue their productive lives.

An example of legislation with respect to an employee unable to continue to work may be found in the *pinkas* (minute book) of the community of Posnan, central Europe, in the year 1643: "Mr. Shlomo Shamash Segal has performed all his duties faithfully and satisfactorily. Now in his old age, his hands and feet have became enfeebled, so that he is no longer able to stand the burdens of his office. The community will keep watch over him and not reject him, but rather supply his needs."[44]

There are two halakhic opinions that provide a legal basis for the obligation of the employer to pay a pension to his aged worker.

Rabbi Benyamin Rabinowitz argues, "By virtue of the long term employment the worker acquires the rights to a grant similar to that of the Hebrew bondsman. In both cases, what has been sold is the time rather than merely his efforts, contrary to the case of the casual or short term employee. For that reason, he has to be paid for the time of his old age when he cannot work any longer."[45]

He adds that even were this not so, then justice would demand that the employer maintain him, and not simply discard him as some used up article or piece of equipment.

Rabbi Eliezer Waldenberg, in present-day Jerusalem, provides a different perspective regarding the pension of a long-term employee:

> It is an accepted custom throughout the entire Diaspora of Israel that ritual slaughterers, teachers and other public employees must be supported even when they are no longer able to work. All their needs must be provided, without reducing their wages by very much, even though they no longer work. [This is likened to the rule that even those who guard the camp during a battle have the right to part of the spoils, even though they did not participate in the battle.] And the custom of Israel becomes law. . . . When he originally hired the worker, the employer undertook to provide for him in his old age as in his infirmity, since he understood that it is not possible to be employed for a long period without aging or becoming infirm.[46]

Partial Employment or Assistance

The provision of pensions and retirement benefits may cushion the elderly worker against the economic loss of his earning ability. Nevertheless modern medicine, improved nutrition, and health care have drastically prolonged the lifespan of many workers, which presents serious economic and social problems in all the modern economies. Many people may still be gainfully employed beyond the mandatory retirement age of sixty or sixty-five, yet at the same time pressures exist for even earlier retirement, both in order to cut production costs and to provide employment for new, younger workers. Many of the older workers suffer both physically and mentally from the sudden feeling of being redundant, while possessing skills and experience that society no longer values.

Welfare agencies provide for the social and cultural needs of some of these pensioners, while private enterprise, through retirement villages or similar facilities, provides for the needs of others. Judaism's insistence on lifelong Torah study may similarly alleviate part of this problem. Yet it seems that in general none of these, of themselves, present a viable solution.

There exists, however, in halakhic sources, both in the legislation of the autonomous Jewish communities and in the rulings of rabbinic authorities, an additional provision that would seem to be a far more substantive contribution, applicable even to non-Jewish corporations. This obligates the employer either to provide assistance to the aged worker who is able to be gainfully employed, albeit partially, or to supply him with less strenuous work.

The concept of an assistant is clearly spelled out in the gloss of the Rama on the *Shulchan Arukh*:

> A cantor [hired for a long period of time] who has become old and wishes to appoint his son to assist him from time to time [may do so on the basis of the responsum of the Rashba]. This is the case even where the son's voice is not as pleasing as that of the father, yet he is able to perform all the other duties properly. The son has precedence over all others [in accordance with the ruling of Maimonides regarding all public positions where the son is competent to fulfill his father's obligations].[47]

The *Arukh HaShulchan* rules that "since he was hired for a long period or for life, this is as though the community agreed to provide assistance whenever necessary as is customary when people become older [through hiring an assistant], which he can do at their expense."

Alternatively, the employer would be obligated to continue to provide the aged worker with less strenuous work. Regarding the Hebrew bondsman, Rabbi Sheshet in the Talmud holds that if he was ill all the six years of his indenture, nevertheless he may go free, even if he only did the lightest of work.

Rabbi Wallenberg maintains that, in accordance with the view of the halakhic authorities, "this means that as long as an aged teacher or a slaughterer or a worker are capable of doing some portions of their job, even if these are the least complicated or least difficult ones, the employer is obligated to retain him without any deductions to his salary."[48]

This solution is widely practiced today in the Israeli *kibbutz* movement, where elder members are gradually given easier jobs and shorter hours.

II

Private Property, Economics of Enough, and Social Obligations

5

When Less Is Better than More

CREATION OF A MORAL SOCIETY

Ethical issues in economics, as well as the halakhic categories of forbidden or permitted actions in business, are unfortunately seen primarily as relating only to the creation of wealth. This is because the methods whereby people acquire money, create economic assets, or accumulate wealth in other forms lend themselves so readily to immorality, oppression, and exploitation. Ethical sensitivity and equity are readily and relatively easily aroused to minimize such moral and social injustice within any society. However, this aspect of economic morality is in fact only one facet, and perhaps even the less important one, of the whole spectrum of ethical issues related to the marketplace. In reality, the primary moral challenge of wealth flows from its use, which not only affects the social fabric of society and a wide spectrum of interpersonal relationships but also, ultimately, determines the degree of wealth-creating activity and the methods whereby such activity is executed.

Patterns of consumption, the relationship between wants and needs, and the accepted levels of living standards are the primary factors in the demand for goods, services, and increased savings. In this way they serve to determine the amount of time and effort that society and individuals devote to earning money or creating wealth. Meeting the needs of the poor, the weak, the old, and ill requires using part of our wealth for voluntary charity or coerced taxation to cover the costs of the social-welfare items in the public-sector budgets. Both damage and conservation of the physical environment affect and are affected by the use to which wealth is put. Even the degree of competition and regulation in the market is conditioned primarily by social mores and the culturally accepted use of wealth. It this use of wealth and the role it plays in any society that will determine and make viable the moral parameters of business activity and economic order.

A society that sees wealth solely as a means to satisfy insatiable needs of the individual and family possessing it will find it difficult to construct any form of morality. It may well possess a legal system preventing fraud or theft that functions efficiently with a patina of morality, but it is not sufficient for real morality in which the needs of the people can be satisfied.[1] For this purpose, some educational method or spiritual guidance is needed that will be able to curb appetites, to guide part of the legally obtained wealth into socially constructive channels, and to recognize the claims of others or even of future generations to part of that wealth. Unless society and individuals are able to do so, it is difficult to conceive of how any moral framework for economic activity can exist. Since the egoism and selfishness of people are unlimited, in the long run even the purely legislative system becomes inadequate to prevent oppression. According to the Rabbis, in the mishnaic *Ethics of the Fathers*, "One who says, 'What is mine is mine and what is yours is yours,' this is the mark of a mediocre person; alternatively this is the mark of Sodom."[2] According to Jewish tradition the egoism of the Sodomites became normative behavior and the basis for their legal system, in contrast to other nations where it remained a matter of individual choice. The *Midrash* tells of a Sodomite custom to give the poor money marked with the sign of the giver. When the storekeepers refused to honor the currency, the poor died of starvation and the owner reclaimed his wealth. The same source tells of the court case of Eliezer, the disciple of Abraham, against a Sodomite who had bashed his nose causing it to bleed. The judge held that since bloodletting was beneficial, Eliezer had to pay his assailant. In reply Eliezer stepped forward and bashed the judge telling him to pay his fee to the Sodomite. Since the laws of Sodom were immoral, life could only proceed through bribery and corruption. Realizing that theft was not legally punishable if the stolen object was less than a *shaveh prutah*—a small copper coin—

each Sodomite, man, woman, and child, took one bean from a storekeeper's bag until the bag was empty—legal yet immoral.[3] So Sodom as a society was doomed to Divine destruction.

The other symbol of immorality and corruption in Judaism is the Generation of the Flood, who called down upon themselves the wrath of God. Midrashic sources make it quite clear that a primary cause of this corruption was the "mine is mine" attitude of the whole generation, which spread from mankind even to the beasts and the birds. As the number of people on earth multiplied, fear of having to share limited natural resources with others became rampant. Violence, theft, and crime became a way to preserve one's quality of life and standard of living, at the expense of others whose very existence threatened the resources available. There was an increase in the proportion of weak and unproductive men and women and a suspected degeneration of the animal species now called upon to provide for an increased population. The earth was deemed to be unable to provide as bountifully as before, so means were sought to prevent economic catastrophe. Limitations were placed on population growth, and only the finest and strongest of all species, mankind and animal alike, were allowed to procreate. As alternative sexual lifestyles, homosexuality and bestiality—both nonprocreative sexual relations—became rampant. Man, as the spiritual leader of the universe, taught the rest of Creation to follow in his footsteps, as reflected in biblical phraseology, "the whole earth became depraved."[4] Echoes of their concern for limiting population as a protection against economic scarcity may be found in societies ranging from ancient Sparta, in which the weak and old were killed through exposure, to the modern world's advocacy of population control. This finds its practical application in a policy of sterilization in India, strict regulation of the right to have children in Communist countries, and the "final solution" of Nazi Germany.

The fear of having to share became so obsessive to the Generation of the Flood that robbery and theft became rampant. Previously, even though idolatry and sexual immorality had been rife, economic honesty had enabled them to retain social harmony. Now crimes against property spread, bloodshed and murder became commonplace, as corruption and immorality became the hallmark of society; therefore God decreed destruction through the waters of the Flood.[5]

Recognition of the impossibility of maintaining a moral and ethical society within the parameters of "more is better than less" and without acknowledging man's egotistical uses of wealth determine much of Judaism. It has made the moral parameters of the limited use of wealth the pillar of its religious, spiritual, and communal tradition.

The *Aggadah* tells of the gentile who came to study Judaism with Hillel the Elder, whose school of Torah represents the definitive basis of the *Halakhah*. The gentile's condition for such study was that it be given while he stood on one foot. Unhesitatingly, Hillel answered, "That which is repugnant to you, do not do to your fellow; That is the basis of the Torah, now go and learn its implementation."[6]

The Book of Leviticus (chapter 19) commences with the biblical portion of *Kedoshim* (Ye shall be holy) in the synagogal annual cycle of public Torah reading. The Rabbis found it remarkable that this section, which includes all the basic tenets of the Jewish business morality, had to be taught to the whole congregation as strikingly distinct from the priests or elders, as is the case in most other laws. They explained that this was necessary since most of the basic injuctions and teachings of the Torah are found in *Kedoshim*, where the verse "Thou shall love thy neighbor as thyself" appears. Rabbi Akiva taught that this verse is the essence of the whole Torah.[7] This is the pillar, as it were, on which the Jewish treatment of the use of wealth rests.

The essence of such treatment lies in the ability of the individual and society to understand and accept that there is a stage of "enough" regarding economic activity and wealth. When the patriarch Jacob met his brother, Esau, he sent him a magnificent gift of flocks and herds, representing much wealth. Esau protested, saying, "I have much." This however did not prevent him from wanting more and accepting the gift. Jacob, on the other hand, replied, "I have everything."[8] It can be shown that society's willingness to deal with social issues, the individual's ability to meet the demands of economic equity, and all the considerations of environmental protection presuppose the acceptance of this attitude of the patriarch Jacob.

WAIVER OF LEGAL RIGHTS

People's sense of obligation, pity, or fairness prompts them to extend charity to others and to participate in the funding of communal social obligations. Far more difficult, however, is the voluntary renunciation in the course of business activites of one's legal property rights for another's benefit, even though this has exactly the same economic effect as the charitable acts.

The Maharal (Rabbi Loew of Prague, seventeenth century, perhaps the foremost Jewish mystical philosopher) explains that this is inevitable. Material things in life, including economic assets, are finite, even though they might always be increasing. Desires however are infinite. While only one Adam was created, the whole world was his, so that there was no boundary to his ambition and his longing, a state that has been bequeathed to his descendants.[9]

Jewish recognition of this human need for private property and its corollary of legislation protecting such property have been amply demonstrated in part I of this book. However, Judaism does not view anything as unlimited, no matter how beneficial or essential to human happiness or development it may be. Regarding wealth, the often proclaimed tenet of the market that "more is better than less" makes the increase in wealth a selfish major aim of life limited only by the parameters of efficiency and legal rights of others. In contrast, Judaism presents a wide variety of actions and legal concepts aimed at weaning people away from this unlimited "more is better than less," toward a social system within which it is possible to say, "This is enough." Such systems presuppose the voluntary renunciation of legal rights and the acceptance of regulation of the market.

The *Sefer HaChinukh* (Barcelona, Spain, fourteenth century), in discussing the ideology of the biblical commandment, "But during the seventh year [*shmittah*] you shall let your land lie fallow" (Exodus 23:11), writes, "This is to teach us the attribute of [the voluntary] renunciation of property and the resultant generosity that flows from this attribute. God wanted the Jews to develop charitable characteristics, that they should become used to helping others and to become accustomed to giving away something that actually belongs [legally] to them."[10]

This is not the same as asceticism. Judaism quite clearly spells out the enjoyment of God's bounty, given to satisfy the needs of all His creatures, first and foremost mankind. The nazirite, who vows to abstain from wine and the fruit of the grape, has to bring a sin offering at the termination of this vow, inter alia, because he has not found pleasure in that which God created.[11] Maimonides rules that a pleasant wife, a pleasant home, and beautiful utensils expand man's horizons.[12] There is no Jewish ceremony without food or wine, while a scholar who wears soiled garments is considered to deserve the death penalty. Clearly there is no spiritual problem involved in using the wealth one has acquired morally and fairly. At the same time, educating toward a mental framework of "enough," which flows from an understanding of God as the source of all wealth and the trust in His Divine Providence, enables people to operate in this marketplace, and yet allow for the economic efforts and needs of others.

MODESTY

The records–*pinkas*–of the autonomous Jewish communities all refer to sumptuary laws or enactments that came to limit consumption. It is easy to assume, as indeed many researchers have done, that these were simply meant to prevent the jealousy of the surrounding hostile gentile societies being aroused by conspicuous consumption. While it is obvious that such an element did exist, nevertheless there is enough evidence to show that these limitations flowed primarily from a basic religious encouragement of the "economics of enough."

The devotion of time to the study of Torah, which is obligatory on all Jews, irrespective of their age, intelligence, and status, is an unlimited one. This demands a limitation in time on the efforts spent in business activity, so that restraints on demand, which make such limitations possible, are an essential and integral part of the Jewish economic framework.

Furthermore, modesty, usually considered to refer to modes of dress, applies equally to standards of living. "Thou shall walk modestly before thy God" is a spiritual demand by the prophet Amos. This is reflected in the simplicity in furniture, clothing, and lifestyle of Jews throughout the centuries, a simplicity that has always been an integral part of Jewish living. Maimonides, in describing the characteristics of the *talmid chakham*–the Torah scholar and ethical role model in Judaism –lays great stress on moderation in eating, clothing, and personal consumption.

> He provides for his family according to his means, yet without excessive devotion to this. His clothing should be neither that of kings nor that of poor men, but rather pleasant, ordinary clothing. The Torah scholar should eat his normal meals in his own house and should not participate in public feasting, even with scholars. It is fitting for him to eat in public [which is more expensive and conspicuous] only those meals associated with a religious precept, such as the marriage of a scholar to the daughter of a scholar.[13]

These rulings of Maimonides flow from the discussion in the Talmud that preceded the persecution of Jews in Christian Europe.

In present-day Israel, the *Admor* (spiritual leader) of Gur, who numbers many thousands of *chasidim* among his followers, has recently limited the number of participants at weddings to 300 in order to curb conspicuous consumption, social competition, and often financial deprivation (or economic immorality). Both he and the *Admor* of Belz have encouraged their followers to move away from Jerusalem, with its high cost of housing, to areas such as Ashdod, where homes are more reasonable. A recent group of secular schoolchildren were particularly impressed by the simplicity in which Rabbi Shach, the leader of the Lithuanian *yeshivot* lives, despite the political power he exercises.

An educational process alone, however, is not sufficient to inculcate such a generous nature, so halakhic forms are provided that obligate such acts, until they indeed become second nature. All of them concern the renunciation of those property rights that are uncontested and perfectly legal.

PE'AH

The Bible (Leviticus 23:22) obligates the Jewish farmer to leave *pe'ah*, the corner of his fields, for the poor, the widows and orphans, and the stranger. A primary difference between *pe'ah* and other forms of assistance or charity is that the owner is obliged to relinquish control over this corner. It is true that the poor may not reap it until the owner has completed his harvest, nor may they trample any of the surrounding crop; that would be theft. Nevertheless, the owner cannot "acquire" the *pe'ah*, either by harvesting it or preventing the poor from reaping it, in order to give it to a particular person or persons; ownership has simply been renounced.

Furthermore, the *mitzvah* of *pe'ah* is introduced, quite irrationally at first glance, into the list of the festivals in Leviticus. At the outset these are presented in their order, Passover, Shavuot, but are then interrupted by *pe'ah*, only to continue with Rosh HaShanah, Yom Kippur, and Sukkot. This intrusion is a glaring one, since there is no festival related to *pe'ah*. Further consideration, however, will show an important moral lesson related to economic behavior. On Shavuot, the festival of the first fruits, the farmer is proud of his economic success demonstrated by these fruits. He struts in contemplation of his wealth, confident of his ability, and reflects on how smart he is. Yet, these very first fruits (easily translated into the annual profits of any modern corporation) had to be seen solely as the result of the bounty of God. So the farmer had to go to the Temple in Jerusalem, take his first fruits with him, and there recite *viddui* (confession) in which the Divine origin of his wealth is acknowledged. The next festival in the Jewish calender is Rosh Hashanah, when the King God sits in judgment on the world and all in it. In order to bring the Jew from the economic self-satisfaction of Shavuot to the humility and awe of the Day of Judgment, the Torah interjected the law of *Pe'ah* to teach the importance of a certain waiving of property rights.[14]

LIFNIM MISHURAT HADIN

The renunciation of property rights is also the basis for the rabbinic concept of business actions that are beyond the letter of the law, *lifnim mishurat hadin*. Actually, this is a third stage in Jewish commercial law. In Part I of this book, the obligation of the rabbinic courts to adjudicate business disputes and to ensure economic justice was clearly demonstrated. In fact, Jewish communities to this day have consistently rejected recourse to non-Jewish courts for this purpose. Inter alia it has been argued that, in view of the Divine origin of Torah, where the non-Jewish law differs, it may lead to the illegal transfer of money from one person to another, which would constitute theft.

Nevertheless, there are often circumstances where for various technical or legal reasons the obligations of the parties cannot be enforced by the courts. In such circumstances, the Rabbis maintained that it was still necessary for one to clear oneself before Heaven, so that the parties concerned could be obligated to certain actions.

> One who leaves embers in the possession of the deaf or retarded or minors [who are considered to be halakhically irresponsible] who subsequently cause a fire to spread to the haystack of a neighbor, is not liable [cannot be forced to pay for the damage since he did not actually cause the damage according to the laws of men]. However, he is liable before the laws of Heaven [and is morally obligated to pay since he is responsible to a certain extent for the damage.] In the case where he left in their care an actual flame, he is responsible [and can be forced by the courts to pay] since he in effect caused the damage].[15]

The Meiri writes, "One who does not pay what is required in order to be clear before Heaven cannot be considered to be a valid witness before the rabbinic courts."[16]

In all the cases where, even though the courts cannot rule, there still remains some monetary damage to others, one is obligated to repair that damage in order to be clear before Heaven. However, there are cases where pious people will perform acts that are beyond the demands even of the heavenly law, *lifnim mishurat hadin*. Since the role models developed by Judaism are such people, these *midat chasidut*, acts of righteousness, are presented as a constant in all the commercial transactions of the Jew in the marketplace. The *Mishnah* in the *Chapters of the Fathers* classifies one who says regarding his wealth, "What is yours is yours, and what is mine is also yours," as a righteous man.[17]

Conversely, the strict prosecution of one's legal right is considered to be a socially destructive force. The Talmud argues that the reason the Second Temple was destroyed some two thousand years ago was that the Jews in that generation "insisted on the exact fulfillment of the law."[18] This was in contrast to the First Temple, which was destroyed in 586 B.C.E. because of the three cardinal sins, idolatory, adultery, and bloodshed.

Maimonides sees these *midat chasidut*—righteous actions beyond the letter of the law—as being the symbol of the market behavior of the *talmid chakham*—the Torah scholar who is the Jewish role model in all walks of life.

> The commerce of the *talmid chakham* has to be in truth and in faith. His yes is to be yes and his no, no; he forces himself to be exact in calculations when he is paying but is willing to be lenient when others are his debtors. . . . He should keep his obligations in commerce even where the law allows him to withdraw or retract, so that his word is his bond; but if others have obligations to him, he should deal mercifully, forgiving and extending credit. One should be careful not to deprive one's neighbor of his livelihood, even where this is legal and efficient, so that one does not cause hardship and anguish. He who does all these things is the one referred to by the prophet Isaiah when he said in God's name, "You, Israel, are My servant, in whom I take pride" (Isaiah 49:3).[19]

In the usual halakhic fashion, this type of business behavior was not seen as that of exalted, yet marginal, personalities but was reduced to legal decisions meant to be applicable to all observant Jews. Such behavior was either enforceable through forms of punishment, or alternatively through peer pressure or rabbinic persuasion.

One such classic case concerns Rabbi Yishmael ben Jossi, one of the Sages at the time of the redaction of the *Mishnah* (c. 200-250 C.E.). The Talmud tells of his meeting a man on the road who temporarily had to unload the bundle of wood he carried on his back. In accordance with the Mosaic law, Rabbi Yishmael was required to help him raise his burden. However, being an old man, this was considered halakhically as not befitting for him, so the rabbi inquired as to the worth of the wood and paid the man its price! Then, in order to save people from theft, he declared the wood ownerless. At this stage, the man, shrewdly enough, acquired possession and asked Rabbi Yishmael to help him load. The story was repeated until the rabbi renounced ownership to all and sundry, except the porter. In the ensuing discussion, the Rabbis taught that even though Rabbi Yishmael was neither obligated to assist the man because of his old age nor to pay for the wood, he did so, *lifnim mishurat hadin*. As the Tosafists point out, this was only so because while he himself was not obligated, everybody else was; this defines *lifnim mishurat hadin* as those actions done by one who is normally free from an obligation that falls on everybody else.[20]

The following ruling in the code of the *Arbaah Turim* gives clear legal expression to the concept of *lifnim mishurat hadin*. "A porter who breaks a cask while moving it from one place to another on a level path is guilty of negligence and is liable to pay for the damage. This applies even in the case of a unpaid bailee [who is liable in Jewish law for negligence]. Nevertheless, it is a *mitzvah* to act *lifnim mishurat hadin* and give the porter his hire if he is poor." [The Bach adds that if, however, the porter has enough to eat, it is not necessary to pay him the hire, even though he is not liable to pay the damage because of his poverty.][21]

There are numerous other cases in the Talmud and in the codes reflecting the application of *lifnim mishurat hadin*—beyond the demands of the law.[22] The following responsum of the Tzemach Tzedek (Rabbi Krochmal, Moravia, sixteenth century) reflects this method of rabbinic commercial reasoning in his ruling in a case of competition.

> Reuven has been selling liquor for thirty years and has many dependents. Now Shimon, who is wealthy and has other businesses but no dependents, wishes to open a simiar firm.

In this case, the law is that Reuven cannot prevent him. However, the question remains whether we can force Shimon to operate beyond the letter of the law and refrain from opening the proposed store. This would be in accordance with the ruling of the *Bach* (*Bayit Chadash* of Rabbi Joel Sirkes, section 12) that where the newcomer suffers no loss from the restraint [preventing one from thereby earning a profit is not, halakhically, the same as causing an actual loss, still] his competition is an act of Sodom [which can be prevented by the courts]. Even were this not so, the courts should at least use verbal pressure to persuade him not to open the competing store.[23]

ONE HAS A BENEFIT AND THE OTHER SUFFERS NO LOSS

The primary example of how the *Halakhah* imposed legal rulings and communal patterns of behavior that force individuals to give up some of their uncontested property rights for the use of others is the concept of *zeh neheneh vezeh lo chaser*—one has a benefit from something yet the owner suffers no loss. This concept stands in stark contrast to the laws of trespass and riparian rights, which exist in almost all Western legal codes. Yet in Judaism it is a primary method for ensuring that in those cases where no financial loss is caused, people will do favors for others. These favors, it must be borne in mind, are not performed for the poor or needy but for all and sundry. They are economic applications of "You shall love your neighbor," and the refusal to apply them is seen in Judaism as a characteristic of the people of Sodom. Such refusals can be counteracted by the courts since "we enforce [preventing of] *midat Sodom*."[24]

The Rabbis of the Talmud saw in the social covenant entered into by the Twelve Tribes on their entry into the Land of Israel, after the forty years of wandering in the desert, the expression of this form of social policy. Maimonides codifies this as binding law.

> Joshua and his *bet din* regulated ten enactments when they allocated the Land [to the Tribes of Israel]:
>
> It is permissible for everybody [without permission or payment] to graze small cattle [sheep] in a forest [even though the forest is private property] with mature trees [since the grazing does not harm the trees]. It is forbidden, however, to graze large cattle [cows or steers] in these forests. [Needless to say] one may not graze either small or large cattle in a forest of under-

> developed trees [since even small cattle can cause damage] without the permission of the owner.
>
> It is permissible for anyone to collect wood from his neighbor's field [without permission or payment]. This includes only that which is of little value and those considered thorns. They have to be green [otherwise the owner could use them for firewood] and attached but not rooted.
>
> Everybody may catch fish in the Kinneret [which belonged to the tribe of Naftali], provided they only use a line and hook [in which case the amount of fish taken is insufficient to cause a loss]. However, they may not use a net or use a ship [since they would be depriving the owners of substantial quantities] except for the members of the tribe in whose territory the sea exists. [The Tur argues that even that tribe cannot spread nets that impede the movements of ships, even though the sea belongs to them.]
>
> A *met mitzvah* [an indigent person who does not have anyone to bury him] acquires the ground on which he lies [for burial, even though it belongs to somebody else]. If he dies on a boundary or within the city limits, then he is buried in the cemetery.
>
> [All these enactments, of which only a few have been presented here, limit the property rights of the owner and permit others to benefit from the property, provided no damage or loss to the owner occurs.][25]

These cases permitting trespassing in order to do other people a favor with wealth that undoubtedly belongs to the owner are paralleled by the law of *bar metzrah*—the adjoining owner. According to this law, real-estate transactions are guided not only by markt forces, which are legitimate, but also by considerations of *zeh neheneh vezeh lo chaser*—one has a benefit from the owner's property, yet the owner suffers no loss. This concept is clearly enunciated in the code of *Arukh HaShulchan* (Yechiel Michael Epstein, Lithuania, nineteenth century):

> The sages have commanded us that when one sells ground or a house or a store, then if the adjoining neighbor wishes to buy it he has precedence [the first right of refusal] before all other people. This is conditional on his paying the market price. The authority for this law is the verse "You shall do that which is honest and good in the sight of the Lord." It is His desire that people do to each other that which is good and honest and there is nothing more honest or correct than this since the seller suffers no loss by giving preference to the neighbor.[26]

The neighbor has a benefit since this law gives him the chance to obtain a larger unified tract of land, with all the consequent efficiencies.

At the same time he has to pay the price that others are prepared to pay; to rule otherwise would impose a loss on the seller. So, too, the law of *bar metzrah* does not apply to bona fide gifts, where the giver suffers a nonmonetary loss by not being able to give gifts to those he wishes to. Those cases where the sale is caused by a lack of liquidity on the part of the owner are also exempt from the law, since under pressure he may suffer a loss if he is unable to sell to the first available buyer. This lack of symmetry is essential, since the concept of *bar metzrah* is based on the obligation to help others with one's property, but this does not give other parties the right to cause the owner any loss. To obligate one to suffer such losses would not only be immoral but also counterproductive since this is something beyond human nature. Judaism has always demanded of people only that they sanctify acts with which human beings are able to live. At the same time, within these restrictions, *dina debar metzrah* is not allowed to be merely a friendly gesture motivated by kindness but carries with it legal consequences that may invalidate a sale made to another party, as in the following ruling of the *Shulchan Arukh*.

> One who sells ground to another, irrespective of whether it is sold directly by the owner, or through an agent or through the *bet din*, the neighbor whose property adjoins this land can pay the purchaser [the price he had paid] and remove him [to take possession]. This is true even where the buyer is a *talmid chakham* [who is usually given preferential treatment in the market; a form of subsidy to Torah study] and the neighbor is an *am haaretz*—an ignoramus.[27]

Maimonides rules, "This law does not apply to minor orphans [as purchasers], since the concept of good and noble in regard to orphans exceeds that demanded in the case of normal owners" [so that the neighbor would have to waive his right of *bar metzrah* in favor of the orphans].[28]

Human nature being what it is militates against this idea of giving somebody a benefit even if it does not cost the giver anything. As often as not, the seller of real estate would prefer to sell to anybody and everybody, except the neighbor who would thus have a free benefit. This is evident in many aspects of the marketplace. Closely held or family-owned corporations often list their shares on a stock exchange, primarily because the various shareholders cannot agree to sell their shares to each other in view of the advantage this may give to one or other of the owners. One of the reasons for registering offshore corporations is to conceal the real identity of the owners, which if known, could cause their potential customers to demand higher prices or not to deal with the corporation at all. So, too, in real life it is possible to evade the "one has a benefit and the other suffers no loss" concept by creating conditions in which the neighbor is unable to execute his halakhic right. This possibility arose in the case discussed by the Netziv of Volozhin (Naftali Tzvi Yehudah Berlin, Lithuania, nineteenth century).

> Reuven left his town to go and dwell in another city. He sold his land to another on condition that after eight years he would have the right within two years to buy back the field and any building which the buyer erected. When this sale/lease transaction, became known, the neighbor came to dispossess the buyer. . . . The seller maintains that if the neighbor would have been willing to agree to the conditions of the sale, he would have been willing to sell the land to him. . . .
>
> The Shach (R. Shabbtai HaKohen, classical commentator on the *Shulchan Arukh*) explains the *Shulchan Arukh*'s ruling (section 175, subsection 38) that the neighbor of one who sells his house in order to move to another city does not have any rights:
>
> This is illustrated by the case of the man who sold an inferior field in order to buy a superior one [in which case preventing the owner from selling it on the open market may have caused him to suffer a loss]. Even though there is no difference between one who wishes to move to another city and one who wishes to sell in order to move to another sector of the same city, the *Shulchan Arukh* is referring to a case where the buyer happens to be from the city to which the seller intends to move [which presents him with an opportune buyer]. This is similar to the ruling of the Rosh that where one sells all his goods at the same time, the protection of *bar metzrah* does not apply, since it is difficult to find one buyer who will buy them all and by giving the neighbor first refusal, we may be causing the seller a loss. From all the above, it seems that the neighbor in our case does not have the right to evict the buyer till after the ten years [eight of the contract and the two-year grace period agreed upon] have elapsed and the seller has not utilized his buy-back options. After that period, the neighbor can claim the law of *bar metzrah* and evict the buyer [upon payment of the purchase price]. If, however, it can be shown by the neighbor that the whole sale/lease contract was only made to evade the rights of the neighbor, the court is required to immediately evict the buyer.[29]

The concept of "one benefits and the other suffers no loss" may under certain circumstances permit somebody to live rent-free in another person's property. The *Mishnah* lays the basis for this when it says that one who stays in a house belonging to another and causes it no damage is not required to pay if the owner's usual practice was not to hire it out.[30]

It must be stressed that this is a limitation on the rights of the owner to the rental. In no way is it a carte blanche for squatting. The squatter is, as we have seen previously, considered a robber, since he takes by force property that belongs to another.

Following the principle of doing "that which is good and honest" affects all the aspects of commerce and business, so the following two examples should suffice to demonstrate the possible implications of this principle for everyday economic behavior.

> Since Reuven was unable to pay his debt, the *bet din* transferred his fields to his creditor Shimon. If after some time the debtor, Reuven or his heirs, acquires money and is able to return the sum of the debt to the creditor, they are able to dispossess him and regain possession of the field. [This ruling of the *Shulchan Arukh* is explained by Rabbi Yechiel Michael Aharon Epstein as flowing from the obligation to do that which is honest and good.] It is fitting that ground that is taken from somebody against his will, even if done legally at the order of the court, should be returned to him if he is able to pay the money [the creditor suffers no loss since he is now being paid his debt in full and the debtor has a great benefit] because of the sorrow suffered since every person has great affection for his property.[31]

While the concept of *bar metzrah* is confined to real estate of all forms and anything attached to it, this authority argues that there are other areas in which the same principle applies.

> In the case of partners in a business dealing with movable property, should one sell his share to an outsider, then if the courts agree that the other partner is not compatible with the buyer, then they can prevent the sale. This is not because of the law of the adjoining neighbor but because one is not permitted to cause damage to his partner and this is doing that which is good and honest. So too, in the case of partners in a credit corporation where the premises are not primarily for purposes of storing goods [which would make them liable to the law of *bar metzrah*], nevertheless if the court sees that the sale of one of the partner's shares is to the detriment of the others, the sale can be prevented.[32]

This principle should therefore apply to the sale of shares in family-held corporations or in those with a small number of shareholders, irrespective of the nature of the firm's business. Of equal significance is the application of this principle to the corporate mergers that characterized the 1980s in western Europe and the United States. It is difficult to envisage that many of them would occur if any sale by one shareholder would have to be scrutinized to determine that no damage or inconvenience is caused to the other shareholders by the sale.

PREVENTING DAMAGES

Any review of a society's attitude to ecological issues has to be concerned with the moral obligation of people to prevent causing damage to others, either through their assets or their persons. The Jewish perspective on this issue is dealt with in chapter 8 of this book. Of equal importance, however, is the degree to which one is expected to invest time, effort, and money in the prevention of that damage to others, caused by exogeneous factors over which one has no control.

In many modern societies, even the wealthiest and most sophisticated of them, people are taught to mind their own business, and so to refrain from interfering when others are in potential or actual danger of financial or bodily harm. The Jewish value structure stands in complete contrast to this, as may be seen in the moralistic literature and the legal codes aimed at inculcating in the Jew a sense of duty to assist others even where he is not the source of damage. Not to do so in the economic sphere is seen sometimes as a function of robbery and sometimes as rejection of the biblical commandment "You shall not stand idly by your brother's blood" (Leviticus 19:16). This may sound overly melodramatic, yet closer examination of the realities in the marketplace lends credence to the comment of Rashi on Deuteronomy 6:5 that material goods are often more precious to people than their own lives.

The Bible reiterates in a number of places that one is obligated to return lost articles to their righful owners, and this is codified as law.

> If one finds a lost cow, he is obligated to care for it and return it to the owners, even if this is not in accordance with his honor since he began the *mitzvah* [and is obligated to complete it]. Even in those cases where

> the cow ran away after being returned, he is still obligated to return it—even if this happens a thousand times, as it is written, "You shall surely return it" [the repetitive form used in the Hebrew text is considered by the rabbis to refer to the repetitive obligation].[33]

The obligation to return lost articles does not apply only to animals, movables, money, or clothing. Land, which obviously cannot be lost, can nevertheless be destroyed and, therefore, to all intents and purposes, lost to the owners. So one has the obligation literally to return it, actually to prevent the loss, as ruled by the talmudical Sages in *Baba Metzia* codified in the *Mishneh Torah*, *Arbaah Turim*, and *Shulchan Arukh*.

"One who sees water in flood threatening the building or field of his neighbor [even where the building is not in danger of being swept away but only damaged] is obligated to shore them up [or to build embankments to prevent the damage]."[34]

It is interesting that the Talmud prohibits one from obeying one's parents when they instruct one not to return lost articles, since God's law obligates them as well.

Perhaps it is in this light that one should view the halakhic ruling that one is obligated "to bring in the implements [left standing exposed in the fields] of the idolators [normally any such help would be considered to be assisting evildoers, either since all men are not allowed to worship idols or because the idolators do not have a moral legal system] for the sake of peace."

Since the Torah also warns against not returning the articles, one who keeps them for himself is considered to be a robber, while one who, in view of the trouble and cost incurred, ignores the article violates a negative precept.

This legal obligation created by the Bible and quoted from Maimonides contrasts with the cultural framework embodied in the Anglo-Saxon saying "finders are keepers and losers are weepers," as well as with the legal power of rulers in many societies to confiscate goods found by their subjects.

Yet the morality of assisting others is extended far beyond the simple scenario of lost property. Reflecting centuries of rabbinic teaching, the *Shulchan Arukh* places the onus for saving other people's property, and even their lives, from a wide range of danger clearly on the shoulders of every Jew.

> He who sees his neighbor drowning or being attacked by robbers or by wild animals and is able to save him himself or to hire others to do so [the Tur rules that later the person being saved has to repay the expenses involved if he is financially able to do so] and did not do so; or if he heard people plotting against his neighbor to do him harm or to inflict damage on him and did not inform his neighbor [who would then be able to protect himself]. . . . Whoever does all these and similar things is guilty of transgressing the biblical commandment, "You shall not stand idly by your brother's blood" (Leviticus 19:16).[35]

The positive religious obligation of the Jew to save others from harm is to be carried out even at the expense of killing the pursuer, regardless of whether the latter's purpose is bodily harm or sexual rape.

Further rereading of the sources will show the special relevance of the *Shulchan Arukh*'s ruling for conduct in the marketplace. The *Midrash* states, "One may not withhold knowledge or evidence that may cause a loss of his fellowman's money, as it is written, 'Do not stand idly by your brother's blood.'"[36] We are also obligated to inform others of shoddy workmanship or loss suffered through a business deal in order that others not suffer the same loss. This is not considered to be *lashon hara* (talebearing), which is strictly forbidden. So, too, if one hears somebody plotting to cause another harm, one is obligated to tell them, so they can prevent it, or alternatively, one should persuade the plotters not to carry out their plans.

The prevention of damage is not only directed to individuals, but applies also to public welfare as may be seen from the comment of the *Arukh HaShulchan*, "Even more so, is one obligated to prevent damage to the public. Therefore, if one knows that people intend to do such damage, one has to protest to the best of one's ability."

These injunctions would seem to have special significance for those possessing knowledge of planned corporate takeovers that are to the detriment of the shareholders, as well as for workers who have knowledge of fraud within their corporation, to make their knowledge public. Modern whistle-blowing would seem to be in keeping with these rabbinical injunctions and was even institutionalized in many communities.

The *Be'er HaGolah* (eighteenth-century commentary on the *Shulchan Arukh* written by Rabbi Moshe Rivkes of Vilna) tells of community actions meant to prevent immoral business actions by individuals that endanger the Jewish community.

> The custom has spread whereby the leaders of the community are vigilant in their efforts to prevent members of the community from defrauding the public. They publicly announce and so spread the names of those who borrow or buy on credit with no intention of repaying. This announcement is a correct and proper custom which sanctifies God's Name. It should be emulated in other communities so that the nations will recognize Israel as a nation that glorifies Him. It also includes those who create counterfeit money and other forgeries.[37]

This religious obligation to prevent others from suffering bodily or financial harm as an expression of love for one's fellowman is explained by the *Sefer HaChinukh*, the magnificent thirteenth-century Spanish study of the ideology behind the *mitzvot*. Regarding the biblical command "If you see the donkey of your enemy straining under its burden . . . you shall surely help him [unload]" (Exodus 23:5), he writes:

> It is a religious duty to help unload a man laden with a burden as well. [The verse uses the donkey only as an example of carrying burdens, which is the usual purpose of a donkey.] Furthermore, even if the owner only suffers the loss of his goods and possessions, it is a religious obligation for us to take pity on him. At the root of this precept lies the obligation to teach our spirit the quality of compassion, which is a noble trait of character. Not only does one have a duty to take pity on a man who is suffering physical pain, but one also has a duty to one who is sorrowed by the loss of his property.[38]

6

"Thy Brother Shall Live with Thee" (Leviticus 25:36)

INTRODUCTION

The effects of greed and the fear of uncertainty, which lead to economic crime and theft, may be limited by the understanding of God's role as the real provider of all the needs of His creatures. This, however, is not sufficient to create a moral economic system. All too often, faith in God's bounty as satisfying all the needs of men leads to an evasion of social responsibilities. This piety can easily degenerate into the moral corruption of telling the poor, the weak, and even one's competitors in the marketplace to trust in God's bounty, using it as an excuse for not sharing what we receive from Him. It is because of this ease with which people are able to find reasonable and rational reasons for not giving charity that the Tur in his opening statement to the laws of *tzedakah* uses a repetitive form, writing that "one is obligated to be very, very careful in giving charity."[1] By these laws, the belief in Divine bounty as a source of all wealth creates in Judaism a concept of stewardship, whereby part of that wealth is given to assist others.[2] The religious concept of *bitachon* (trust in God) may be applied only to ourselves and may not be projected as the means to solve the economic problems of others. One of the chasidic masters said that he was taught this lesson when he found a ten ruble note. "I put it under a stone and wrote on the stone, 'Thou shall not steal!' When I returned, I found a five ruble note in its place and written on the stone was the verse 'Thy brother shall live with thee.'"

The *Mishnah* classifies one whose attitude to wealth is "What is mine is mine and what is yours is yours" as being a mediocre person. Such a person is prepared to respect the property of another and operate within the framework of the law. However, he is not prepared to assist others, nor does he recognize a social obligation in view of the wealth in his possession. "Some say," continues the *Mishnah*, "this is the mark of the people of Sodom."[3] The people of Sodom have been the archetype of an evil community deserving of destruction ever since biblical times, primarily because of their selfish economic behavior. The Malbim (Rabbi Meir Lebush, Hungary, nineteenth century) comments that their sin lay in their refusal to share their wealth with the surrounding nations.[4] It should be noted that while the *Aggadah* is replete with stories of their inhospitality to strangers, the men of Sodom welcomed Lot, Abraham's nephew. Lot was a wealthy man, and it was only poor strangers who were not welcome in Sodom. The Sodomite view of absolute private property rejects any obligations to assist others, which is contrary to the Jewish concept of limited private-property rights.

Hearing that in the World to Come evildoers would be punished by not being able to bend their arms, a *chasid* queried Divine Justice, saying that this was no punishment. "Well, they will not be able to eat," answered his master. But the *chasid* countered, "Let them sit opposite each other and then they can feed one another with their outstretched arms." "That, however, they refuse to do. That is their evil way even as it was in Sodom."

However, what made it necessary to destroy Sodom was not the individual selfishness of its citizens, but the fact that this had become an integral part of its communal culture. While a society can exist with cruel and selfish individuals, the moral decay that sets in when cruelty and callousness become hallmarks of that society marks it for Divine retribution. Rashi, commenting on the verse in Amos "They who sell the poor for a pair of shoes," highlights this communal aspect. He notes the difference between a sandal, which is open, and a shoe, which is closed and possesses in Hebrew the same grammatical root as lock. This is what the rich did. They closed in the poor farmer's field and then forced him to sell—a perfectly legal but immoral use of societal legislation. So Judea had to be destroyed. In Sodom they gave charity generously. However, all the money was secretly marked so that the storekeepers refused to accept it. When the poor died of hunger, each Sodomite reclaimed his money—legal but abhorrent. Cruelty and callousness are expressed not only in relationships with the poor and weak but also in those between buyer and seller, employer and employee, and even competitors in all spheres of business activity.

When a *chasid* came to his *Admor* to complain that his competitors were encroaching on his livelihood, the master told him the following story:

> A horse, pausing to drink of the waters of a lake, was astounded to see the head of another horse, bending to drink of his water. In anger, he lashed out with his hooves to chase the other horse away. When, indeed the waves drove away the intruder, the horse put his head down into the water once again to drink, only to find that the other horse had returned. Once again he lashed out with his hooves. You, my friend are a man not a horse. The God who provides for you, provides also for the needs of your fellowmen.

If people really believed that all their needs would be satisfied as a result of God's mercy and providence, then they would not hesitate to share their wealth with others. Indeed, the refusal to share wealth with others is a denial of trust in God, a rejection of God's merit as the provider of the needs of man, and an assumption that that wealth is the result solely of one's work, ability, or luck. The selfishness of the people of Sodom and their imitators in all societies is actually a form of idolatry, since it negates the Divine Source of all wealth.

The rabbinic treatment of one of the laws of the *Shmittah* (Sabbatical year) can easily illustrate this. The Talmud, commenting on the sequence of the biblical verses in Leviticus 25 foretelling the punishment for those who trade in such produce, states:

> Rabbi Jossi bar Chanina says: Come and see how severe [are the consequences of] the dust of *Shmittah* [the rabbinical injunction against trading in produce of that year]. A man trades in the fruits of the Sabbatical year, this leads to [a punishment wherein he has to] sell his movable goods [relating to verse 14], then he has to sell his fields [verse 25], then his home [verse 29], then he has to borrow money at interest [verse 35], then he has to sell himself because of his poverty [verse 39], and finally even to be sold to an idolator or to idolatry [verse 47].[4]

Querying the severity of the punishment for this trade, the Torah Temimah (Rabbi Baruch Epstein, Lithuania, early twentieth century) points out that after all, trading in the produce of *Shmittah* is only derived from the additional phrase in the Bible stressing that the produce may be eaten, that is eaten and not sold, in contrast to the biblical injunction that forbids only agricultural work such as plowing and sowing. This should in theory make trading less serious than the sin of agricultural work. He answers that the trader, seemingly only a marginal factor, is actually denying God as the source of all wealth, to the same extent as one who works his land. All reject the words of God, "For all the Land [wealth] belongs to Me, says the Lord," which conclude the Sabbatical and Jubilee laws.[5]

Faith in God as the source of all wealth and in His ability and undertaking to provide for all is therefore the basic tenet on which the whole Jewish concept of the economic forms of "Thy brother shall live with thee" rests.

JERUSALEM AND ROME ON CHARITY

Turnus Rufus, the Roman governor of Judea during the second century of the Common Era, argued that it would have been better for the Lord to care for the poor, the weak, the aged, and the inefficient, rather than place this onus on the shoulders of other men. The ensuing discussion in the Talmud between the pagan governor and Rabbi Akiva provides a concise description of the basic concepts of mutual responsibility that have always characterized Jewish living.[6] They may be summarized as follows.

Imitatio Dei

In Judaism, man is considered to be able to emulate God, and his whole life should be considered to be one vast opportunity to do so. This emulation is inherent in the very essence of man's nature, as may be seen in the biblical account of the Creation. God, about to create Adam, said, "Let us make man in Our Image." To whom was this addressed? The Baal Shem Tov, founder of the chasidic movement, taught: "This was addressed to man himself. 'Come,' said the Lord to man, 'let us make man together, for without you I cannot make man.'"

Yet, in a talmudic discussion, a rabbi asked how one can emulate God and be so presumptuous as to assume that one can walk in His ways. After all, He is eternal, He is all-consuming fire, He has neither shape nor form. To this the rabbinical rejoinder was, "Just as God is all-merciful so man should be merciful; just as God is kind and righteous, so man should be kind and righteous; just as God is careful to look after all the creatures in His world, so should man be." Rabbi Simlai taught, "The Torah begins with an act of *chesed* (loving-kindness) and ends with an act of *chesed*. At the beginning of the Torah, it is written, 'The Lord God made garments of skin for Adam and Eve and clothed them' (Genesis 3:21). At the conclusion of the Torah, it is written, 'He [God] buried him [Moses] in the valley in the land of Moav'" (Deuteronomy 36:6).[7]

Assisting God

The world was created in such a way that, God's bounty not withstanding, man's needs are not satisfied through miraculous means, but rather through plowing, sowing, reaping, grinding, building, buying, and selling. Already at the dawn of history, man was placed in the Garden of Eden to work it and to guard it, thus completing God's creation through his own efforts. So, too, he is required to alleviate the sufferings of others through his own acts of righteousness, as a means of extending the bounty of God. This assistance, which men give to each other, is similar therefore to Divine worship.

Giving away wealth is, as it were, giving a loan to God, so Maimonides links the legal status of the gifts that a man gave to the Temple (*Hekdesh*) to the status of social obligations, in this way transforming the latter into a means of serving God. In *Hilkhot Mekhirah*—laws of buying and selling—he states a basic Jewish legal principle:

> A man cannot legally transfer ownership, either through a sale or as a gift, something that does not have tangible reality about it. So, a man cannot sell the taste of this honey; or the smell of this apple. He is required to actually sell the house, the tree or the honey itself. However, those things that a man sanctifies to the Temple, the gifts to the poor, and the oaths that one takes on oneself, do not have the same legal status as that of the commerce of individuals. So, if a person says, "Whatever will be born to my animal will be a gift to the Temple . . . or I will give it to charity," then even though the object does not yet exist, nevertheless, he is obligated to execute that which he took upon himself. It is thus written, "Every [word] that his mouth utters, he shall fulfill" (Numbers 30:3). Similarly, if a man is lying on his deathbed and he says, "All the produce of this field or of

> this tree will be for charity or the rent of this house will be for the poor," then the poor have a legal claim [even though all of these assets will only be created in the future].

Furthermore, Maimonides continues to link the spiritual significance of the Temple offerings to the religious nature of the objects given to charity when he insists on the equality of the beauty and quality required of both of them.

> And this is [also] the law regarding all those things that one consecrates to God. They must be of the best and the most beautiful. If a man built a synagogue for prayer, it should be more dignified and beautiful than the house in which he lives, when he feeds the hungry he must give them the best and sweetest food which he serves at his own table, when he clothes the naked, it should be with the finest of his own clothes.[8]

It was for neglecting to do just this that the offering of Cain was rejected. The Bible (Genesis 4:4) tells us that he brought of the fruit of his labor, whereas in the case of his brother Hevel (Abel), we are told that he brought the best of his flocks. Therefore, the sacrifice of Hevel was accepted, whereas that of Cain was rejected.

All Men Are Brothers

Rabbi Akiva, in the discussion with Turnus Rufus, maintained that since all men are God's children, they are all brothers and are all equal before Him. In the *Mishnah*, Rabbi Akiva further taught, "Blessed is man for he was created in the Divine Image."[9] The *Midrash* taught that only one man was created so that no one could say, "My father was created before yours," and no one could say, "My father was created of better substance than yours."[10]

It is true that men are different from each other physically, culturally, and mentally, but this is not a rejection of their Divine Creator or of their resultant brotherhood. On the contrary, these are only signs of His greatness. "See how superior He is to flesh and blood," taught the Rabbis. "A human artisan makes one mold and all the coins are identical. He created one man in His image, yet all men are different."[11]

The Brotherhood of Man is a horizontal relationship of mutual responsibility fostering acts of righteousness and personal concern. The

Fatherhood of God is a vertical linkage between man and God. Just as the vertical relationship between God and the Jews always exists even in exile, so too does the horizontal one, even in cases of individual impoverishment.

Turnus Rufus, however, envisages only a vertical relationship. There are the gods, or there is chance or there are supernatural powers, all of which hold men in perpetual subjection or as playthings to their whims or fancies. Since there is no Fatherhood of God, there can also be no Brotherhood of Man. For him, the world is a large household inhabited by a mass of unrelated individuals with neither community of interest nor any obligations to one another.

Coercion

All acts of *chesed* (loving-kindness) and *tzedakah* (charity or righteousness) are not left to the individual's sense of responsibility or to his feelings of pity for the weaker or the poor. There is an entire network of legal obligations that translate Judaism's emphasis on righteousness into practical everyday actions, irrespective of the personal feelings of the individuals. Rabbinical courts have the right to force people to do such acts, while the community may pass economic legislation that in effect makes righteous acts obligatory. This should not be surprising since coercion and legislation at various levels are an integral part of Judaism in all aspects of life. Jewish prayer is communal and of a fixed form, irrespective of one's personal emotions, likes, or dislikes. So, too, are the other aspects of Judaism relating to food, sex, clothing, and social organization. All of them are translated into permitted or forbidden acts, rather than left to the results of individual behavior. If this were not so, then by and large people's good intentions and their basic decency would remain in the realm of pious wishes and visions.

At the same time, this framework of clearly defined obligations and legal coercion may sometimes suffer from a diminished spontaneity and a weakening of the individual's participation. However, closer examination of the halakhic system shows that this problem seems to be more speculative than real. There exists in Judaism a tension between prophetical, spiritual, and the soulful, on the one hand, and legal, formalized, permitted, and forbidden acts, on the other hand. It is this tension, however, that makes of Judaism a religion of here and now, while at the same time permeating life with godliness.

With regard to charity, this positive tension is clearly shown when we examine the two biblical verses describing this obligation. The first verse (Deuteronomy 15:7), which reads, "Thou shall not close thy hand from your poor brother," is a negative injunction forbidding one from withholding assistance from those who require it. The following verse, which reads, "Thou shall surely open thy hand to him and give him either a gift or a loan to satisfy all the needs he has," refers to positive financial and nonfinancial acts of righteousness. At the same time, the first verse comes to obligate one to answer the weaker person's call for help, while the second one is a cry for one to provide assistance, even before the needy request it. One refers to injunctions to alleviate suffering, while the other may be seen as stimulating these efforts to prevent suffering. The two verses therefore present two aspects of Jewish charity, one a communal ability to force its members not to refrain from extending assistance to the poor, the weak, the aged, and even the lazy according to their ability, while the other relates to the individual's feelings of mercy and caring. The existence of these two aspects stimulates private concern and charity, while at the same time provides assistance, even in those cases where the individual does not feel that he has obligations or that he has to fulfill them.

There are two words in Hebrew that, while they have the same grammatical root, denote these two twin strands of coercion and feeling. *Tzedek* refers to justice, achieved through the rabbinic courts and communal legislation. *Tzedakah* refers to personal acts of mercy and righteousness.

Limitations

While acts of kindness and righteousness, whether *tzedakah* or *tzedek*, are obligations flowing from the Divine source of wealth, they are not unlimited ones. Rabbi Yehudah HaLevi, poet, philosopher, and doctor, describes this in the *Kuzari*, a classic philosophy of Judaism written in the form of a dialogue between a wise Jewish Sage and the king of the Khazars, a nation living in the Crimea who converted to Judaism. HaLevi writes, "The increase in wealth is not a sin nor is decreasing it [through excessive charity] piety."[12] This idea of limiting charitable acts obviously does not flow from a philosophy of selfishness but rather from a realistic understanding of life. Maimonides codifies this as *Halakhah* when he writes:

> A person should never donate all his money to *mitzvot*. . . . To do so is not an act of righteousness but stupidity, since he will waste all his wealth and become dependent on the charity of others, for he is one whom the sages classified as a stupid pietist [referred to in the Talmud as one who sees a woman drowning and says, "It is forbidden to look upon a woman and therefore I cannot save her." In our case, by giving away all his wealth and embracing poverty, he is simply substituting one poor man for others, but not solving anything].[13]

Furthermore, although the poor acquire property rights in the charity that others give them, the receipt of such assistance is neither an entitlement nor a desired status. The assistance is by and large limited to necessities, and Jews are urged to do everything in their power not to be welfare recipients.

"A man should rather flay a carcass in public [considered to be a degrading occupation] rather than be dependent on the charity of others."[14]

These five factors described above, the spiritual framework for the owners of wealth, create an economic system in which, in addition to devoting efforts to increasing their wealth through legitimate means, men are also involved in meeting their social obligations, since in Judaism there are no rights without obligations. Even if poverty and inequality are pervasive and perhaps endure forever, one is halakhically bound to mitigate suffering and injustice. This is irrespective of whether one considers these to be a form of Divine punishment (since we are not called upon to sit in judgment) or the result of determinism. There is no place in this spiritual framework for a feeling of condescension toward people who always seem to be singled out for failure.

These five basic concepts relate to a wide variety of human relationships. The most outstanding of them, the education toward and the emphasis on acts of charity for the poor, the weak, the aged, the widows and orphans, and the inefficient, is only one aspect of the mutual responsibility of people. In the course of life, there are many scenarios in which entrepreneurs and those with economic assets are faced with decisions that go beyond these acts of charity. The Brotherhood of Man in Judaism, therefore, includes communal intervention in the marketplace in order to protect weaker elements of society, an obligation to extend interest-free loans, and a concept of "one has a benefit and the other suffers no loss," which enables others to have free use of property that undoubtedly belongs legally to another. It has been shown that the biblical injunction to return lost articles to their owners has an important impact on business practices, as does the obligation to love one's neighbor.

TZEDAKAH

Acts of righteousness and charity have been interwoven into the very fabric of Jewish national consciousness ever since its inception. They remain characteristic of the Jews, both individually and collectively, until this very day.

The patriarch Abraham, at the dawn of our history, is granted a covenant with God since "He will command his sons and his house after him and they will keep the way of the Lord to do justice and righteousness" (Genesis 18:19). Lot deserts Abraham, the symbol of *chesed*, and goes to live in Sodom, whose people are "exceedingly evil," yet Abraham pleads for them before the Lord. Moses protects the Midianite daughters of Jethro from the persecution of the shepherds, even though he himself is a stranger and virtually defenseless. When he shepherds the flocks of Jethro, Moses spreads out the sheep so that the older ones can find suitable grazing and the younger ones will be close to water. The Torah itself echoes this with laws wherein the corners of the field (*pe'ah*), the gleanings (*leket*), and the forgotten crops (*shikhechah*) will be left for the poor, the orphans, the widows, and the stranger. Interwoven in its verses are those forbidding the oppression of the poor, widows, orphans, and strangers. God Himself is phrased in our prayers as the Father of Orphans and the Advocate of Widows, while we are to remember the stranger, since we were strangers in the land of Egypt. It is not remarkable, therefore, that the Sages of the Talmud taught, "If one does not do his fellow a favor, it is doubtful that he is a descendant of our Father Abraham."[15]

Tithing and Taxation

These good attributes and interventions are codified into law by Maimonides, repeated in all the codes, and form the basis of the responsa on this subject.

> It is a positive commandment, incumbent on every Jew, to give charity, as it is written, "You shall surely open your hand to him" (Deuteronomy 15:8)

> and, "You shall support the stranger, and your brother shall dwell with you" (Leviticus 25:35). He who sees a poor man begging and ignores him, refusing to give him charity, transgresses a negative commandment [which makes him liable to physical punishment by the rabbinic courts], as it is written, "You shall not harden your heart and you shall not close your hand from your poor brother" (Deuteronomy 15:7).[16]

In order to fund this charity, Jews are obligated to tithe their wealth annually. Since there are numerous halakhic questions regarding the income from which the tithe has to be made and the purposes for which the tithe may or may not be used, recourse has to be made to a competent rabbinic authority. The discussion here pertains only to general principles.

Some rabbinic sources see the present-day obligation to tithe as an implementation of the biblical injunction "Every three years [that is the third and the sixth years of the *Shmittah*, Sabbatical year], take a tithe of that year's crop and leave it for the Levite . . . the stranger, the orphan and the widow . . . when they then eat and are satisfied, the Lord your God will bless you in all the work of your hands" (Deuteronomy 14:28-29).

Elijah, the Gaon of Vilna, the most famous and authoritative of the scholars of eastern Europe in recent centuries, apparently holds this view when he writes to his family: "For God's sake, set aside the one-fifth as you have been commanded and do not detract from it, even as you have been warned, for [giving] less than this, one transgresses every minute on a number of negative and postive commandments and it is as though one voids and negates the entire Torah."[17] The Gaon's remarks, it would seem, are based on the statement in the Jerusalem Talmud that "It is a *Halakhah* from Sinai that one is obligated to give a fifth to the poor."[18] This also seems to be the opinion of Maimonides.

However, the majority of the authorities hold either that tithing of money, at the present time when the vast majority of the Jews do not live in Israel, as distinct from the produce of the fields, is only a rabbinic injunction or that it is primarily a custom that the Ashkenazi Jews have taken on themselves.[19]

Even though the source of a law, whether of Sinaitic origin, rabbinic injunction, or custom, has important implications for rulings of a rabbinic court, nevertheless, in practical everyday terms, the obligation to tithe one's annual income is and has been a feature of Jewish life throughout the centuries. It continues to be considered by all halakhic authorities to be a binding one today.

The *Shulchan Arukh* reflects this when he rules that:

> The rate of charitable giving is in accordance with all the needs of the poor, if his means are equal to it. If not, then the *mitzvah* is to give one-fifth of his possessions, the most precious of them. [Tithes of] one-tenth are the mark of a mediocre [spirit]. Less even than that is [the act of one who possesses] an evil eye [defined by Samson Raphael Hirsch as one who will rejoice when others suffer loss and sorrow, grief and misery (*Pirkei Avot* chapter 2, *Mishnah* 14)]. The fifth of one's income referred to here has to be deducted from the equity in the first year and then from the income in each following year.[20]

It should be noted, however, that the *Shulchan Arukh*, and indeed all the authorities, stressed that any limitations on the proportion of wealth given to charity and communal needs are only a function of their effect on the well-being of the giver. Only in those cases where excessive giving could lead to impoverishment do the limitations of one-tenth or one-fifth exist. Beyond that, there is no halakhic justification for limiting either one's donations to charity or communal needs.

People have an aversion to giving away any part of their wealth, so it is easy perhaps to sympathize with the following story, which, according to the *Midrash*, Korach used to incite the people of Israel against Moses.

> There was a widow who sowed her field with wheat. When it ripened, Moses came and said that the corner had to be left for the poor. When she reaped the remainder, she had to give *terumah* (one-sixtieth) to the Kohen, *terumat maaser* (one-tenth) to the Levite, *maaser oni* to the poor [during the third and sixth years of the *Shmittah* cycle] or *maaser sheni* to be eaten in Jerusalem [in the other years]. When she ground the wheat into flour, part had to be given to the Kohen. In anger, the woman sold the field and bought sheep. However, the same story was repeated; the firstborn sheep, as well as the first fleece of the shearing, went to the Kohen. So the woman slaughtered the sheep, thinking to escape the Mosaic taxation. In vain, the law now claimed the Kohen's share in the carcass. "I declare it ownerless," shouted the woman before Aharon. "In that case, it all belongs to the Kohen" was the rejoinder.[21]

Regarding the basis for tithing and the permitted deductions, one should consult one's rabbi. Yet it seems that as a general principle, tithes, whether one-tenth or one-fifth, should be deducted from the total income. This would include income from business ventures, after deducting business expenses, from interest received, dividends, refunds from income and other taxes, capital gains, pensions, rents, royalties, unemployment compensation, Social Security benefits, and so forth. One may deduct state or government taxes levied on any of these forms of income, excepting those taxes that in effect are savings, such as Social Security or IRA or retirement plans. Where these have been deducted at source, it is necessary to add them back for purposes of tithing.

Some of the following permissible deductions from the "taxable" income are similar to those allowed in most countries for income tax purposes. Nevertheless it seems that in part the halakhic rulings are more stringent.

It seems that one may deduct losses or expenses from one transaction from the total income,[22] even though there are opinions that one may not do so.[23] It seems that there are also differences of opinion as to whether an accrued or cash basis has to be used, which obviously would lead to a different *maaser* base with regard to credit sales and the methods used to evaluate inventory. So, too, there exist differences of opinion regarding depreciation of assets. Some allow normal accounting methods, whereas others permit immediate deduction in the year of purchase, and yet other authorities permit the deduction only when the asset is sold. One may not depreciate assets that do not actually depreciate, as distinct from allowable depreciation. In all these cases, it is important to refer to a rabbinical authority. They have been mentioned here only in order to present some idea of the scope of the problems involved.

There is, however, an area of business conduct that requires perhaps even greater scrutiny for purposes of *maaser*, primarily because almost all fiscal systems have found it difficult to police and therefore have tended in practice to act leniently, thus creating a gray area of unaccountability. Various studies show that some firms, primarily those not listed on a stock exchange or not owned by institutions, do not distribute dividends, allowing the shareholders to draw their return on capital in the form of expenses. These expenses are limited in effect only by the imagination of the managers and the ingenuity of their accountants. They range from managerial salaries in excess of the market, traveling and entertainment expenses, which include the personal ones of the owners and their families, interest on loans made by the owners to the firm, yet included in the general interest payments of the firm, and general expenses, which often include household expenses.[24] The motivation for this form of nondividend distribution of profits is to evade the double taxation that exists in most tax systems whereby profits are taxed, and then when they are distributed as dividends, taxed once more. In Jewish tax law, it is interesting to note, most authorities hold that the same income dollar may not be taxed twice.[25] However, since these expenses are in effect either in part or completely the same as dividends, they have to be treated as such for purposes of *maaser*. Thus, for example, when one stays in a luxury hotel during a business trip, or entertains or buys an expensive motorcar for personal/business use, then one may not deduct the total expense incurred. One would have to calculate that part of the expense that is not essentially business related. This could involve the difference, for example, between a three-star and five-star hotel, the cost of the owner's meal, or perhaps the "perk" involved in driving one's family in the most luxurious car. These would then have to be added back to the *maaser* base.[26] Naturally, the wages of family members fictitiously added to the payroll, excessive wages paid to the manager-owners, or interest payments paid on their loans have to be added back to the *maaser* income base, even if the general tax authorities recognize or ignore them. It should be noted that in many countries adding back the "dividend" contained in these tax-deductible expenses has been found to increase the actual profit by between 75 and 100 percent.[27]

In the same way, most halakhic authorities do not allow one to deduct from the *maaser* base those household expenses that are not related to the business. These include medical and dental expenses or interest payments on mortgages or nonbusiness loans.[28]

The question of whether one may deduct the cost of child support will depend on the ages of the children. Parents have a halakhic obligation to support their children until the age of six years.[29] Since one may not deduct obligatory costs from the *maaser* base, these expenses too may not be deducted.[30]

Today, unlike during most of the past centuries, it is common practice for parents to provide for their children beyond six years of age, in fact until they are able to earn their own livelihood. This makes their support an extension of the parental obligation and therefore is considered by some authorities not to be deductible from the *maaser* base.[31] This would be strengthened by the legal requirements of the general society in many countries, placing the obligation on the parents until the late teens. The major codes, however, consider the support of older children to come under the category of charity, as discussed in the Talmud.[32] The situation of these children from the aspect of *maaser* becomes easier, in the view of those who consider household expenses to be deductible or those who view the *maaser* as only a custom that these individual parents did not take upon themselves.

Even though an adult child is obligated to give his parents' honor, he is not obligated to use his own money to support them. It would seem, therefore, that he could deduct such support from his *maaser* payments as an act of charity. The *Shulchan Arukh*, however, rejects this and argues that unless it causes great financial hardship, a child should regard the support of his parents as an obligation and not as an act of charity, which would mean that one could not deduct it from his *maaser* base.[33] The Rama, in his gloss on the *Shulchan Arukh*, writes that "if his financial situation permits it, only evil comes to a son who supports his parents from the money set aside for charity."[34]

While one may view tithing as voluntary self-assessment, Jewish charity comprises another element that is communal and coercive. It is not surprising, therefore, for the Talmud to argue that it is in the power of the *bet din* to enforce acts of charity, literally to force one not to perform "acts of Sodom."

This is reflected in the ruling of the *Shulchan Arukh* that:

> The people of a city may force one another to [pay for the costs of building] a wall, gates and locks for the city and to build a synagogue, to buy a *Sefer Torah*, Prophets and Writings [*Tanakh*] . . . [The Rama, in his gloss, adds "all the necessities of the city . . . to provide hospitality for travelers, give them charity and contribute towards charitable funds."][35]

In another section, the *Shulchan Arukh* spells out clearly the right of the community to tax its citizens for purpose of charity, ruling that "one who gives less than his due [according to the communal assessor], the *bet din* forces him [and] applies corporal punishment until he pays what he has been assessed. They have the right to seize his assets for the amount of his debt to the charitable funds, even on the eve of the Sabbath."[36]

Since the Napoleonic Wars and the emancipation of the Jews, first in western and later in eastern Europe, the communal autonomy crumbled, and Jews found themselves in voluntary religious or social groupings, similar to their non-Jewish neighbors. Nevertheless, it would seem that even devoid of legal autonomy, forms of communal peer pressure still exist that would help to maintain the coercive power envisaged by the halakhic sources in respect to charity and other acts. Even were this not the case, the principles of Jewish taxation regarding charity contain important guidelines similar to the voluntary self-assessment and so are included in the following discussion.

Scope of *Tzedakah*

Communities, like individuals, have limited budgets, and therefore it is necessary to have a system of priorities according to which money is allocated. Nevertheless, communities have a wide range of uses to which their tax money can be put, and these are halakhically binding, provided they are decided by majority vote of all the members or their elected representatives. While we have already seen that there exist limitations as to what is considered charity for purposes of *maaser*, such communal decisions are obligatory on all the members even when they go beyond these limitations and a majority can force its will on the minority.[37] This applies also to taxes levied by the non-Jewish authorities. Maimonides rules that if a tax is regulated by a legitimate ruler, is not arbitrary, and applies equally to all the citizens, it is halakhically binding.[38] In our own day, Rabbi Moshe Feinstein (New York, twentieth century) ruled that since the government of the United States is a benevolent one, permitting the Jews to live in peace and equality while pursuing the teachings of their religion, one is halakhically bound to pay all its taxes, and tax evasion thus becomes contrary to Jewish law.[39] Similar decisions have been rendered in other countries.

The question has been raised as to whether there is a limit to the percentage of income that may be taken as taxes. It has been suggested to the author that, following Joseph's tax of 20 percent on the Egyptians, this amount should constitute a halakhic cap on taxes. This would be similar to the reservation of the Rabbis mentioned previously regarding tithing. Since that reservation is meant to apply only where further charitable donations would impoverish the individual, it would seem that the same should apply to the group.

Regardless, however, of the question of the limitation on taxation and of the leeway given to the communities, there are certain categories of public need that may not be evaded either by individuals or by communities (even by majority decisions) seeking to lower their tax obligation. Neither they nor the individual is excused from paying for the needs of Torah education or for the charitable needs of the society.

Torah Education

Originally, parents had the obligation to teach Torah to their children. In mishnaic times, however, this was made a communal one. Rabbi Yehoshua ben Gamla, a high priest during the days of the Second Temple in Jerusalem, ruled, "The community is obligated to provide elementary school teachers in every state and every province and city."[40] This is in accordance with the rabbinical tradition that in the biblical commandment "Teach [the Torah] diligently to your children. Talk of them when you sit in your house and when you walk by the way, when you lie down and when you rise up" (Deuteronomy 6:7), "children" refers to all pupils, extending beyond one's immediate family.

The cost of this education was theoretically to be borne by the parents. Salaries were usually paid, in practice, by a mixture of taxation that applied primarily to the poorer children and by the recourse to private tutors for those of the wealthier ones; this was in addition to the tax burden shared by the latter parents. Other costs such as buildings and other facilities are also considered part of the *maaser* and communal tax.

Torah education is not limited to children, but extends to adults, as expressed in the obligation "Devote yourselves to its [Torah] study" (Joshua 1:8). Naturally, this obligation brings in its wake financial burdens on members of the community to finance teachers and facilities. The Rama rules that rabbis (and teachers) should not be paid out of the general charity funds, since this is insulting. "Rather the funds should be found from other sources."[41]

Adult Torah education, as often as not, was conducted and financed through the existence of special *chavurot* (fraternal groups) in almost all Jewish communities throughout the centuries. In addition to the donations of their members, funding was available from the communal funds and from the *tzedakah* of individuals. In addition, throughout the centuries, the communities made great efforts to attract scholars through different forms of assistance, since they were regarded as important communal assets. Such assistance included not only housing and salaries, but also preferential treatment in the market, such as buying goods from their stores rather than from others or granting monopoly rights on the sale of various articles.

So essential is the existence of Jewish educational facilities that the Rabbis maintained that a person is not allowed to live in a town or commuity that does not provide them, just as he is not allowed to live in one that does not have a doctor.[42]

This centrality of Torah education as a priority in charity funds, both private *tzedakah* and communal taxes, is clearly reflected in the ruling of the *Shulchan Arukh*:

> The charity of supporting poor boys in the study of Torah or of giving to the needy sick is more important than the maintenance of a synagogue. Charity funds given for a synagogue or a cemetery may be diverted to the needs of a *bet midrash*, House of [adult] Learning or a school even against the will of the donor [in contrast to the usual ruling that money cannot be diverted from the purpose for which it was given without such consent] except in those cases where the needs of the school are being met satisfactorily.[43]

So, too, Maimonides rules that "it is permitted to sell a synagogue [used only for prayer] in order to erect a *bet midrash*, since one has to ascend in the scale of holiness [and the study of Torah is considered spiritually to be higher than that of prayer]."[44]

Scholars also have a priority in the allocation of charity funds relative to other needy people as can be learned from the continuation of the ruling. Regarding the choice between allocating charity when there are insufficient funds for all, between a High Priest who is nevertheless an ignoramus and a *talmid chakham* who is a *mamzer* (born of an incestuous or forbidden marriage), the *Shulchan Arukh* writes that the latter has precedence, even though priests normally have precedence over ordinary Israelites of legal birth and most definitely over *mamzerim*. In the same way, when one has an opportunity to retrieve a lost article belonging either to one's father or to one's rabbi, and one is unable to do both, one's teacher takes precedence.[45]

Charity to the Poor

> One is obligated to give the poor person all that they need. If they lack clothes, one clothes them, if they do not have household goods one buys them. If a man does not have a wife, we are obligated to help him get married. [The Talmud in *Ketubot* explains that this is deduced from the phrase in the Torah "that which he lacks," namely a wife, even as God said, "I will make him a helpmate." So too] if the poor person is a woman, we are obligated to help her get married. [Great emphasis has always been placed especially on assisting orphans to marry, as we learn from the continuation in the *Mishneh Torah* of Maimonides:] "An orphan, who they are helping to marry—they rent a house for him, buy bedding and all the household utensils and then make the marriage." [*Hakhnasat kallah*, funds for dowering poor brides, is considered to be one of the acts of charity for which no limitations similar to the 10 percent of *maaser* were made. One of the boasts of a sixteenth-century author was that "in the whole area of Poland and Galicia there never were any cases of brides being unable to get married because of a lack of funds."][46,47]

So the Tur can rule "one is obligated to give to everyone who extends his hand [to ask for charity]. This includes gentiles [and idolators] since one is obligated to support the gentile poor together with the poor of Israel."[48]

There is, however, a type of need that poor people have that is not financial, yet nevertheless it is a real and valid need. Maimonides includes it in the obligation of giving charity.

> [If the person had previously been rich] so that it had been the custom of this poor man to ride on a horse and have a servant to run before him [a sign of nobility and status] and now he had become poor, then we are obligated to buy [out of charity funds] a horse for him to ride upon and a servant to run before him [thus restoring him to his former status] even as it is written (Deuteronomy 15:7) all his needs which he lacks.

The Rama in his gloss on the *Shulchan Arukh* rules that the individual only has an obligation to bring it to the notice of the communal funds.[49]

Over and above the poverty involved, people who were formerly better off also suffer personal and psychological damage from the fact that they have lost their former standard of living. One of the severe problems of unemployment, beyond the financial one, is the harm that is done by telling somebody that he is redundant or by the shame that the employee feels before his family and his friends when he is unable to maintain his standard of living. Refugees, dismissed workers, bankrupt businessmen, disposed farmers, and evicted homeowners all often suffer the same twin effects of poverty: loss of income and psychological hurt. They all too often fall therefore within the halakhic definition of one whose need includes "even a horse to ride upon," and that lack must be provided.

It should be noted that even when there is no money left in the communal funds or when one has already distributed all the tithes (a function of the size of the one's income), there is still an obligation to give assistance to the poor. So Maimonides writes:

> If the poor asks of charity of you and you have nothing in your hand then at least comfort him with words. One is forbidden to rebuke the poor [taking him to task for his indolence or his inability] or to raise one's voice to him, since his heart is broken and despondent. It is thus written (Isaiah 57:16), "Revive the spirit of the lowly and to enliven the heart of the oppressed."

Maimonides then goes on to rule that one has to give at least some small contribution to the beggars, who prefer this to having to go to the communal funds, and one is not allowed to turn away the poor empty-handed. Furthermore, while it is permissible to check the validity of requests for clothing from the poor who are unknown to one, requests for food have to be met immediately without any examination. However, in the case of those known to be poor, one is obligated to clothe them according to their honor, and one is not allowed to examine their requests, thus preserving their dignity.[50]

These, however, are not philanthropic acts or those of personal charity, but rather the result of obligations enforceable in rabbinic courts. In fact, the halakhic treatment of debts owing to the charity funds parallels that of debts owing to commercial creditors. In both cases, the courts have the right to search out the assets of the debtor, evaluate them, and force the sale of that portion owing to the creditor or the charity funds. This action may be done even, on Friday, *Erev Shabbat*, the Eve of the Sabbath.[51]

Furthermore, this obligation is a function of wealth, so that the charitable burden is spread progressively, with the rich contributing relatively more. The following reponsum of the Rashba (Rabbi Shlomo Ben Aderet, North Africa) was subsequently codified by the *Shulchan Arukh* as law:

> You write that the poor have become numerous and the wealthy members of the community argue that they should beg from door to door [rather than be funded from the communal funds]. The middle class, however, argue that they are not to beg but that their upkeep be provided by the community, according to [a tax on] wealth. The law is with the middle class, since charity is always paid for on a basis of wealth [rather than a per capita tax or a users tax]. . . . In all the communities, the poor are supported by the charitable funds [taxed] according to wealth. If in addition, the poor wish to go from door to door, they may do so and each person will give them according to their understanding and their will.[52]

Even the poor who receive charity are obligated to give something to other poor people; after all, a prime consideration, as explained in the conceptual framework of charity, is the spiritual education of the giver.

Unfortunately, persecution and expulsion of Jews simply because they are Jews have been an all too common feature of national life, and one that continues even to this day. It was only a short while ago that the Jews of the Soviet Union and the Falashas were unable to emigrate, being in effect captives, and the Jews of Syria are, at the time of writing, still in this position. Individuals and communities are reduced to poverty or forced to pay ransom to save themselves. This creates demands on the communal and individual wealth of other more fortunate Jews. Here, too, there exists a halakhic obligation, which cannot be ignored, to find the funds for this form of charity. The reasoning is very simple; the hostage and the captive suffer all the problems of the poor, in addition to the danger to their very lives, making them preferential candidates for assistance.

Halakhically, *pidyon shevuyim* (redemption of captives) has first priority over feeding and clothing other poor, since in the words of the Talmud, "the captive is more unfortunate than all others, because he has all their troubles, and he is in the hands of the gentiles who can do with him whatever they wish, give him life, death, starvation."[53] One who refuses to provide funds for the redemption of captives transgresses a large number of *mitzvot*, negative and positive, in addition to those of ordinary charity, such as:

"You shall not stand idly by your brother's blood" (Leviticus 19:17) because he is in mortal danger.

"He, [the servant] shall not be oppressed through rigorous work before your eyes" (Leviticus 25:53), and now other Jews are witnessing the oppression of the captives.

"Your brother shall live with you" (Leviticus 25:36).

"Love your neighbor as yourself," which includes all the *mitzvot* between man and his fellow.[54]

So it is not surprising to find such rabbinic decisions as "one may use funds collected for a synagogue or sell building material bought for that purpose, or a *Sefer Torah*, in order to redeem captives."[55]

Naturally, the major impact of this ruling regarding *pidyon shevuyim* is on the community directly faced with the arrival of individual captives, when these were, for example, sold as slaves. A modern parallel is the victims of hijacking or the taking of hostages in other forms. Of greater consistent import, however, would seem to be the responsibility posed by the danger of oppression or persecution to whole communities.

Halakhically, this danger demands the financial support of other Jews, even if they are geographically distant. Indeed, this support has been forthcoming even down to modern times, when Jews in freer, more prosperous societies have intervened to ransom captive Jews whether it be in Tzarist Russia, the Ottoman Middle East, pre- and post-Holocaust Europe, the Soviet Union, or Ethiopia. An example of this halakhic obligation is found in the following responsum of Rabbi Joseph Colon (Pavia, Italy, fifteenth century):

> The rabbinical council at Nuremberg has instructed all the communities surrounding Regensburg to come to the assistance of the seventeen members of the community of Ratisbon who have been accused of killing a Christian child before Pesach. These have appealed to me whether this obligates them. It is lawful that the neighboring communities be called upon to contribute to the forthcoming expenses [bribery, etc.] to avert the evil decree.
>
> A similar case is to be found in *Baba Metzia* 108a. Rabbi Yehudah says, "If the upper reaches of a stream dry up or are impeded by stones, the owners of the fields down river have to contribute to its restoration as they,

> too, need the water to irrigate their fields." [In our case, this hints at the future danger to all the Jews if the blood libel in Ratisbon succeeds. This makes the assistance of the surrounding communities a form of insurance. So Rabbi Colon proceeds:] And even if the surrounding communities will object, saying that the libel which has brought so much misfortune to the Jews of Ratisbon will not be brought against them formally and therefore there exists only a distant possibility of their being affected, nevertheless, they are still obligated, since it is the duty of the Jews to assist one another.[56]

Sometimes one would like to differentiate in this matter, and in all matters of charity, between those who become needy because of factors beyond their control and the other people who, because of their own indolence, weaknesses, or inabilities become thrust on the benevolence of others—the deserving and the undeserving poor. Halakhically, there does not seem to be any distinction of this nature excepting in the case of fraud and misrepresentation, which bring in their wake the very poverty and suffering simulated to earn charity. So the codes include among those eligible for funding not only people captured through no fault of their own but also those imprisoned by gentiles for economic crimes.

> One who borrowed money from gentiles and then is imprisoned because of nonpayment is to be redeemed [with monies taken from communal funds or from philanthropic donations]. If he persists and repeats this, he is again to be redeemed. The third time, however, we will not redeem him [this is willful exploitation of the obligation of others]. If, however, there is danger to his life, then he is to be redeemed even [if he repeats this behavior] a thousand times.[57]

Priorities in *Tzedakah*

In all societies, the social functions financed out of public funds and the policies meant to finance them are determined not by some invisible or undetermined factors but solely by the ideological concepts of the society. In the same way, the priorities of Jewish *tzedakah* and the method of funding them are also determined by the religious value structure of Judaism. These priorities are presented here in two major groups, the first based on the eight degrees of charity formulated by Maimonides and reproduced in the *Shulchan Arukh*, and the second on the ranking of those eligible for the various types of charity.

Eight Degrees of Charity

The highest degree of charity—above which there is no higher one—is he who strengthens the hand of his poor fellow Jew and gives him a gift or [an interest-free] loan or enters into a business partnership with the poor person. [Interestingly, Maimonides within the internal allocation of this degree proceeds from the lower rank to the higher. The loan is a higher form of charity than is the outright gift since the poor are not shamed thereby (Rashi on *Talmud Bavli*, *Shabbat* 63a), while the business partnership is more praiseworthy than the loan or any other form of charity.] By this partnership the poor man is really being strengthened as the Torah commands in order to strengthen him till he is able to be independent and no longer dependent on the public purse. It is thus written, "Strengthen him [the poor] so that he does not fall [as distinct from one who has already become poor] and become dependent upon others" (Leviticus 25:35). [In modern terms, these are all charitable actions aimed at breaking the poverty cycle and enabling the poor to establish themselves as independent and productive members of society. For this reason, there is no halakhic objection to the poor working while they are receiving their basic needs from society. By the same standards, guidance regarding budgeting, financial planning, consolidation of loans, and so forth, would be included in this highest form of charity.]

A lower standard of charity is one in which the benefactor has no knowlede of the recipient and the latter has no knowledge of the individual source of the charity—*matan beseter*. This is practicing the *mitzvah* of charity for the sake of the *mitzvah* [since the benefactor has no benefit, social or egoistical]. Such charity is like the courtyard in the Temple where the righteous used to place their donations secretly and the poor would benefit from them in secret. Similar to this secret courtyard is the act of one who puts his money into the charity box [or funds].

Below this rank is the case where the recipient is known to the benefactor but the latter is unaware of the source of the charity. [Since the benefactor may have, subconsciously, pleasure and a sense of power over the recipient, this detracts from his act and makes it less meritorious than the previous standard.] This is what the sages used to do when they would go in secret and place their gifts at the door of the poor. It is fitting to do this and meritorious in those cases where the officials in charge of the communal charity do not behave righteously.

Where the recipient is aware of the source of the charity but the giver does not know to whom the money is being given, the degree of charity is lower [since the recipient, knowing who gave him the money, feels beholden

> to him and ashamed in his presence]. Yet, there is merit since the poor are saved from direct shame.
>
> Of lesser merit is charity where both are known to each but [at least] the gift is made before the poor asks for it. [In this case the giver is showing care since he anticipates the needs of the poor. The Patriarch Abraham does not wait for the stranger to come to ask for his assistance, yet runs toward him and begs him to share his hospitality; this is the archetype of Jewish righteousness.]
>
> [Clearly] where one gives charity after being asked for it is of a lower degree. [Since the method of giving charity is an integral part of charity], one who gives less than what is fitting but with good grace [is of higher merit than] one who gives unwillingly.[58]

Priorities in Charity

Even though people are allowed latitude as to which institutions or to which individuals they wish to give charity, there exist certain types of charity–Torah study and charity to the poor–that are obligatory, and within them there are definite priorities.

The precedence of scholars has already been discussed as well as the greater claims of the newly poor. There are, however, other priorities as well, as may be seen from the ruling of the *Shulchan Arukh.*

> Providing for one's adult children so that the sons will study Torah and the girls follow a straight path and the granting of gifts to his father where they [children and the parents] are needy . . . these have precedence over all other . . . this applies also to one's relations who have precedence over other poor . . . the poor of his own family have precedence over the poor of his town . . . the poor of one's town have precedence over those of other cities. [The Tur defines other poor as nonresidents who have come to the city.] Jews of *Eretz Yisrael* have precedence over the poor of other countries.[59]

It is interesting to note that the Rama, in his gloss on this section in the *Shulchan Arukh,* writes that a man's own sustenance has precedence over the needs of others, so that one is not obligated to give charity before he has arranged his own livelihood. The same ruling applies to the redemption of captives, so that if a man is held for ransom and he has the means, he has the obligation to ransom himself before the others.[60] Indeed, the *bet din* can sell a person's assets to redeem him even against his will. This is in accordance with Jewish law that one may not commit suicide or even place oneself in danger in accordance with the verse in Deuteronomy 4:15, "Guard your lives exceedingly carefully." One's life takes precedence over that of others, since we are not able to judge the value of different people.[61] So, too, does one's livelihood (not only because to deem otherwise would be contrary to human nature and therefore not viable, but also because to rule differently would simply mean substitution of one poor person for another, which would be irrelevant).

The financial status and opportunities of the poor also play a part in deciding how to allocate scarce resources. A modern responsum written in Jerusalem holds that one may refuse charity to a person who does not accept employment.[62] This would not, however, apply to those cases where there was a danger of starvation, in view of the Jewish sanctity attached to life. One of the chasidic *Admorim* would not agree to charity being used to provide housing for newly married couples in Jerusalem when cheaper housing was available in Ashdod. The following *mishnah* is the basis for the Codes and responsa regarding ineligibility for charity.

> One who has two hundred *zuz* [considered to be sufficient for a year's sustenance] may not take [of the agricultural gifts to the poor], *leket* (gleaning), *shikhechah* (forgotten sheaves), and *pe'ah* (the unharvested corner of the field) and *maaser ani* (tithe of the poor). [The codes extend this to the charity funds]. . . . If, however, [the money or assets] are security for a loan or for his wife's marriage contract, he is allowed to receive charity.[63]

In addition to this, the Codes ruled, on the basis of the talmudic discussion, that where a person had assets of two hundred *zuz* or more, he could be forced to sell them and reduce his standard of living before becoming entitled to public charity. However, he could not be forced to sell them at a loss.

It may be argued that the two hundred *zuz* requirement was made in the light of the economic conditions of previous generations, and that since living standards are far higher today, the poverty level has to be raised. Even then, the principle of a minimum level of support is clearly defined in Judaism, in contrast to the modern welfare concepts of a reduction of inequalities or of a poverty level close to the average standard of living. Such concepts have led to unemployment payments and welfare benefits that are so close to average wage levels that they promote unemployment, with all the negative social consequences.

Over and above defining the financial obligations imposed on the Jew and determining the charitable priorities, rabbinic sources throughout the centuries have insisted that the frame of mind of the giver is of primary importance. It is this frame of mind that ultimately determines the uniqueness of Jewish social philosophy.

Care has to be taken to spare the poor from shame and to make access to charity as easy as possible. So the *Mishnah* in *Pe'ah* teaches that the times for collecting the agricultural gifts were not dependent on the convenience of the giver but designated by the Rabbis in view of the needs of the poor themselves.

> At three distinct times in a day [the poor have permission to harvest the *pe'ah*—the corner of the fields that the farmer is obligated to leave for them]—at daybreak [in consideration of the mothers whose children are still asleep so that this is the most convenient time for nursing mothers who need to eat early in the day], at midday [for the children of the poor who sleep late and are not able to reach the fields early] and in the afternoon [especially for the aged who walk slowly and cannot arrive earlier].[64]

Maimonides rules that "he who gives charity to the poor with an angry countenance or over the bowed head of the poor, even should he give a thousand golden coins, has no merit from it [actually only a slight merit, as Maimonides himself pointed out in the final of his eight levels]. Rather, the charity has to be given with a pleasant demeanor, with joy and with commiseration for the recipient's trouble."[65]

Already in the *Chapters of the Fathers, Pirkei Avot,* the ethical and moral treatise of the *Mishnah*, Rabbi Jossi ben Yochanan of Jerusalem taught, "Let your home be wide open [so that the hungry, the poor and the weak may enter and] let the poor be as the dwellers of your house; [a family relationship rather than a bureaucratic officious transfer of funds]."[66]

The ease with which the communal officers or philanthropic individuals are able to ignore the suffering and problems of the poor, even while assisting them, was pointed out by one of the chasidic masters. He told of an official who said of himself:

> When I first began to busy myself with charitable acts, I shed tears every time I spoke to the orphans and the widows and the poor. After a while, I became more accustomed and so was able not to weep, yet still found it difficult to eat or drink. As time passed, I found myself able to eat, though unable to enjoy my meals because of the tragedies and sorrows I had witnessed. Only years later, was I able to enjoy my meals. Today, however, I cannot eat or drink or even live a normal life, unless there are crowds of hungry, homeless, wretched people knocking at my door.

The custodian concept of wealth, teaching that one of the purposes for which Divine bounty is granted is for assisting others, is a major weapon in preventing just such a frame of mind.

7

"Thou Shall Not Lend Thy Money at Interest"

The relationship between borrower and lender, the role of interest, and the morality of banking reecho in the social, political, and religious lives of men in all generations and in all societies. Nevertheless, for both Jews and non-Jews alike, there seems to be a special Jewish dimension, which is reflected in almost any discussion of Jewish business ethics and economic morality. Such discussions often reflect the distortion of anti-Semitic literature, racial memories of persecution, and religiously induced bigotry. Jewish teachings concerning interest cannot therefore be restricted solely to the halakhic parameters of money and banking, but must of necessity deal with many of these misconceptions if activities in the financial and money markets are to be viewed in a correct Jewish perspective.

All the strands of Jewish thinking related to wealth, business, and economics discussed in the previous chapters merge in this discussion to an extent not found in any other area. God as the source of all wealth, faith in His Divine bounty, the collective nature of Judaism, the wide-ranging definition of dishonesty, the injunction to do righteousness, and the necessity for constant reexamination of every transaction for moral lapses all form the Jewish framework for lending and credit.

Within this framework, Jews as individuals and as communities have lived for many centuries, weaving righteousness and justice into their financial institutions and their monetary affairs. The authentic picture, therefore, of the Jew as a banker and the role of credit within the Jewish community is a complete negation of the Shylocks, Guggenheims, and anti-Semitic imagination. This is true, even if many Jews, too, accept the fraudulent image. Such acceptance flows either from an ignorance of Jewish source material or from a willful distortion of Jewish economic history in order to satisfy non-Jewish social, cultural, or political ideologies.

As in the other chapters of this book, the emphasis will be on the moral and ethical issues involved and possible Jewish answers. Since interest is considered to be a primary religious concern and is also probably the most problematic of halakhic economic areas, authoritative answers to specific situations have to be referred to competent rabbinic authorities. This is of especial relevance in view of the sophisticated and volatile forms of financial instruments and relationships in the modern economy.

RIGHTEOUSNESS AND MERCY

In different verses in Exodus, Leviticus, and Deuteronomy, the Bible forbids Jews to lend money to other Jews in return for interest. This repetitive yet varied emphasis, involving a number of different religious injunctions that are violated in every transaction involving interest, is ample evidence of the seriousness with which Jewish law and homiletical literature have viewed the subject down to the present time.

Maimonides maintains that everybody connected with interest-bearing transactions is liable to infringements of numerous *mitzvot*, thus highlighting that what is involved is of spiritual significance, not primarily economic. Even those parties who have not benefited from it and even the borrower who is getting credit with which to earn money are involved in these violations.

Just as it is forbidden to lend money at interest, so too is it forbidden to borrow (based on the Talmud's understanding that the verse in Deuteronomy 23:20 refers to causing another to lend at interest [*Baba Metzia* 70b]). It is also forbidden to serve as an intermediary in interest-bearing transactions. Even those who are guarantors, scribes, or witnesses transgress a negative injunction (since without them the transaction could not be completed), as it is written, "Thou shall not put on him interest" (where the word Thou expressed in the plural is the source for including all these parties. In addition, the intermediary is guilty of putting a stumbling block in the path of the blind, since it was his actions that caused the lender to sin).

So we learn that he who lends his money at interest violates six negative injunctions (Exodus 22:24, Leviticus 25:36-37, Leviticus 19:14), including "putting a stumbling block in the path of the blind [the borrower]." The borrower transgresses two commandments [including a stumbling block in the path of the blind—the lender who is being encouraged to act against the Torah].[1]

From the verses in Exodus and Leviticus prohibiting the lending of money at interest and the related rabbinic legal and spiritual teachings, it is quite clear that the element of charity is involved, rather than an antimonetary philosophy or acts of theft and robbery.

> If thy brother becomes poor . . . then shall thou support him, the stranger and the sojourner too, so that he may live next to thee. Take thou from him no usury or increase and fear thou thy God; and thy brother shall live next to thee. Thy money mayest thou not give him on usury [interest at any rate—not the usual English understanding of exorbitant interest rates]. . . . I am the Lord your God who brought you out of the land of Egypt to give you the land of Canaan, to be your Lord (Leviticus 25:33-35).

These verses in Leviticus follow the injunction regarding the Sabbatical and Jubilee years, and must be seen in the same ideological light. It is quite obvious that Judaism sees nothing wrong with plowing, sowing, and harvesting; these are, after all, the normal way to produce agricultural goods, both for consumption and sale. Yet in the *Shmittah* year, both production and sale become forbidden. In this year, economic activity is to be superceded by a spiritual dimension. It is normal for farmers and others to buy and sell land, and there is no evidence that the Torah forbids such sales. On the contrary, the Talmud devotes much discussion both to the sale of real estate and to the transfer of ownership in other forms as inheritance or in payment of debts. What is forbidden on spiritual grounds is the permanent sale of land, so that the Jubilee year brings with it a relocation of all land to the original owners.

There is no objection in Judaism to payment for the hire of capital in the form of draught animals (similar in economic terms to the present-day leasing of equipment and vehicles) or to the payment of rent for the use of capital in the form of housing. It is only in regard to capital in the form of money that the Torah demanded that this be done without that fee or charge that economists called interest, even though that term applies equally to money received for the use of capital in other forms. This demand is made in full cognizance of the benefits of banking and interest, both to the borrower and the lender. It is quite clear from any reading of the halakhic sources that not only is there no denial of the legitimate function of capital in economic development, but that the contrary is true.

Commenting on the phrase "Your brother shall live with you" (Leviticus 25:36), which concludes the biblical injunction against interest, the Torah Temimah writes, "For the money [credit and capital] is an essential part of life and business and the use of interest is beneficial both to borrower and to lender, 'Your brother shall live with you' applies to both of them."

Even a casual glance at our modern economy will support the contention of the Torah Temimah. The rapid increase in home ownership in the United States and England in the past decades can be attributed partially to the growth of a pool of mortgage money available to the prospective home owner. In contrast with this, in Israel and other countries where motgage banking is less developed, home ownership creates great problems, since newly married couples and their families have to fund the major portion of the costs involved from savings or expensive short-term loans. The standard of living in all societies would be much lower than it is were it not for the availability of consumer credit and installment buying. In the business world, the benefits of interest-bearing credit is as obvious as it is in the field of consumer consumption. The expansion of existing firms has been shown to be slowest when there is reliance, primarily, on share capital and accumulated profits, while periods of rapid growth, both of individual firms and of an overall economy, are characterized by increased borrowing. New firms, small and large alike, find start-ups to be either impossible or delayed because of the unavailability of credit.[2]

The rabbinic understanding of the benefits of interest is shown by the ruling that a debtor cannot freely agree to pay the interest for the loans that will contribute to his welfare. This is in contradiction to *onaah* (price fraud), where, as discussed previously, the acceptable level was set at one-sixth of the market price on the assumption that people are prepared to ignore such overcharges. So, too, a person may waive his property rights in favor of a thief or robber who has stolen his goods. He may not, however, forgo the protection against interest that may have been expected if Judaism viewed that interest as intrinsically evil.

The interest forbidden by *Halakhah* has to be direct, between borrower and lender. Those cases, where Reuven pays Shimon a fee for arranging a loan from Levi, are not considered to be a transgression of halakhic interest. If this were a crime, no such intermediary would be permitted, as is indeed the case of theft or damage, since one could become an agent for forbidden acts, *ein shaliach ledavar aveirah.*

Perhaps the best proof that taking interest is not regarded as being evil per se, but rather only forbidden because the Torah said so, is the rule that while one may not take interest from other Jews, it is permitted in regard to non-Jews. There is even the opinion of Maimonides that in that case, it is a *mitzvah*.[3] This distinction between Jew and non-Jew does not exist in any of those laws dealing with intrinsically evil or immoral actions. Both Jew and non-Jew are forbidden to worship idols, and it is forbidden for Jews to rob, steal, or kill non-Jews. These are fundamentally and clearly evil acts. One is obliged to bring in the tools and implements of non-Jews from the fields in order to prevent them from being damaged by the elements; to neglect to do so would be close to theft. The poor of the non-Jews have to be supported together with those of the Jews; to do otherwise would upset the symmetry of peace. The Codes, *Mishneh Torah*, *Arbaah Turim*, and the *Shulchan Arukh*, forbid *geneivat daat* (the stealing of another's mind, misrepresentation). One of the examples of such fraud is selling non-slaughtered meat to a gentile, who is halakhically permitted to eat it, as though it were koshered meat. We have seen that *lifnei iver* applies to selling goods to non-Jews that are harmful to them spiritually or physically, even as it is to Jews. The permission given to lend and borrow money at interest from non-Jews—either as individuals or as corporations—must therefore be understood as an act that is neither harmful nor immoral.

If indeed there is nothing morally wrong with interest-bearing transactions or if interest is even considered to be mutually beneficial, why did the Torah forbid Jews to lend or borrow money for interest from one another? It would seem that it is possible to view this injunction only as an expression of the Divine demand for acts of mercy and righteousness.

Although at first glance the injunctions prohibiting interest seem to have no relationship to the Exodus from Egypt, closer consideration will show that it is this element of mercy and righteousness that is implied in the linkage between the two found in Leviticus. The prime message of the Exodus is God's mastery both over the natural forces of the world and the affairs of men. This Lordship is expressed inter alia in the Divine source of wealth and in Divine Providence for providing for the needs of all creatures. Men are meant to increase their economic assets through their own efforts, yet have to realize that God can be relied upon to satisfy their needs. One who lends money at interest is demonstrating his worry that if he does not do so, he will not have enough for the future and cannot rely on God's bounty. The interest charged is a sign of refusal to do for others the acts of mercy that God does for him, so the Sages said, "He who lends his money at interest denies the Exodus from Egypt."

Perhaps it was this ideological consideration that led the authors of two of the major codes in Judaism, Rabbi Yechiel ben Asher (*Arbaah Turim*) and Rabbi Yosef Caro (*Shulchan Arukh*), not to place the rules of interest as part of the laws of borrowing and lending, as did Maimonides, which is their logical framework. In both codes, interest is to be found between the laws against idolatry and those of *nidah* (family purity).

The Sefer HaChinukh expresses the opinions of the rabbis in all generations when he writes: "According to the normal morality of the world, one should be entitled to charge for the use of one's capital [in the form of money as well]. However since the whole purpose of all the *mitzvot* is to spiritually refine the Jew, [He] instructed us to give up that which is acceptable by normal moral standards [and perform acts of charity]."[4]

Indeed, many of those authorities who maintained that one should refrain from lending money at interest to gentiles, even though the Torah permitted it, were expressing this aspect of righteousness rather than an anticapital bias.

So Ravina in the talmudic discussion regarding lending to gentiles related it to the problem of social and general intercourse between the Jew and the non-Jewish world. Moneylending should be limited, since it led to personal relationships through which the Jew may assimilate and adopt un-Jewish mores and practices.[5]

The Mechilta deRabbi Ishmael (an aggadic work of the talmudic era) extended the obligation of the interest-free loan shown in Exodus 22:24

to non-Jews. This would be in accordance with the principle that Jews are obliged to act with righteousness and kindness in their dealings with non-Jews, even when such behavior is not biblically obligatory. In effect, this places the interest-free loan into the category of *tzedakah*, where as we have seen, it really belongs. Maimonides considered the granting of a loan to be the highest form of charity. The Tur, while following the general part of Maimonides, altered the internal rating of this highest grade of charity. He placed the interest-free loan a rung below the creation of a partnership with the poor, since in this case, the new partner was free of the shame attached to being a recipient of something for nothing.

The talmudic sages made this Jewish view of interest as a normal and justified economic act, forbidden only because of the demands of mercy and charity, quite clear. "Hoarders of produce [in order to profit thereby during subsequent periods of scarcity] those who lend money at interest . . . are those to whom the prophet Amos refers when he says, 'The Lord has sworn by the strength of Jacob that He will never forget their actions.'"[6] One does not have to be an economist to understand the economic wisdom of buying basic goods during times of excess supply, storing them, and then reselling them at times of increased demand. The foresight of such dealers would be rewarded in the marketplace, yet the Rabbis condemned it since it would be at the expense of other, weaker, less efficient members of society, with whom we are commanded to deal in mercy and righteousness. In the same way, the desire to avoid the loss involved in lending money to others free of charge by charging interest is almost logical and understandable. The linkage between the understandable speculation and the equally valid economic demand of payment of interest for funds lent demonstrates the moral injunction in both cases to move beyond these considerations, substituting others of mercy and charity.

This understanding that the biblical injunction against taking or giving interest is primarily concerned with righteousness and charity led the Chafetz Chaim (the primary Jewish moralist of the twentieth century) to the following explanation of why people find it so difficult to fulfill these injunctions.

> When one has capital of hundreds of rubles, it is not valid or feasible to demand that he lend this to others rather than invest it in order to earn profits. So, some should be lent interest free, and the rest invested in

> halakhically legitimate ventures. However, everybody, even those who only have a few rubles or even one, cannot bring themselves to lend it free of interest, and seek ways to invest it so as to earn [a marginal sum of] interest?[7]

Perhaps the words of the Chafetz Chaim may also explain why, if refraining from interest is such an important act of righteousness, a Jew should be allowed to lend his money to non-Jews for interest. To demand this would obviously be laudatory and noble, yet so ingrained in human nature is the objection to letting others have a benefit from our money while we suffer a financial loss, the end result would be the complete negation of such an injunction. Judaism, in all avenues of life, makes demands that are difficult and costly, yet makes no demands that are so contrary to human nature that only angels are able to fulfill them.

The negative attitude of the Torah to interest-bearing transactions as a spiritual refinement shaped by considerations of mercy and *chesed* is also reflected in the moral limitations placed on realizing the undoubted legal rights of the lender. The *Halakhah* accepts the validity of loans secured in the form of a lien on the assets of the borrower, as well as the right of the creditor to verify that the assets are still extant. At the same time, however, ethical considerations limit these rights. The Bible (Deuteronomy 24:6) forbids the taking of a millstone as security for a loan, while in Exodus (22:25-26), basic necessities like a pillow or a cloak had to be returned each night. Without the millstones, the debtor's family would be without food, since the grinding of wheat or barley into flour would be impossible were the stones pledged to the creditor. The ruling of the Codes and of the halakhic authorities throughout the centuries prevented the use of all items essential primarily for food, shelter, or for earning a living, such as the tools of an artisan as security for a loan. Creditors are not allowed to enter the borrower's home without his permission, nor to press for payment when he knows the borrower cannot repay it. "Thou shalt not be to him as a creditor," of the Bible, is understood to create a negative injunction against this, so that even though there is no legal way to prevent the collection of a due debt, the moral disapproval is clear.

Maimonides expresses all these moral and psychological aspects of credit and lending when he presents the following rule regarding the case of loans made to a widow.

"It is not permitted to take a pledge from a widow, irrespective of whether she is rich or poor, neither with her permission nor without it. [In his commentary to the *Mishnah* in *Baba Metzia*, which is the source of this ruling, Maimonides explains that possession of the pledge creates a special relationship, understood by the commentators to refer either to possible forms of coercion and sexual immorality or to evil gossip occasioned by the contact between borrower and lender. Thus, the financial situation of the widow was irrelevant.] As it is written, "Thou shall not pledge the cloak of the widow" [Deuteronomy 24:17]. . . . If she then admits to the debt, she is obligated [by the court, even against her will] to pay the debt" [since, adds the Kesef Mishneh, the Torah did not say that it is not permissible to claim debts from the widow. We collect these debts from her even as from all other debtors.][8]

IMPLEMENTING HALAKHIC INTEREST

Halakhic Definition of Interest

The halakhic treatment of *issur ribit*—the injunction against taking interest—in daily life is a direct consequence of how such *ribit* is defined. Those actions that do not constitute *ribit* are permissible, those that constitute *ribit* are forbidden, and others are permissible within certain parameters and legal forms. Basically, there are two concepts of interest, *ribit mide'oraita*—interest forbidden by the Written Law—and *ribit miderabbanan*—interest forbidden by the Rabbis in those cases that, while not identical, are nevertheless close conceptually to biblical interest. This was done in order to prevent people from possible transgression due to the similarity of the two types. Biblical interest is also referred to as *ribit ketzutzah*—apportioned interest, while rabbinic interest is referred to as *avak ribit*—literally, the dust (fallout) of *ribit*.

The Bible in Leviticus (25:36-37) uses two different Hebrew terms for interest—*neshekh* and *tarbit*, a repetition seen by the Rabbis as meant to stress the severity of the act by making the participants liable on two counts for the same transaction. The *Midrash* uses the different terms to refer to the effects of the interest-bearing loan. *Neshekh*—literally, a bite—makes the debtor's situation similar to that of one bitten by a snake. At first, he suffers only slight discomfort, but later serious pain and suffering, even as the debt of the borrower mounts in severity and cost. *Tarbit*—increase—refers to the growth of the capital of the lender.

In the Talmud, however, the terms are used to present the two different definitions of *ribit*. *Neshekh* is *ribit mide'oraita* and *tarbit* is *ribit miderabbanan*.

So Baal HaTanya, Rabbi Shneur Zalman of Lyady (founder of the Lubavich trend in Chasidism, eastern Europe, eighteenth century), writes in his *Shulchan Arukh*:

> And the principle of interest is when one takes from his fellow any reward for delayed payment of the debt which he is owed. If the payment is made simply for the delay and not through trade or investment then this is *ribit mide'oraita* [referred to in the *Mishnah* in *Baba Metzia*, chapter 5, *mishnah* 1, as *neshekh*] even if the terms were not decided on at the time of making the loan. . . . In those cases where the reward [the interest] is paid for a transaction [selling or investing] then this is *avak ribit* [or *tarbit*] and is forbidden by the rabbis. Wherever one erred, and took *avak ribit*, he has to return the interest if he wishes to clear himself before Heaven.[9]

In the case of *neshekh*, the creditor is being paid for the loss of the alternative use of his funds or *hamtanat ma'ot*, literally waiting for his money. Anything therefore that involves simply this element is *ribit mide'oraita* and is forbidden. Other factors usually associated with this type of interest are the terms of repayment and increment, which are stipulated in advance, and the lack of any risk for the creditor. Not only is monetary compensation for *hamtanat ma'ot* forbidden, but so are all other kinds of benefits to the creditor. The creditor may not dwell in the debtor's house free of charge, nor may the latter teach his children without payment. The Rabbis even forbade the borrower from greeting the creditor unless this was their usual practice before the loan. Any transaction, therefore, wherein the creditor receives any payment or benefit simply on the basis of his loan is considered biblical interest and forbidden.

Avak ribit or *tarbit* is far more complicated and pervasive than biblical interest. It covers all the transactions so prevalent in the modern economy of buying and selling, investment, and financial instruments, in which credit, inactive investors, or future benefits are included. Here the return on capital is not being paid simply for *hamtanat ma'ot*, but is received for participating in transactions or other market-related activities, which takes it out of the *ribit mide'oraita* category. Not only is it difficult to distinguish between the loan element involved and the commercial elements, but also the form of financial arrangements and the nature of available financial instruments are subject to rapid change. *Avak ribit* or *ribit miderabbanan* is therefore one of the most complicated areas of halakhic involvement in business. The discussions in the following two sections are therefore presented only as an attempt to clarify the thought process that lies at the base of halakhic decisions and to illustrate the range of problems involved.

In both types of interest, the rate of interest is not relevant to the religious injunction even though the term *ribit ketzutza* (biblical interest) is used in modern Hebrew to denote usurious rates of interest. It is the moral imperative to use one's wealth to assist others that permeates the laws against *ribit*, and therefore the interest rate involved in negating them is quite irrelevant.

There are, however, important legal differences between the two types of halakhic interest primarily as regards the ability of the debtor to use the *bet din* to reclaim the interest paid or to avoid paying it.

While rabbinically prohibited interest cannot be reclaimed in the courts, the *Shulchan Arukh* rules:

> *Ribit mide'oraita*, which is paid in return for a loan with specified repayments, can be reclaimed [by the borrower] through the court. The court will force and beat him [the lender] until he expires [or pays back the interest. This is similar to the transgression of all other *mitzvot* that the *bet din* can physically punish]. [When the interest is] less than a *shaveh prutah*, [one transgresses a] negative injunction of interest, but it may not be reclaimed through a court. [The Ramah, quoting the *Tur*, writes that *ribit*, even if less than a *shaveh prutah*, is forbidden, irrespective of whether it is in the form of a loan or in the form of commercial transactions.][10]

Present-Day Issues in Rabbinic Interest

The following *Mishnah* is the basis of the rabbinic discussion regarding those types of ventures that are forbidden because of *ribit miderabbanan*—rabbinic interest.

> One may not give a storekeeper [who fulfilled many different functions such as banker, money changer, or a trader on behalf of others in addition to his normal activities even as is the case in many underdeveloped countries and certain areas even of developed countries to this day] [produce to sell on one's behalf at market prices] in return for a half share of the profits or losses nor may one give him money to buy goods [for resale] in

> exchange for an equal share in the profits [or losses. The goods are seen as partially representing a loan and partially as a pledge for which the storekeeper accepts responsibility for damage or a decline in prices. If they share equally in the profits the storekeeper is paying for the pledge with that part of the profits that flow from the loan, which constitutes rabbinic interest]. If the storekeeper is given payment as an employee [so that the inactive partner, the lender, does not share equally in the profits], then it is permissible [as this sharing flows solely from the business venture and this is permissible].[11]

This has implications for almost the whole gamut of financial activities, presenting halakhic problems in hire-purchase agreements, credit sales, mortgages, savings schemes, and the issuing of corporate bonds. Actually, the real scope of the problem is almost unlimited, and it is only possible to deal here with some examples.

The final sentence of the *Mishnah*, whereby the storekeeper is paid a salary before the allocation of profits, thus creating a joint venture, is the basis for the *heter iska*, a rabbinic legal format that came to regulate *iskot* (transactions), so as to permit business ventures that would otherwise transgress the laws of rabbinic interest.

In addition to agreeing that the investor participate in the risks and profits in unequal proportions to the active partner, the former could forgo his share of the profits, his right to a current financial report of the venture, and other claims, in return for a fixed sum.

Contrary to widespread misconception, the *heter iska* does not legalize the taking of biblical interest—that is the earning of money or a loan given for a certain period of time. Furthermore, the *heter iska* is not a charm, magically transferring forbidden transactions into kosher ones, a sort of fraud against God. There has to be a genuine business venture for it to be valid. For example, a modern responsum by Rabbi Moshe Feinstein holds that the *heter iska* must state that the money advanced is being used for ventures that may reasonably be assumed to yield profits of at least twice the amount of the interest. In this way, the venture will yield the entrepreneur more than twice the anticipated profit to be earned on the investor's share of the goods, that is the interest.[12]

A closer examination of many business practices will show that what appear to be moneylending, and therefore forbidden are in fact ventures in which the supplier of capital shares the risks and is paid for that and not only for *hamtanot ma'ot*. Therefore, the *heter iska* is in fact only a validation of a business transaction and not a shield behind which interest-bearing loans are permitted. Where this is not the case, the *heter iska* is valueless.

Some forms of credit, which at first glance look like simple personal loans and therefore not covered by the *heter iska*, will on closer examination be found to be actual business ventures, both in the halakhic and economic sense. For example, loans taken for university tuition or to pay for professional training of any kind are in effect being used to finance an investment that will yield income in the future. The "interest" being paid to the creditor is his share of the future profits.[13]

The activities of modern banking fall into two major categories: business loans and consumer loans, which are radically different from each other in this regard. Business loans today, as distinct from money-lending, which characterized banking until the nineteenth century, are in effect investments rather than simple loans against collateral. Banks place the same emphasis on the debtor's financial reports, his profitability, and future viability as do investors. In the case of large lenders, they may often behave as shareholders, demanding a seat or a nominee on the board of directors, while in many economies, such as Japan and Israel, the share of assets represented by loan capital is greater than the owner's equity, making the creditor in effect an owner, if not in the legal sense, at least in the commercial sense. It would seem, therefore, that the *heter iska* is simply a rabbinic recognition of this aspect of modern commercial banking.

At the same time, however, none of this applies to consumer loans, or to the employees whose wages are automatically deposited in a bank account, and so forth. In these cases, there seems to be no venture or no sharing of risk, only payment for the use of money, which is *ribit mide'oraita* and would seem to be beyond the provisions of the *heter iska*. There has been an argument proposed that since the bank views the clients' business as one whole operation, the consumer loan, being part of the overall activity, would be covered by the business elements, to make the *heter iska* viable. Most consumer loans, however, are made to people whose only business with the bank is these loans and the deposit of their paychecks. It seems a bit farfetched to view these as a venture, so that the question of the consumer loans has to be seriously reviewed.

Since the injunctions against interest taking require that the transaction be direct, between two Jews, some have argued that they do not apply to the corporate structure, in view of its legal identity separate from that of the shareholders. We have discussed this issue at length in a previous chapter. Here it suffices to repeat that most authorities maintain that a bank, finance house, or trading corporation in which Jews own the majority or all of the stock either requires a *heter iska* or is forbidden *ribit mide'oraita*, even as an individual is.

Mortgage Payments

Though mortgage payments are such a common part of our lives, they have to be reexamined in the light of halakhic rules. The simple scenario is where Reuven buys a house and borrows a major part of the required funds from Shimon. As security he gives Shimon a lien or mortgage on the property. Actually, this is a rerun of the case in *Baba Metzia* where one person buys a field, takes possession, and pays for it later.[14] The seller [who provides in effect the funds, similar to the Shimon case] is not permitted to have any benefit from the field or from the buyer. In our day, Rabbi Moshe Feinstein argued that the *heter iska* cannot apply here unless a special format is used.[15] Others argue that no *heter iska* can be used at all, since the whole nature of the mortgage is a straight loan for a specific period of time and rate of interest and is risk free in view of the value of the house. These are the characteristics of *ribit ketzutzah–ribit mide'oraita*, in which the lender is getting paid only for the loss of the alternative use of the money.[16]

Other authorities argue that only *ribit miderabbanan* is involved, so that a *heter iska* is applicable. Some authorities have suggested to me that the homeowner is saving himself rent, and so on, and this makes it a venture. This has some validity since, until recently, countries like the United Kingdom and Israel levied taxes on an imputed value of rent for homeowners as a form of income.

Installments and Credit Purchases

In all Western economies, most consumer goods are bought on credit. Such credit takes two major forms. One of them is the extension of unsecured credit—usually for nondurables like food, clothing, services, and entertainment, either in open customer accounts or through the use of credit cards. The other form of consumer credit, usually used for the purchase of durables like motorcars, major appliances, furniture, and so forth, is granted, like mortgages, in return for installment repayments and a lien on the goods; in case of default, the seller can repossess the goods sold. Similar types of credit are extended by manufacturers to other firms at different stages of the production cycle and to wholesalers or to retailers. This interfirm credit shares most of the economic characteristics of consumer credit.

All these forms of credit present serious halakhic problems since even though they accompany business transactions, the seller is extending credit and being paid for *hamtanat ma'ot*. Furthermore, the terms of repayment are almost always clearly spelled out, violating another halakhic principle.

A *heter iska* would seem to reflect general practice in the case of unsecured credit since here the transaction is in fact a real business venture. Evidence for this may be found in the results of empirical research in many countries that show that unsecured trade credit and consumer credit, in general, are far more expensive than ordinary bank credit. The higher interest rates charged for such credit is a rational economic expression of the high risks undertaken by the unsecured lender. Statistics showing that the default rate on consumer credit is far higher than on bank credit is ample evidence of this increased risk.

The *Shulchan Arukh*, in his ruling on credit purchases, makes a distinction based on the pricing policy of the market.

> It is forbidden to sell to someone for twelve [coins] an article worth ten [coins], in order that he [the seller] should wait [for payment]. Based on *Tosafot* in *Baba Metzia*, 63b [we may ask] in which cases [this is forbidden? The answer would be] for those goods which have a fixed market price or whose value is known, like pepper or wax [in our day perhaps commodities traded on a public exchange or those sold by a monopolist who is able to set and maintain prices]. However, a cloak or similar items which do not have a known value or a fixed price may be sold at a higher price [for credit. Perhaps the credit is to be considered variable just as the price is, minimizing the interest effect].[17]

Nevertheless installment credit as distinct from unsecured credit would seem to constitute a more serious difficulty. Here the loan implicit in the credit extended is made under clearly defined conditions against the security of the pledge—the motorcar, equipment, or other durable asset—which serves as the halakhic *pikadon*—and the creditor is being paid for *hamtanat ma'ot*, which are the characteristics of *ribit mide'oraita*.

These functions would make the use of the *heter iska* problematic, even as it is in the case of mortgages. An interesting halakhic ruling suggests that the interest charge be included in the initial price. In those cases where an original price without credit terms has been agreed upon, the transaction can be canceled and the new price substituted. This would only be applicable in special cases where the two parties are able to write special agreements but does not solve the problem in the free market, where individual trade contracts are not possible. The State of Israel presents an opportunity to organize all installment agreements according to halakhic principles, even as all banks in that country employ a *heter iska*.

Nevertheless, even according to those authorities who take a lenient view of the mortgage loan and the installment agreements enabling items to be covered by a *heter iska*, a serious moral problem exists and needs to be addressed. Much consumer credit is given to poor or economically illiterate people. They are tempted by the chance to obtain goods or services immediately, without being able to calculate whether they are able to meet the payments or what the exact cost to them will be. As a result, people slide into debt from which they cannot extricate themselves and repossession by the seller often occurs. Naturally, resale of the repossessed assets yields more profits to the lender. In many countries, protection is offered through legal requirements for explanatory advertising regarding interest payments and total costs compared to the cash price. It would seem, however, that a halakhic treatment is called for. Is the seller guilty of *lifnei iver*—giving bad advice to one who is blind to the real implications of the advertised credit? If so, is the community obligated to use the halakhic power invested in it to make *takanot* (rulings) to implement the moral imperative of *lifnei iver*? Since the explicit advertisement of the comparative cash and credit prices makes the role of the *heter iska* complicated, would we need to seek a separate system of interest-free loans, *gemilut chesed*, for the purposes of consumer credit in an autonomous Jewish economy?

Inflation, Devaluation, and Changes in Price Levels

Changes in the prices of goods and services may flow from two factors: changes in price levels while the currency remains nominally steady, as in times of inflation, and changes in price levels due to a devaluation or revaluation of the rates of exchange. In both cases the value of our incomes and our wealth change. On the one hand, during inflation or devaluation of the currency, we suffer a loss since we now require more money to buy the same basket of goods and services. This applies not only to current expenses, but also to the pension funds, retirement schemes, or insurance policies, which lose part of their value. On the other hand, as borrowers we enjoy a profit since we now require less money to repay our loans and debts. Nevertheless, the lenders obviously suffer a loss to the same extent. All concerned seek naturally to protect themselves against the effects of inflation and devaluation in various ways, some of which create halakhic problems. Investments are made in real assets, antiques, precious stones, gold, and other rare metals, which have been found to preserve their value even during the changes in the price levels, thus protecting the equity of the investor. It seems that these investments do not pose any moral or halakhic problems. There are however other protective measures, such as the linkage of loans, wages, insurance policies, and pension funds, either to a stable foreign currency or to a specific basket of goods and services, as for instance the consumer cost-of-living index. These cause serious problems, since the creditors are getting more than their initial loan or investment, and this may be either biblical or rabbinic interest. Furthermore, inflation has moral and ethical effects over and above the economic sphere, and these must also be considered in a halakhic perspective.

The basic key to much of the halakhic discussion in this respect is the Rabbis' concept of money in which they distinguish between means of payment and goods.

Money and Goods

A clear distinction is made between means of payment considered *mamon* (money) and goods (*peirot*—literally, fruit or produce), which is not considered money for halakhic purposes. In order to constitute "money" the object needs to be legally recognized as a means of payment, easily transferable, and of constant value. Goods are considered to be those objects that are not legal tender, difficult to use as a means of payment, and above all, subject to fluctuations in price. For example, in the bimetallic system used during mishnaic and talmudic times, while gold coins in regard to produce were considered to be money, they were regarded as goods in relation to silver coins. The latter, in turn, were seen to be goods relative to copper coins, owing to the latter's easier exchange and transferability. In all these cases, the value of the more expensive coin fluctuated relative to the cheaper one.

A halakhic problem arose, however, with regard to the paper currency that came to replace bullion and metallic coins. This currency has no actual intrinsic value over and above that of the paper on which it is printed. In earlier centuries, the banknotes were seen to be backed by an equal value of gold or silver, but when this backing was abandoned, earlier in the century, they still remained promissory notes issued by the government. Since promissory notes are not considered, halakhically, to be anything more than an acknowledgment of debt, rather than a means of exchange, the question arose as to whether the banknotes could be regarded as money for halakhic purposes, primarily concerning interest. In this respect, there are two definitive decisions on which most rabbinic rulings have been based. The Chatam Sofer maintained that the banknotes are money, since the law of the land mandates that they are legal tender, so that nobody can refuse to accept them as payment for goods or sevices or debts.[18] In our own time, the Chazon Ish in Bnei Brak, Israel, ruled that since everybody accepts the banknotes, trades in them, pays their debts with them, they constitute halakhic money.[19] These two opinions, as explained before, have important implications for questions of devaluation and changes in the exchange rates.

The distinction, as may be seen from the following quotation from the *Shulchan Arukh*, between money and goods is clearly made in the codes and responsa, which deal with loans of goods more strictly than with loans of money, the former being forbidden while the others are permitted.

> It is not permissible to lend a measure of wheat against a promise to return a similar measure even though no time has been specified for its return [based on the *Mishnah* in *Baba Metzia*, chapter 5, *mishnah* 9]. The same

> applies to all goods except silver coins, which [in his days were] legal tender [and in ours would apply to paper currency] and not *peirot*—goods. [The reason for the stricter rule toward goods is the concern that] perhaps the price of the wheat [or other goods] will rise [before the loan is repaid] and the borrower will thereby be returning more than he borrowed [and this will constitute interest, which is forbidden].[20]

This injunction of *se'ah bese'ah*—lending a measure of wheat in return for a repayment of the same measure in the future—is one of the bases for rulings that do not permit the linkage of debts to an index of the consumer cost of living. However, almost all the halakhic authorities permit the borrowing of household goods or similar items, even though changes in their price level may occur before payment, in view of their marginal value.[21]

Linkage to a Basket of Goods

The linkage to the consumer cost-of-living index or to other such measurements of price stability is meant to enable the parties to buy the same basket of goods and services as previously. At the end of the period, the creditor, investor, or saver will receive a monetary sum larger than that invested—the nominal sum invested plus the incremental rise in the consumer cost-of-living index. In actual fact, however, the investor is only getting back the same purchasing power and so may not consider the increment to be interest or profit. Indeed, such profits are, in economic terms, illusionary ones, even as are increased sales or wages where the increase is only equal to the rise in the cost-of-living index. Nevertheless, most halakhic sources do not allow linkage of loans to such an index, seeing this as interest, since, while the value of the money (*mamon*) remained stable (by definition), what has declined is the basket of goods due to inflation. Since one may not lend goods in order to receive back the same amount of goods, as explained, precisely because of the possibility of price changes, such linkage requires a *heter iska*. Rabbi Goren, a previous Chief Rabbi of Israel, argues that in times of inflation the roles of money and goods are reversed, so that it is really the goods that remain stable while the *mamon* declines, so that such indexation should be permitted. However, this is not accepted by most other authorities for a number of other reasons, which may be summarized as follows.

1. The consumer index is not a specific good but rather a theoretical basket of goods, which does not apply to any single consumer or transaction, and therefore, it is not possible to link the loan to it.

2. One cannot buy or sell something that does not yet exist, so that linkage to a future basket of goods whose existence is not known is not permissible.

The vast majority of authorities, therefore, require the existence of a business venture and a formal *heter iska* to permit this sort of indexation.

Linkage to a Foreign Currency

It is possible to borrow *mamon* (money as distinct from goods) and repay the debt in another currency. This is so since the value of money is considered not to fluctuate. Reuven can therefore borrow dollars and repay an agreed-upon sum of pounds sterling, even where the relative rates of exchange have changed. In this way the lender can protect himself against any changes in the value of the dollar. This arrangement, however, is dependent on two factors—both currencies have to be legal tender and Reuven must possess some sterling at the time the loan was made.

Government Changes in the Currency

Governments have, since ancient times, devalued their currency, causing, inter alia, problems for borrowers, lenders, and investors. When actual metallic coins were used, the content of precious metals was changed, while in our time, the actual rates of exchange are not always left to market forces but are changed by government action. The rabbinic discussion as to the legal status of loans or commercial transactions centers on the question of whether the increased value of the debt constitutes interest or not.

The halakhic attitude to such government changes is usually to insist on payment of the nominal sum borrowed. So if Reuven borrowed one thousand dollars and the government devalued the dollar in regard to other currencies, Reuven would not be obliged to repay Shimon at the new rate of exchange, even if no condition were made to the contrary. The government decision in this regard is considered to be the same as the issuing of a new currency, in which case the obligation is to pay the new legal tender since no agreement of linkage was made. However, since such decisions impose sudden hardship, the rabbinic authorities argued that perhaps the lender should be obligated. So, for example, Dayan Weiss, the late head of the *bet din* of the *Eidah Chareidit* in Jerusalem, held that it is not clear whether or not in the case of the devaluation of the Israeli lira the borrower is not required to pay at least the rise in price levels generated by the devaluation.[22] In those cases where the issue regarding the element of interest is not clear, one is permitted to pay the increase in order to be clear before Heaven of the damage caused to the lender. This is parallel, it would seem, to the ruling of the Raivad that where one wishes to clear oneself before Heaven in those cases where one is not sure of the amount of the debt, one may pay the higher sum without fear of interest "but the borrower has to forgive the lender so that he should not be guilty of theft and of transgressing the injunction against interest [by taking the increased sum]."[23]

Over the centuries, a pattern emerged of a compromise whereby the profit or loss resulting from government devaluation would be shared equally by borrower and lender or buyer and seller, even though this was beyond the requirement of the law. Such compromise is to be found both in the enactments of the Jewish communities and in halakhic decisions, all of which stress the moral as opposed to the legal basis of the compromise.

One of the earliest of such enactments is that of the community of Fez in North Africa in 1614.

> The constant changes in the value of the coins have led to much communal strife, since the claimants want to collect the increased value while the dependents want only to pay the nominal value. We [the communal council] have decided to enact a new rule whereby they will share the increase between them.[24]

Rabbi Avraham di Boton (Salonika, 1625-1700) presents another view of the reasoning behind the communal enactments, seeing them as a means whereby the judges can make an ethical judgment. "So I have said that the leaders and important people of our town have done well to provide [through the enactment] a compromise in these matters. After all, the legal situation is not clear, so that is best that the parties compromise and each one will depart in peace, since the compromise is a judgment of peace."[25]

These communal enactments figure prominently in the halakhic decisions where they acquired the force of law. Rabbi Yechiel Basson (Constantinople, seventeenth century) adjudicated a case according to such a communal enactment of the town regarding the payment of a women's marriage contract after divorce or death of the husband.

> Rabbi Eliyahu, the son of Rabbi Chaim, enacted an edict here in Constantinople whereby the difference [in case of devaluations] should be divided equally [between the heirs who are liable to pay the widow's marriage contract out of their inheritance and the widow]. Therefore all those *ketubot* which were written when 60 silver coins were worth one gold coin, should be paid 90 silver coins, now that one gold coin is worth 120 silver ones.[26]

The idea of these compromises as being *lifnim mishurat hadin* is clear from responsa such as the following one of the same rabbi.

> Reuven agreed to pay Shimon on a specified date a certain sum of *groschen*, irrespective of whether their value relative to the silver coins rises or falls. This is a matter of halakhic dispute. Maimonides and Rabbi Yitzchak Alfasi (Rif, Fez, North Africa, tenth century) hold that this is *se'ah bese'ah* [a loan of goods for other goods since the *groschen* are goods relative to the silver coins, which are halakhic money as explained previously]. Other authorities disagree, so that if their value falls, then Reuven would be liable to pay more. Reuven can argue that he wants the court to rule according to Maimonides and the Rif, in which case he would only have to pay the original debt. I, however, rule that the good and righteous way is for the *bet din* to force both sides to do as we do here in Constantinople and divide the increase between them.[27]

Inflation as a Moral Problem

For the individual, inflation and devaluation are primarily questions of protecting himself against erosion of his savings or investments. So, too, the primary halakhic concern has been whether such protection constituted interest, rabbinical or otherwise, and its effect on the debtor- creditor relationship. There are, however, serious moral issues resulting from inflation, and it would seem that viewing them in a Jewish perspective makes a contribution to business ethics, even if the individual is not able to affect the course of inflation directly.

Taxation

Inflation may be considered from an economic view to be a form of taxation.[28] The government, in order to finance its activities, raises the necessary funds through loans and taxation, but also by devaluating its coinage or through inflation. In both of these cases, the state is reducing its obligations to the holders of the currency and the government paper, so that it is in effect taking money from them, even as it does when it levies direct or indirect taxes. The question to be discussed, however, is to what extent is such taxation morally justified?

We have seen in Part I that all communal legislation requires either unanimous approval or at least that of a majority of the constituents or their representatives. It is possible to argue that the majority vote in the legislative bodies meets this requirement with regard to taxes, even as it does to other acts of legislation. Inflation, however, poses a special problem. By voting for the budget from which the degree of inflation may be deduced, it would seem that the representatives of the people have accepted such inflation. This is only so, however, if we may assume that all those voting are fully aware of the inflationary effects of the budget. Given the level of economic knowledge of most legislators, it is doubtful that such an assumption is valid.

Even, however, were it possible to accept such an assumption, there still exists a further difficulty. It is extremely difficult, if not impossible, to forecast accurately the full impact of the inflation arising out of the provisions of a specific budget. This means that an inflationary tax, or at least part of it, is being leveled without the knowledge of the legislators and therefore without their explicit consent. In effect this is a secret tax imposed on society, similar to the methods used by the Stuart kings in England, which led to the revolt of Parliament in the seventeenth century. Is this tax then invalid from a Jewish point of view?

Furthermore, almost all the halakhic discussions provide a mechanism for the allocation of the tax burden according to capital, according to utility, or a combination of them.[29] Although the levying of taxes and the allocation of the tax burden have been traditionally left to the "secular" communal leaders, the *bet din* or halakhic authority serves as a review court to see that the tax is being allocated according to Jewish law, in order to prevent social injustice.

It has been found that the prime sufferers from inflation are the weaker members of society—the poor, the pensioners, the sick—so that *tzedakah* would make such a moral review mandatory. Unless this is done, there are serious risks that the taxation through inflation becomes arbitrary and socially irresponsible.

Morality

Perhaps the most ignored and overlooked effect of inflation is its relationship to the moral standards of society. It is true that the relationship may not easily be proved through the statistics of crime. Nevertheless, it can be shown that there occurs an erosion of the general moral level of any society exposed to long periods of steady inflation or even, in the case of hyperinflation, relatively short periods of time.

Economic historians have argued that the decline of the Roman Empire in ancient times and the collapse of the Weimar Republic in modern Germany are both to be attributed to the moral decay that resulted from their inflationary policies.[30] There is no reason to doubt that these historical experiences are repeated in our own societies.

Inflation affects the moral conduct of a society in a number of ways:

1. The existence of a stable monetary system provides an impartial and consistent value to goods, services, property, and even injured body parts of people. By devaluating the currency, inflation distorts this value until no objective measuring rod remains, so that the cost of damage to property or to body becomes subjective and not easily measured.
2. An escape from money to goods, whether needed or not, is seen as the only way to preserve one's income or wealth. Saving becomes pointless, further encouraging consumption and waste. Instant gratification becomes the way of living. People try to increase their wealth at the expense of others by borrowing more, hoping to pay back in a devalued currency.
3. As wages are eroded by inflation, the work ethic disappears and people try to get by with giving as little as possible, in return for a decreasing real wage.
4. Governments, unchecked by the discipline of the budget, find it easy to pander to the demands of the people, whether these are feasible or not. "Bread and circuses," to be paid for at the expense of future generations, become the normal means of ruling.
5. The whole society spends a major part of its time, energy, and

brain power in manipulations attempting to preserve their own real wealth, often at the expense of the less wary or more vulnerable part of the population.

The conditioning through inflation toward immediate gratification or enriching oneself at the expense of the creditor, employer, or neighbor, and the neglect of property, one's own and that of others, spreads until it destroys the moral fabric of society.

Since immorality is indivisible, this immorality does not remain restricted to economic affairs, but soon is reflected in sexual behavior and crimes of violence. According to the Rabbis, the destruction of the Generation of the Flood was only sealed when they were guilty of robbery. Unlike the cardinal crimes of murder, idolatry, and sexual immorality, robbery does not invoke a death penalty, which seems to question the talmudic decision. The chasidic master Shmuel of Sochochow explains that when robbery becomes prevalent, all the other sins follow.[31]

It is true that all these moral issues apply to non-Jewish societies just as they apply to a halakhically based one. In other societies, however, moral issues are primarily the domain of the individual. Even in those cases where they lead to legislation, the moral basis is a voluntary one, dependent on a consensus that is in constant flux.

This voluntary, noncoercive nature of modern morality, as widespread as it is, conflicts however with a Jewish concept of morality. Here it is normative rather than relative and part of the structure of obligations incumbent on the individual and on the collective. Just as the individual has obligations, so too can the community be obligated both to legislate moral behavior and to implement such legislation. It is accepted halakhic policy that it is as necessary to legislate against wrongdoing as it is to punish the wrongdoer. So communal enactments to prevent mingling of the sexes to prevent promiscuity, to promote modesty in consumption, and to minimize gambling are to be found in many Jewish communities, bolstered by the halakhic authorities of their time. The many examples presented throughout this book should suffice to show that it is similarly appropriate from a Jewish viewpoint to prevent the moral decay brought about by inflation either by preventing it in the first place or by taking social action to limit the ethical side effects.

In the State of Israel, it would seem, therefore, that rabbinic authorities would have to devote attention not only to the problems of interest arising out of changes in the price levels but also to the role of the government in causing such changes, in view of the moral effects resulting from these things. Outside of Israel, it would seem that these same issues have to be approached and suitable ways found to prevent the moral damage that accompanies inflation.

GEMILUT CHESED–THE INTEREST-FREE LOAN

Restrictions on interest-bearing loans or transactions, irrespective of whether they constitute rabbinic or biblical interest, are only one aspect of the Jewish perspective of the debtor–creditor relationship. Just as in all other aspects of business activity, or for that matter of daily life, positive acts–*mitzvot asei*–are as important as the injunctions preventing unethical behavior. Furthermore, these positive acts, by their very nature, show the individual's ability and willingness to improve his spiritual behavior, in its Jewish framework, to sanctify his behavior and make it holy.

Already in mishnaic times, the Rabbis expressed the religious and spiritual value of *gemilut chesed*, acts of righteousness, one of the most outstanding of which is the granting of interest-free loans.

Shimon HaTzaddik was the last of the *anshei Knesset HaGedolah*, the men of the Great Assembly, who guided the Jews from the time of the return from the Babylonian Exile (c. 600 B.C.E.) until the time of the conquest of the Land of Israel by the Greeks under Alexander the Great. He used to say, "The world stands [is based so that should they be missing the world cannot exist] on the Torah, serving God, and active loving-kindness [promoting the welfare of our fellow men]."[32]

Rabbi Samson Raphael Hirsch comments, "If a person omits *gemilut chesed* he will be without that characteristic which is the very first act of godliness. Instead of being God-like in acting as a creator of happiness and prosperity for his fellow man, he will harden his heart in callous selfishness and mankind will lack the bond of brotherhood and loving-kindness."

Gemilut chesed includes all those acts that do not flow from an obligatory or contractual relationship with others. They may be done with one's body, as for instance, visiting the sick or burying the dead, or with wealth through the interest-free loan. Acts of righteousness are conceptually different from charity, since they relate not only to the poor, but also to those who do not qualify for charity but nevertheless are in need.

A proper perspective of the importance within any economic system of the interest-free loan may be seen in the fact that Maimonides in his codex–*Mishneh Torah*–legislates this obligation at the very outset of the laws of credit and borrowing.

> It is a positive *mitzvah* to lend [interest-free] to the poor of Israel [The *Shulchan Arukh* and the *Arbaah Turim*, following the talmudic discussion, write that this obligation applies also to the rich who are temporarily illiquid], as it is written, "When you lend money to My People, to the poor, who are with you" (Exodus 22:24). [The superfluous phrase "to the poor" is understood by the Rabbis only to give them precedence, but not to limit the *gemilut chesed* to them.] Perhaps this is not obligatory but only admirable [since the Hebrew word *im* can mean both "if" (permissive) and "when" (obligatory)] yet the Torah teaches us (Deuteronomy 5:8), "You shall open your hand to him and also surely lend to him."[33]

Such an obligation is not merely important for the financial well-being of the borrower, but also for the spiritual development of the lender, who is using his God-given wealth to help others and in that process forgoing part of his legitmate right to earn a profit on that wealth. This is explained by the Sefer HaChinukh.

> The root of this *mitzvah* lies in the Divine wish that His creatures be proficient in this attribute of righteousness and that acts of mercy shall become ingrained. By means of attuning their bodies [in this case, their wealth] to such good traits, they become as vessels to receive Divine bounty and through the wealth which He grants to the righteous, His desire to deal kindly with the world becomes realized. If not for this, God would give the poor all their needs without our intervention. Through this mercy, however, we are able to become His instruments [to implement this kindness and thereby] become [spiritually] refined. The righteous God desired the [economic] development of the People He chose, and therefore commanded us to remove an obstacle thereto, in order that they should not devour the possessions of the other in a manner whereby he is not aware, for such is the nature of interest [bearing loans]. The warnings of our sages against ignoring this obligation are many and repetitive, seeing one who does so as being abhorrent, perverted and abominable even as he who worships idols [since he is in effect denying the Divine source of his wealth].[34]

Rabbi Samson Raphael Hirsch, commenting on the verse in Exodus, maintains that the Hebrew word for "loan," *loveh*, is used in many other instances to refer to the attachment of one person to another that furthers the welfare of that person, as for instance, when the matriarch Leah names her third son, Levi, since "This time my husband will become attached to me" (Genesis 29:30). Furthermore, since the object of the loan is not only the individual, but also My People, through it one is really creating a community, thus fostering a social life dedicated to God.[35]

It must be stressed that such halakhic instruments permitting what would otherwise be rabbinic interest as the *heter iska* do not free one from this obligation—to make interest-free loans. One who is extremely cautious not to transgress the biblical injunction against the interest-bearing loan, even in the many varied situations of modern commerce discussed previously, is similarly not free of this obligation. One who does not make interest-free loans is deficient Jewishly in his business activities.

Repeatedly, the interest-free loan is seen, because of the tendency to view the Bible as relating to a primitive agrarian economy, as a stop-gap measure meant to provide for the short-term difficulties of farmers caught between harvests. As such its relevance for present-day business behavior would be limited. However, the extension of this concept to include a much wider range of eligible individuals and uses makes the concept of the interest-free loan a primary contribution to modern social thinking and an important instrument for welfare policy.

That the interest-free loan is not meant in Judaism merely to provide assistance to the poor or for funding the purchase of consumer goods is quite clear from talmudic discussions, from halakhic commentators, and from all the codes.

In the Talmud, Rabbi Abba said, "One who gives a loan is more meritorious than one who gives charity, while he who funds a business venture with the poor is even more meritorious." Rashi explains this ranking by pointing out that preference is given to the venture, since in this case, the poor suffer no humiliation as the investor is sharing in the profits. However, in the interest-free loan, there is a certain shame attached even as in charity, as the lender is receiving no benefit for his money.[36]

The role of the interest-free loan as a means of preventing people from becoming poor or enabling those already poor to break out of the poverty cycle is stressed by all the codes. They point out, as in the language of Maimonides:

> The pinnacle [of charitable acts] beyond which there is no greater is he who supports one of Israel who has become low [poor] and gives him a gift or a loan [interest free] or enters into a business venture with him or who offers him work, so that he not become dependent on others for charity. [We are commanded to] support him so that he does not become impoverished [literally—to fall] and become needy.[37]

These interest-free loans, either funded by individuals or part of the charitable framework of communities, have been a constant feature of Jewish economic history. In the nineteenth and twentieth centuries, the waves of Jewish immigration to western Europe, the United States, and other countries created a financing problem, solved partially, at least, by such funding. The immigrants had neither the equity nor the trading results that would qualify them for commercial loans or credit. Even without any racial discrimination, credit officers would have been hard-pressed to make funds available to them, in view of the higher than normal risk posed by the immigrants. This is a problem faced by many minority groups even today in the United States and United Kingdom. The Jew, however, has been able to avail himsel of the interest-free loan funds established by other Jews. These funds enabled the Jewish immigrant to establish businesses, acquire basic equipment and inventory, and operate successfully until he was able to avail himself of funding from the regular markets. Hard-pressed Jewish businessmen and new entrepreneurs are able even today, in almost all countries, similarly to avail themselves of such interest-free loans. It is a pity that Shakespeare's Antonio could not avail himself of similar funds from his friends and coreligionists.

BANKRUPTCY

Bankruptcy, both of individuals and of firms, is not a new phenomenon, but one that stretches back into the beginnings of economic history. Like all economic phenomena, it poses moral issues over and above the purely commerical and financial ones. In the main, these can be categorized as follows:

1. Morality is involved in the debtor not being able to repay money given to him by his creditors.

2. The creditor has the ethical dilemma of whether to demand payment or to forgo his property right to the debt.

3. In macroeconomic policy, importance is often given to public-sector intervention to rescue failed firms or dying industries in order to prevent large-scale unemployment. It is necessary, therefore, to consider the morality of using public funds for this purpose.

Close examination of attitudes toward bankruptcy and a society's treatment thereof will show that what are actually being discussed are attitudes to charity or a specific case of welfare. So the differences in approach between a Jewish understanding of the subject and that of other faiths or cultures flow from the basic theological differences regarding the role of wealth, private property, charity, and justice.

The experience of modern social policy over the past fifty years has shown that rescue policies aimed at "bailing out" inefficient firms in order to prevent unemployment, or establishing nonviable industries or firms in order to provide work within the shortest possible time has created moral problems, often no less serious than the unemployment they came to solve.

Public money is often wasted, thus demoralizing the general public's attitudes toward taxation. These policies have been funded by subsidized interest rates or by making money available, which normal financial institutions would not do in the view of the risk factor. At the same time, credit criteria are relaxed, and the monitoring of these loans is usually defective. Entrepreneurs, aware of such social policies, make noneconomic investments on the basis of the available public funding. The workers in such industries have no incentive to productivity, since the public funds will prevent the collapse of the firm. Private-sector creditors make funds available to such firms, since the public-sector funding has reduced their risk. Research has shown that it is the existence of such public-sector lenders, possessing sociopolitical aims rather than profitability, that enables firms to operate with a lower equity base and therefore greater than normal risk to all. Such was the experience of public lending to minority-owned firms in the United States and to specific types of small firms in the United Kingdom. In many developing countries, international agencies have found that obligations to repay the loans are not treated seriously. Fraud and political corruption often follow the casual attitudes toward defaulting, which so often results from the lack of credit screening or normal security requirements.

This moral malaise flows from a blurring of the distinction between justice—protecting the rights of the creditor—and mercy—solving the problems of the poor. It is in this light that the bankruptcy issue, relating to debtor and creditor alike, must be reviewed.

The Morality of a Debtor Not Repaying His Debts

Empirical research[38] has shown clearly that corporate or business bankruptcy is not the result of unforeseen circumstances or unavoidable actions, but rather it is the consequence of poor management, fraud, or incorrect economic decisions. This clearly separates it from the financial distress of farmers overwhelmed by natural disasters, over which they have no control and that they could not foresee, or of employees fired through no fault of their own.

Nevertheless, in regard to their eligibility for assistance, Jewish tradition makes no distinction between these two types of financially distressed people. Neither in the biblical texts nor in the rabbinic sources do we find a distinction between the deserving poor and those who become so because of their own laziness or inefficiency. The agricultural gifts to the poor—gleaning, forgotten sheaves, the unharvested corners of the grain fields, and so on—are available to all the poor. So too are the welfare funds provided from the taxes levied by the autonomous Jewish communities. Eligibility was always a function of income level, not of the factors causing the poverty.

At the same time, the bankrupt businessman and the discharged worker do have a special status in Jewish welfare. In addition to the financial embarrassment or economic difficulties they face, they incur a severe spiritual or psychological loss. They have to adjust to a lower standard of living, which also requires social or mental adjustment. There is often the anguish of failure and, in the case of the discharged worker, being told that one is redundant to society. The rabbinic codes recognized this and therefore waived the stringent limitations on the amount of charity to be given, as discussed in the previous chapter. There it was pointed out that communal welfare funds are obligated only to provide the poor with minimum assistance—"Two meals a day, a pallet to sleep on, and some form of housing"—or in the words of

Maimonides, "We are not obligated to make the poor rich, only to support them." In the case, however, of a rich person who becomes poor, individuals and the community are obligated to provide him with all the luxuries he was accustomed to previously, "even a horse to ride on." At the same time, a bankrupt person is unfortunately saddled with the same stigma attached to all other recipients of welfare or charity. This is the price he pays for making incorrect business decisions, as explained below. However, there is a further negative consideration involved that is related to the interest-free loan. The same moral code that obligates a Jew to lend money to another obligates the latter to repay his debts. So where a man claims he cannot pay, the *bet din* is required to evaluate and sell all his assets, including his expensive personal belongings and those of his wife and of his family. He is left with the minimum requirements of one who is just above the poverty line.[39] To rule otherwise would be a distortion of justice. In the case of the interest-bearing loan, the attachment of the debtor's assets to the value of the debt, even if it meant leaving him with only the mandatory two meals a day for thirty days, his religious ritual requirements, and simple clothing, also applies. While the debtor may claim protection against paying interest forbidden by the Torah, he cannot escape paying the debt.

In all cases, the creditors intended to make loans, not to give charity, and therefore they cannot be obligated to waive their rights; voluntary renunciation as an act of righteousness is something else and is dealt with in the next section. Naturally, the attachment of the debtor's personal assets is not possible where the limited-liability corporation is concerned. This is a form of business organization where the creditors are able to obtain only the value of the owners' equity, a limitation that is common knowledge and under which the credit was extended. At the same time, there is a distinct moral demand that the debtor repay his debts out of his private assets in order to be "clean before God and men," a moral demand, yet one that cannot always be enforced by the rabbinic courts.

Nevertheless, it seems to this author that the *bet din* could actually enforce such payment even in the case of corporate bankruptcy. The monetary conditions—*tenai bemamon*—which make limited-liablity clauses halakhically binding, do not apply to fraud based on the withholding of relevant data. This can be seen from the following decision of the London *bet din* in 1992, in the matter of Reuven and Aleph Ltd.

Following a hearing on 20 June 1991, and a review of the documentary evidence, THE BET DIN HAS FOUND as follows:

1. The Plaintiffs were engaged by the Defendant's company, Aleph Ltd., to provide professional accountancy services for that company. The Plaintiffs did indeed provide services for the company, for which invoices were rendered but no payment was made.

2. The Defendant acquired another company, Bet Gimel. In October 1990, Aleph Ltd. transferred its assets to Bet Gimmel before entering voluntary liquidation on 27 February 1991.

3. At a meeting held between the Plaintiffs and the Defendant on 16 March 1991, the Defendant affirmed that he held himself as being personally responsible for the monies owed by Aleph Ltd. to the Plaintiffs, in respect of the services rendered.

4. The Plaintiffs therefore claim from the Defendant their fees on two grounds:

A) As a consequence of the meeting set out under Paragraph 3 above.

B) As result of his actions set out under Paragraph 2 above.

THE BET DIN RULES THAT–

i) The claim based on 4a) cannot be upheld. The promises made in that conversation have no binding legal effect in Jewish law.

ii) Where goods or services were provided to a limited company in consquence of which a liability has arisen and the company had subsequently gone into liquidation, there is no recourse in Jewish law to the directors or shareholders. This only applies when there had been no action designed to denude the liquidated company from its assets, prior to the liquidation. If such moves were made, the person so acting would be personally liable for the liquidated company's debts.

Having been satisfied that the Defendant had indeed acted as set out in Paragraph 2, he is therefore personally liable for the monies owed.

The Defendant's contention that the fees charged are excessive is not upheld, since no evidence had been adduced in support of that contention.

Accordingly, it is hereby ordered that the Defendant is to pay to the Plaintiffs, the sum of 5,581.76 Pounds within 30 days of the date of this Award.

In the light of the forecasting models mentioned previously, it seems that this ruling of the London *bet din* would apply to most cases of corporate bankruptcy. It is quite clear that this is not a sudden development, akin to corporate heart failure, but rather the result of a gradual cancerous growth or long-term debilitation. All these models show clearly that the probability of a firm becoming economically bankrupt, even if not legally so, can be foretold at least three to five years prior to the actual event. If this is true of the outside analyst using only financial data, it is obviously even truer of those actually engaged in the everyday affairs of the corporation. When they borrow funds, enter into new obligations, or postpone their existing ones, they have full knowledge of the real financial situation long before they plead legal bankruptcy. Surely this makes them liable for any debts incurred after they have such knowledge?

It is true that large financial institutions are also able to ascertain the risk involved in lending to corporations, using the same predictive models. Their failure to do so may make the debtor less liable to make full restitution. Yet, this surely does not apply to employees, pension funds, trade creditors, or others who do not have access to the financial data needed for such predictive models. In these cases, the fraudulent aspect flowing from nondisclosure may make the officeholders and major shareholders liable halakhically for claims against their personal assets. It has been suggested to the author that a distinction should be made in this regard between the private corporation and one whose shares are traded in a stock excange. The assumption is that the separation of ownership from management in the latter type of corporation reduces the scope of such mismanagement. However, this assumption needs to be examined more carefully in the light of the recent collapse of the Maxwell empire or that of the Bank for Credit and Commerce International.

Waiving the Rights of the Creditor

In recent years, bankruptcy laws in many Western countries have been relaxed in favor of the debtors. Chapter Eleven in the United States and the new legislation in the United Kingdom are two examples of a divergence from the strict debtor legislation that existed for many centuries. These changes allow for greater protection of the debtor's rights and remove, to a large degree, the stigma previously attached to being bankrupt. Some allow the bankrupt firm to operate even though it is unable to meet the current obligations. Others permit a bankrupt person to operate a business even though he has not repaid all his debts.

It seems that *Halakhah* does not approve these lenient trends. After all, the debtor does not possess any moral right that would absolve him from repayment of his debts or legally coerce the creditors to withdraw their claims. Furthermore, the leniency and the removal of the stigma from bankruptcy make it socially acceptable, increasingly widespread, and of great social damage as described above. In contrast, *Halakhah* defines as a form of robbery, the arrangements for part payment in settlement of debt. This is an additional expression of the moral obligation of people to meet their responsibilities in the marketplace. It must be stressed that physical punishment, exile, or imprisonment is foreign to the halakhic system.

However, the twin strands of righteousness and justice in Judaism operate in this respect as they do in all other areas of life. In accordance with this tradition of righteousness, the Jewish creditor was not only educated to be merciful, but he was also legally restrained from exercising many of his normal property rights. The *Halakhah* views as forbidden interest even nonmonetary forms of payment and forbids the debtor to give any services that could be construed as a benefit to the creditor, such as letting him live rent free in the debtor's house, teaching the creditor's children without wages, and so on. Even the expression of thanks by the debtor may sometimes be considered as interest.

A creditor may not enter the debtor's house to demand payment, since this may shame him in the eyes of his family, nor may he press for repayment if he knows the debtor is in difficulty. While the Torah provides for the creditor to secure his debt by means of collateral, this right is limited both in regard to what may serve as collateral and what use may be made thereof. Things essential to the debtor's livelihood cannot be taken as security for the loan; the Mosaic Code forbids the millstone and the rabbinic law, the tools of the artisan. Personal belongings may be pledged but have to be returned when needed—the cloak in the day and the pillow at night.[40] Maimonides codifies as binding Jewish law that one may not take a pledge from a widow, irrespective of whether she is rich or poor, since this gives one a power over her that could lead to sexual harrassment or because people will gossip about the relationship.[41]

Despite the conclusion, aimed at in all these laws and *mitzvot*, that the Lord is the source of all wealth and gives it to man, inter alia, to share with those less fortunate than himself, nowhere do we find a demand that the creditor forgo his debt (except for the seventh-year legislation). *Lifnim mishurat hadin* (beyond the demand of jusice) is a rabbinic dictum to describe praiseworthy action that one should strive to perform, a frame of mind in which one is prepared to forgo one's legal rights in order to cause another pleasure or profit, and a conciliatory attitude toward commercial transactions that the Torah wishes to inculcate. Beyond the demands of justice are mercy and righteousness, yet at the same time justice has to be pursued, so that if the creditor refuses to forgo his rights, the courts have to uphold them, even if the debtor is poor. One could argue that since the creditor is richer than the debtor, society should force the former to waive his rights. Yet the Jewish sources are clear on this point. The Bible tells us that one may not favor the poor in judgment. A woman once appeared in a rabbinic court and burst into tears, leading the judges to excuse themselves from the case, arguing that there is no greater bribery than the tears of a poor widow. Concern for the poor can be bribery, even as fear of the rich and mighty, with the same immoral effects.

The rabbinic courts are therefore obligated to support fully the legitimate claims of the creditor, as may be seen from the continuation in the codex of Maimonides.

> Even if the creditor is wealthy while the debtor is poor and earns his livelihood with difficulty [the judge should not say to himself that since I and the wealthy creditor are obligated to support the poor debtor as an act of charity, I will rule in his favor to erase the debt so that he can provide for himself with dignity (*Hilkhot Sanhedrin*, chapter 20, *halakhah* 4) but rather] we do not have mercy on him in the court. [After all the Torah commanded, "you shall not favour the poor in judgment," and "you shall not favor the person of the poor in judgment."] So the debt is to be collected in full either from his movable or unmovable property even if the latter is mortgaged to his wife's dowry. . . . If the debtor claims that the liquid assets are borrowed ones or held by him in trust or rented from somebody else, the courts pay no attention to this, unless he can provide evidence thereto.[42]

Even the debtor's personal property is to be included in the assets that are to be sold to cover the debt, excepting for the most essential and basic ones. Luxury clothing of the whole family, jewelry, and fine household goods are to be sold. Only basic needs are to be provided for, so everything that is actually an asset rather than a utensil is included in the sale. This treatment effectively prevents the all too common practice whereby the debtor retains his standard of living at the expense of the creditors.

In many modern economies, subsidized credit is made available without any of the normal credit screening or security, in order to promote full employment to disadvantaged ethnic groups or to distressed economic areas. The public-sector lender takes on himself a degree of risk greater than the normal banking one in order to pursue humanitarian or social aims. At the same time, the borrower knows that default will not be met with the same severity as in the marketplace and therefore wasteful investments are made, "white elephants" are created, and fraud is rife. The social and moral implications of clearly separating the demand for charity and righteousness from legal support for creditors' rights would prevent such economic immorality.

Public-Sector Responsibility

Honoring the legal rights of the creditor by forcing the borrower into bankruptcy means that now the debtor is poor and has needs that have to be attended to. If the welfare of the debtor is not the responsibility of the creditor, arising out of the specific creditor–debtor responsibility, then are we to argue that since the banktruptcy is his own fault, nobody has a responsibility for assisting the debtor?

Judaism's answer is a categorical no. The halakhic codes place the social responsibility fully on the communal purse. Naturally, the creditor as a member of the community will be obligated to pay his share of the tax burden, which the community will impose, inter alia, to take care of the poor and needy, including the bankrupt debtor. This is a demand of charity that is financed in Judaism through taxation and not a result of denial of the creditor's legal right to the debt. It may well be that if the creditor who caused the banktruptcy was only a minor claimant to the debtor's assets, but a wealthy man, his tax liability could be far greater than the debt.

The public-sector responsibility to the bankrupt person or to those unemployed as a result of corporate bankruptcy can be met in many ways. Public funds can be used for retraining purposes, for unemployment benefits, or for interest-free loans either to cancel temporary illiquidity or to start up a new firm. Such funds can also be used to continue the operation of the bankrupt firm, so as to provide employment and a livelihood earned with dignity. All those public-sector activities, however, are acts of charity and need to be implemented as such. This contrast to the public-sector "bail out" of distressed corporations, so common in many countries, must be constantly borne in mind. In the Jewish perspective, the "distressed" corporation becomes, through the public funding, a sheltered workshop. This radically changes the role of the shareholders and the creditors, since the funding is meant only for the welfare of the unemployed. Since the likelihood of bankruptcy can be foretold by suitable analysis, the creditors obviously did not make such analysis and therefore should be made to lose their ill-conceived loans. Similarly, the shareholders obviously paid no attention to the management policies, which caused the bankruptcy, and therefore it is fair that they lose their equity. It is reasonable to assume that both groups are not poor and therefore not entitled to charity. Now only the workers are left, and they are entitled to communally funded charity.

THE JEW AS BANKER AND FINANCIER

The truth about the role of the Jew as a moneylender and a banker must be seen in relationship to the previous discussions in this chapter, rather than in the light of more popular misconceptions. Much of the social, political, and historical treatment of this subject is based on the argument that the Jew was forced into these activities. The Christian religious objection to moneylending on the one hand and the restrictions against Jews owning land or entering certain crafts on the other meant, according to this interpretation, that two of the few economic avenues open to them were credit and banking. The cultural motivation, however, behind these theories is to clear the Jew, both for his own self-esteem and to limit anti-Semitism, from the stigma of usury. However, this stigma exists and needs to be explained away only if credit and banking are regarded as evil. It seems that the Socialist and anticapital social philosophies and sentiments of the nineteenth century were the primary source of these apologetic views of Jewish banking; in a world view that sees interest and finance as beneficial, productive, and legitimate, there is no need for apology. Free-market economists and businessmen, however, see clearly the benefits of the interest mechanism, even as Judaism does. Seeing nothing intrinsically evil about taking interest as discussed earlier, the Jew entered the financial markets, primarily because they were profitable ones, generated by the economic growth that marked Europe's emergence from the Dark Ages.

Reexamination of the broad historic facts would seem to bolster this opinion and to minimize the apologetic argument about Jewish involvement in banking and moneylending.

This argument concentrates on medieval Christian western Europe, ignoring the history of the Classical Period, that of the Moslem world, and the development of eastern Europe. Jewish activity in international trade led to their involvement in credit and banking in all these countries, even though they were less restrictive and often even liberal in economic terms to the Jews. In Roman times, there existed credit and money markets involving lending, interest, and investment, and evidence exists to show that Jews were active in all of them, in the Land of Israel, throughout the Roman Empire, and beyond. Exports of textiles and agricultural produce from the Land of Israel to the farthest corners of the Empire are recorded, while their participation in business ventures from Mesopotamia to India is known. So too they were later involved in the widespread banking enterprises of the Moslem world, even though there, too, they suffered little economic regimentation or exclusion. The large-scale emigration of Jews to eastern Europe in the fifteenth and sixteenth centuries followed the invitation of local rulers interested specifically in their financial expertise. It seems, therefore, that the discrimination that prevented them from owning land, bearing arms, or entering certain trades was only a marginal cause of their involvement in moneylending in western Europe. One also has to bear in mind that the feudal system offered even its non-Jewish members few economic opportunities, such as being a serf, a soldier, or a cleric; none of these alternatives seemed to be attractive enough to have encouraged our ancestors to accept them, even if they would have been permitted to.

Even if one accepts discrimination as a factor in Jewish banking, nevertheless, that same involvement reveals major ethical and moral strengths of the Jew, which flow from the Jewish economic man described throughout this book.

Any analysis of Jewish banking activities must deal with the question of how a persecuted, widely dispersed, and politically weak people were able to become successfully involved in such activities. Europe until modern times was a patchwork quilt of conflicting religious and political entities, while international economic activity was conducted under the protection of state power. Nevertheless, Jews from medieval times down to the present have integrated themselves into trade and into the financial and capital markets. It can be shown that the social and moral life of the Jew is a major factor in this integration. This can best be done by an analysis of medieval Europe, since there, the separation of the Jew from the surrounding social and political life was far greater than it is in the modern world. Under those conditions, the specific Jewish element can be more easily seen, even though it exists and continues to play an important economic role even today.

While common language and religion enabled the medieval Jew to communicate with other Jews, even in faraway lands, to a degree not possible for his non-Jewish neighbors, there was more at play. All the factors described in the previous chapters created not only a legal framework for economic activity but also established a moral and social climate without which no market economy can flourish. The mutual responsibility Jews are conditioned to have for each other and the pervasive acts of charity that characterized their communal living also had important economic consequences. A Jew could transmit funds from one country to another without physically transferring coinage, with the resultant risk of robbery, through family and religious associates; it is argued that the first bills of exchange and checks were introduced by Jewish merchants. Travel for the Jew was easier, since lodgings and guidance, not easily available in those troubled times, were provided by the communities en route. The letters of membership granted by the community constituted in effect "passports" for the individual Jew. Even the strict communal regulations regarding weights and measures, truth in trading, and personal liability were actually a moral framework within which banking and credit facilities could be provided easily. The network of rabbinical courts and the extensive halakhic legislation regarding business behavior were maintained by the power of the autonomous communities to police and tax their

Jewish citizens. This made justice available to all, thus providing the legal framework essential to economic activity.

Perhaps this description of the effect of the Jewish moral and ethical framework on the role of the Jewish banker and moneylender may seem exaggerated and a false glorification. Recourse to the Jewish moneylender may well have been a matter of necessity or even as some Jewish apologists would argue the result of the lower interest rates relative to the Italian or German non-Jewish bankers. The very fact, however, that members of the hostile and anti-Semitic society were willing to trust their deposits and financial affairs to the Jew is eloquent testimony to the morality that characterized him.

The prominence of the Jewish financiers in England before the Expulsion in 1290, and in medieval western Europe could only have been achieved if they possessed the character and morality that remains the basis of banking to this day. Even in modern times, this ethical stamp remained. The basis of the Rothschild banking empire was laid when, in the eighteenth century, the Elector of Wurtenburg preferred them to his own coreligionists as a safe haven for his wealth before he left for exile.

8

Community and Social Demands on Wealth

INTRODUCTION

In every society, there are certain functions that cannot be performed by private business or by the individual entrepreneur and so must be provided by the government at various levels. Almost always these include defense and security but, in most modern states, welfare, education, and health services are also provided in full or in part. The extent of these functions is not an economic axiom but reflects the cultural, religious, and social philosophy of each particular society. In all cases, however, they cost money and need to be financed from some source. Primarily they are funded by taxes collected from the citizens, who are therefore faced with moral and ethical issues deriving from this enforced transfer of wealth. These issues will be affected inter alia by the tax rates, the allocation of the tax burden, and the allocation of the funds collected by the government.

However, unlike the individual or communal use of wealth discussed in the previous chapters, the public-sector activity includes not only direct funding but also the formularization of an appropriate economic policy. Over and above the fiscal policy, the public sector necessitates a wide range of regulations, tariffs, monetary formulas, and employment policy. Like taxation, all of them place limits on the individual's use of his own wealth. Judaism's perspective on the use of wealth would be incomplete, therefore, if its concepts of public-sector activity were to be neglected.

The communal nature of Judaism together with its purpose of *Imitatio Dei*, emulating the Divine attributes, forge a public-sector model based on justice, mercy, and human dignity. From the very first days of the loss of national independence at the beginning of the Common Era, the Jewish communities throughout the world constituted in fact mini-states, autonomous in varying degrees from the host gentile societies. The consequent right to tax its members and to judge them according to Jewish law was jealously guarded by the Jewish communities. For example, in 1090 Henry the IV granted these provisions to the Jews of Worms, which subsequently became the basis for Jewish communal life down to the extinction of the Holy Roman Empire in 1806. As often as not, these formed their major demands in regard to the charters or privileges given to them by the non-Jewish rulers. With the additional force of the *cherem* (ban of excommunication), which in effect meant that the individual had no place in the highly stratified Christian or Moslem society, the communities had the power to make the rulings of the codes and the Rabbis operative. In this way, a public sector similar in its variety to those of present-day societies developed alongside a tax structure to finance it. In addition it used market regulation, monetary policy, tariffs, subsidies, and environmental legislation in order to implement it. This sector included defense, education, welfare, social and religious institutions, public health, sewage, and so forth.

It is argued here that such a model could apply and have significance beyond that of an independent Jewish society. Care, however, must be taken not to force Judaism into a pattern that primarily reflects the personal social philosophy of the scholars and thinkers engaged in constructing this public-sector model. Even though it is impossible for the individual to free himself completely from such bias, it must be acknowledged and guarded against as much as possible. This is especially pertinent since the only public sector existing in most Jewish history has been at the communal level within a foreign society, extensive and enduring as this may have been. Though the ideas and experience recorded both in the halakhic literature and in the enactments regarding this communal level provide substantive principles and concepts, great care must be taken in their pragmatic application. In the transition from a limited homogeneous framework to larger national or international societies, errors and distortions easily multiply. Furthermore, the Jewish perspective on public-sector activity in general, and on business and economics in particular, is deeply rooted in religious concepts and principles. The secular divorce of these concepts and principles from their religious roots, as often as not, creates frameworks that, at best, are only partially Jewish, but more often are mere travesties of an age-old tradition.

The acknowledged and accepted obligation of society to provide for the economic and social welfare of weaker elements and to strive for a maximum of economic justice and morality has become an integral part of modern Jewish culture. This is evident in voting patterns in many countries, in much of economic thought and practice in the State of Israel, and in the philanthropic contributions of Jews in all the countries in which they live. Even though other non-Jewish value judgments have been mingled, creating an unbalanced social policy, nevertheless, it is important to recognize these Jewish links.

All of the major figures of the left-wing parties within the Zionist movement drew much of their social inspiration from the pages of the Bible and the teachings of the Jewish prophets and rabbis. Growing up in communities in which mutual help and the emphasis on justice and mercy were integral parts of daily life could not but mold the social philosophies of these men. A. S. Lieberman (the father of Hebrew socialism) could state: "For us socialism is not strange. The community is our existence, the revolution our tradition, the community the basis of the Torah which has been made concrete in the law that the land is not to be sold in perpetuity, in the law of the Jubilee and Sabbatical years, equality and tranquility."[1] David Ben-Gurion, the first prime minister of the State of Israel expressed himself as follows:

> The activities of the State of Israel will not be guided solely by economic and political considerations. We would be untrue to ourselves if we were to ignore the great moral inheritance of our prophets and sages. In that inheritance we inherit the social and humane visions of brotherhood, social justice, and freedom. The State of Israel will be judged ultimately by the loyalty to the sublime dictate of Judaism; "Thou shall love thy neighbor as thyself."[2]

A similar pattern whereby intrinsic Jewish social teachings were erroneously transcribed to a widespread participation of Jews in Socialist, Communist, and other left-wing movements may be discerned in Europe and the United States from the mid-nineteenth century even down to the present. Indeed, for many, such social involvement became transformed into a secular Judaic religion.

It is of interest that Christian thinkers, primarily in the Protestant and evangelical Anglo-Saxon churches, also found much support for their anti-Capitalist philosophies in Old Testament teachings.[3]

This widespread identification of Jewish social thinking with that of socialism is, however, the product either of ignorance of the source material, or willful distortion. Selective aspects of traditional teachings are presented, whereby partial truths are depicted as an integral whole system. Deeply entrenched ideas and practices are divorced from God and separated from halakhic rulings, so that the one-sided economy that emerges is as un-Jewish as is the philosophy of the unregulated free markets. The delegitimization by socialism of private property and wealth creation, the ignoring of the moral obligations of the beneficiaries of public-sector support, and the release of the executors of public policy from halakhic restraints, all contrary to Torah, create as much of an immoral society as that which they come to supplant. In the fourth section of this chapter, the corruptive effects of excessive public-sector control and intervention are discussed in greater detail. Here it is sufficient to point out the extent to which Jewish teachings of equity, mercy, and justice have become an integral part of the cultural and ideological framework of the modern Jew, even if much non-Jewish thinking has distorted and transformed them.

This chapter will attempt to present a more balanced and integrated perspective of public-sector activity, based on halakhic decisions, communal enactments, and the historically recorded character of Jewish social life.

The independent Jewish State of Israel and the existence of large and free Jewish communities in democratic and liberal countries make the study of such a Jewish perspective vital to any guide to present-day economic behavior. In all these countries, the economic and private lives of Jewish individuals impinge on the public sector and are affected by it. At the same time, as citizens they help, through the ballot box and through public opinion, to shape the public sector and its policies. If no Jewish perspective is available, other philosophies and ideologies will determine the outcome.

Following the plan of this book, the emphasis throughout the chapter will be primarily on the effect on the individual and his use of wealth, rather than on the macroeconomic aspects of society's economic role.

TAXATION AND COMMUNAL FUNDING

The Jewish communal-sector economic activity described throughout the previous chapters of this book requires funding that, as in most public sectors, came primarily from tax revenues. By and large, great leeway was given to the lay leadership and to custom in deciding how the tax burden was to be spread and how the tax base was to be calculated.

In the reality of everyday living, the legislators had their own special agendas, the wealthy attempted to evade their obligations, and the masses were easily exploited. The claims and counterclaims were therefore adjudicated before the *batei din* or by leading rabbinic scholars. These also provided citizens recourse against the communal enactments, being in fact courts of appeal regarding not only taxation but all aspects of regulatory legislation.

A voluminous responsa literature exists on the Jewish fiscal system, which enables one to construct a general framework for taxation. At the same time, there is recorded evidence of an extensive public sector funded solely by the Jewish community. Such evidence is more than sufficient to destroy the myth of the Jew as a chronic tax evader. This also applies to those taxes levied by the non-Jewish authorities, except sometimes the special discriminatory taxes, in those periods where those same authorities had anti-Semitic policies aimed at destroying the Jewish communities, economically and often physically.

Legal and Moral Basis of the Fiscal System

Wealth is granted to man to satisfy his personal and family needs but also to meet social obligations. In accordance with Judaism's concepts of enforced morality, possessors of wealth can, therefore, be compelled to give up part of their wealth to fund these obligations.

It would seem that three halakhic concepts converge to provide the practical framework for such funding: the obligations of neighbors, the law of the king, and *dina demalkhuta*—the law of the land.

1. The Obligations of Neighbors

The following *Mishnah* provides the basic formulation in halakhic literature for the rights and obligations of neighbors and the people of a city or community regarding public funding: "[The neighbors in a courtyard] can force any of the dwellers to [pay for] building a gate house [to prevent intruders] and a door for the courtyard . . . [so too the citizens of a town may] obligate each other to pay taxes in order to build a city wall and gates."[4]

This source and the subsequent talmudic discussion provide a primary moral base both for the communal right to impose taxes and the ethical imperative for the citizen to pay them. It starts as a description of the obligations of owners of common property, but then recognizes the individual's financial obligations regarding social costs, beyond those of property ownership. The people of the city, town, or state become, as it were, "neighbors" with mutual obligations and rights deriving from their common citizenship.

So the *Shulchan Arukh* rules that the citizens of a town are able to force each other to participate in funding all the needs of the town.[5] These include defense, provision of a synagogue and *mikveh*, Torah study, and welfare. Furthermore, the citizens of the town have the right and the obligation to enforce zoning laws in order to protect the health and aesthetic pleasure of the inhabitants. This often means relocating industry and introducing ecological safeguards, all of which incur costs and are therefore a form of taxation.[6] The *Talmud Yerushalmi* maintains it is a duty of the rabbinic courts to force the community to perform public works, such as repairing the roads and the streets after the winter rains, cleaning the ritual baths, as well as settling the public needs.[7] Those communal functions mandated by *Halakhah*, as, for example, the provision of a synagogue or welfare, can be imposed by a minority, since the majority cannot escape its Torah obligations. At the same time, however, the citizens of a town can decide to fund other projects, and for these a majority vote is required, or according to another decision, a consensus of the citizens.[8]

This right of taxation flows from the national and collective nature of Judaism, which aims at the creation of a holy nation, a kingdom of priests, rather than merely the spiritual growth of the individual. While recognizing private property, *Halakhah* grants society rights to a share of that property. Society is, as it were, a partner in the wealth of the individual, in order to fulfill those obligations incumbent upon the community. It is not surprising therefore that the communal minute books of the communities and the decisions of Jewish synods show the actual everyday operation of a diversified Jewish tax system.[9] At the same time, it is erroneous to view the autonomous Jewish communities as voluntary religious or social entities, funding social needs through philanthropy. They were in fact ministates, so that the halakhically stipulated provision of publicly financed education, health, and welfare by these communities can provide the moral basis for a modern state-imposed tax system and budget. The communal financing of these services has all the hallmarks of a modern government activity, requiring direct or indirect individual voting, providing recourse to *batei din*, and drawing punishment for tax evasion. These quasi-Jewish states, with fiscal powers similar to those of present-day states, regulated Jewish life not only in small local communities but also were a feature of national and supranational entities.[10] For a thousand years, the Jews of Mesopotamia and beyond were ruled as a separate political and social group by the Jewish Prince of the Exile of Davidic descent. In medieval Europe, councils and synods provided an independent social and organizational framework for the Jews of Spain, Franco-Germany, and Italy between the tenth and sixteenth centuries. *Vaad Arba Artzot* was a supranational government covering Greater Poland, Lesser Poland, Volhynia, and Lvov, into the eighteenth century.

This centuries-old Jewish communal taxation actually gains present-day relevance from the fiscal-political development of the past four centuries of European and later world history. The introduction of democratic states in modern times has placed the fiscal system in almost all countries primarily on a communal-neighbor basis as distinct from the royal-purse concept prevalent since the dawn of history. Under the former system, the citizens agree both on the raising of funds and their allocation, similar to that described in the Jewish fiscal system. In the royal-purse concept, the treasury is the private property of the ruler to be used almost as he sees fit. This change in the role of taxation reinforces the applicability of the halakhic system, with all that it implies, to the modern public-sector financing.

2. Law of the King (*Din HaMelekh*)

"A Jewish king possesses the right to levy taxes, in money, in kind, and in labor."[11] This ruling of Maimonides is a codification of the talmudic decision "that everything expressed in the law of the king, the king may do."[12] The Rabbis were referring to the words of Samuel in which he described to the people the nature of the kingship they requested.

> He will take your sons and appoint them for his chariots, and to be his horsemen, and they shall run before his chariots. And he will appoint them for captains of thousands . . . to plow his ground, to reap his harvest and to make his instruments of war . . . and he will take your fields and your vineyards and your olive plantations, even the best of them, and give them to his servants. And he will take the tenth of your seed and of your vineyards and give them to his officers and his servants, and he will take your man servants and your maid servants and your goodliest young men and your asses and put them to his work . . . and ye shall be his servants.[13]

In addition the king had the right to appropriate private land for public use (a form of taxation even where financial compensation is made). "A king has the right to make a way or to break down walls and one [the owner of the property through which such roads, and so on, pass] has no right to prevent him."[14]

Modern responsa here clearly established that democratically elected representatives have the same power as that provided for by the law of the king.[15]

3. Law of the Land (*Dina DeMalkhuta*)

In accordance with the opinion of the talmudic sage Shmuel, all halakhic authorities recognize the obligations of Jews, wherever they reside, to obey the law of the land in regard to economic and business activity, provided it does not contradict Torah law.[16] All these laws, therefore, become halakhically binding on all Jews. Contracts, agreements, and conditions of employment or trade thereby become part of the Jewish halakhic framework. People may assume that these laws are being kept and could claim in a *bet din* in cases where this is not so. This includes the legal right to taxation. Those taxes placed upon the whole population, Jew or gentile, for the benefit of society are not problematic from a Jewish point of view. All the Codes, *Mishneh Torah*, *Arbaah Turim*, and the *Shulchan Arukh*, rule that "one who does not pay his taxes or evades the customs [of the gentile ruler] is as one who steals the share of the king."[17]

The real problem emerges with regard to discriminatory taxes or illegal taxes enforced by brute force. In this regard, an illegal king or usurper, one who is not accepted by the subjects, or one whose laws are capricious or discriminatory lacks the moral authority to levy taxes.[18]

Throughout the Diaspora, Jews were often faced with discriminatory taxes levied only on them, either individually or collectively. Sometimes those taxes had the avowed purpose of destroying the economic infrastructure of the Jews as a means of converting them or driving them out of the country, as in Tzarist Russia during some decades of the nineteenth to twentieth centuries. As often as not, the Jews were simply seen as an easy source of funds for the royal treasury. In almost all cases, none of these funds were used to finance either the needs of the Jews as citizens or those needs specific to their religion. The enmity of the rulers and the crushing financial burden of the taxes encouraged a mental frame of mind that could make tax evasion acceptable and widely practiced. However it should be stressed that despite the avowed enmity of the rulers and the injustice in taxation, the halakhic authorities insisted that even such taxes be paid, for a number of moral reasons.

First, where collective taxes were levied, those who did not pay were, so to speak, stealing from those who had to make up the communal share.[19] Furthermore, there was the ever-present consideration of *chillul HaShem*, which would flow from revelations of tax evasions by Jews, thereby desecrating and besmirching the Jewish God and People, something that Jews are halakhically obligated to prevent. Anti-Semites throughout the centuries, and even today, have made capital out of portraying the Jew as a tax evader, which has led to expulsion and persecution.

Authorities have therefore ruled that even such immoral taxes have to be paid lest they cause communal and physical damage.[20] Some halakhic authorities even ruled that taxes known to be earmarked for idolatry should be paid, provided the share for this purpose was not specified.[21] This permission runs counter to the usual strict prohibitions regarding supporting or benefiting from idolatry.

A new perspective regarding the Law of the Land has been created with regard to the halakhic authority of the fiscal system of the State of Israel. Maimonides and the *Shulchan Arukh* hold that this law applies not only to non-Jewish kings, but also to Jewish rulers in the Land of Israel, to whom the Law of the King does not apply, since it is reserved for the kings of the Davidic dynasty.[22] However, the Ran, Rabbi Nissim (of Gerondi, fourteenth century), held that this is not so.[23] His primary argument is that the power of the gentile king flows from his absolute ownership of the land and the ability to expel or dispossess his subjects. No Jew, however, has this power in the Land of Israel, where there exists a collective ownership of all the land. So, the Ran maintains that here the principle of the Law of the Land does not apply, which would negate the State of Israel's fiscal policies. Summing up this discussion, a modern authority, Rabbi Ovadiah Yosef, Israel's former Chief Rabbi, has ruled that in fact *dina demalkhuta* applies also to the State of Israel, making observance of its fiscal policies halakhically obligatory.[24]

Important as this discussion is, it seems that regarding taxation it is not of prime concern, in view of the social-contract motive of taxation in the modern democratic state. The treasury is no longer the private property of the king but rather an enlarged communal fund. It is financed by agreement of the citizens through their representatives, and funds not the private pleasures or ambitions of the king, but rather the economic needs, physical security, and social welfare of the citizens. This makes the modern fiscal system primarily a function of the rights of neighbors or the people of the city, as explained above. Indeed, this concept is supported by the ruling of the Rashba and others.[25]

The Conceptual Framework of the Jewish Fiscal System

It has been claimed by many halakhic authorities that there actually is no specific Torah judgment regarding a tax system. Society, therefore, has great freedom to define its own tax system, relying on precedent, custom, and on the wishes of the population. The *bet din* and halakhic authorities serve as a sort of court of appeal to adjudicate the workings of the system and to see that it adheres to principles of justice and equity.

Ben Aderet, the Rashba, in thirteenth-century Spain, authored the most extensive responsa literature on communal taxation and regulation. Even a cursory reference to his responsa will show this diversity in tax law and the power of the various communities to have their own fiscal system.

Replying to a question from the Jewish council of Majorca regarding exemptions from taxation he writes:

You write that since there are people in your community who are very poor and, therefore, unable to pay the tax allocated to them, the parnasim wish to waive their obligation. This, however, is contrary to your communal enactment which forbids the changing or rescinding of any tax regulation, so you ask me what may be done.

There are many communities whose custom it is to free from taxation [as a pragmatic step only] those who are poor. In your case this cannot be done in view of your ordinances [keeping peace and communal harmony often neccessitates preserving regulations even though to some it would seem simply easier to charge them. Much civil dissatisfaction and anger may be seen in modern societies when governments change fiscal policies even when they only have slight electoral majorities].

It is my suggestion that either you collect the taxes from the poor and then return it to them [making clear that the exemption from taxation is an act of charity and not a decision freeing people from their moral obligation to contribute their share to the public need] or to allocate their share of the tax among the other members of the community equally [here too, this allocation is a charitable act and as such falls on all equally].[26]

In Lerida it was the custom to include in the tax base, loans which a debtor had received [since they produce income for him]. However, at a different period in time, the same town levied the tax on the creditor making the loan. They had different [tax] rates for movables—three percent of their value, immovables—one and a quarter percent, and dwelling houses were tax free. Yet in Saragossa, dwelling houses were also taxed.[27]

If one takes into account the different economic systems and conditions within which Jews have lived over the centuries, in so many different countries, it is easy to accept the variety in the range of fiscal systems adopted. This, at first glance, would make a claim of a Jewish fiscal system seem almost irrelevant, were it not for the fact that all taxation raises moral issues of equity in rates, in constructing the tax base, and in the appropriation of the funds collected. In this regard, there are definite binding Torah judgments, legislation, and values. So it is suggested here that there are certain principles common to the fiscal methods developed in all the various autonomous communities, which may serve as a basis for a Torah-orientated taxation. These are presented here in order to highlight the moral and ethical principles so essential for an equitable tax system.

1. The taxes cannot be confiscatory, as for example a tax on a nonincome-earning asset. This will ultimately lead to a destruction of the asset and so constitute theft of private property by the community.[28]

2. It is necessary to have the consent of the taxpayers, either directly, or through representatives. According to some authorities it requires a consensus, and according to others, a majority. In this way a minority could not impose their will on the majority. It is interesting to note that at least one authority ruled that the voting rights should be according to the taxpayers' share of the tax burden. This would justify giving the rich citizens bearing the greater share of the tax burden more voting rights than the poor. The principle of majority rule, however, does not apply to those cases where the funds are to be used for the fulfillment of halakhic obligation, such as *mikveh*, synagogue, Torah education, or welfare; here a minority can force a majority.[29]

3. Taxes can be levied either on a per capita basis, on a wealth basis (a form of progressive taxation), or a mixture of the two. However, there is an important moral imperative that the element of utility be included so that the tax burden will, in one form or another, reflect the individual taxpayer's benefit and his obligation to pay for it.[30] This would place the *Halakhah* in favor of toll roads, user fees, and other forms of utility-related taxation. At the same time, however, this principle may deprive part of the citizens of the use of the facilities, since they are unable to pay for it. Alternatively, if one group uses more of a facility than others, their tax burden could be far greater than their relative income. Equity would then demand either the provision of alternative free facilities, albeit of inferior quality, or a mixture of benefit and ability to pay. Indeed, the halakhic system was based on just this mixture. Perhaps the benchmark decision for this may be found in the talmudic discussion regarding the allocation of taxes for building of a city wall and gate for the protection of property against bandits or robbers. While in the case of protection of life there is always a principle of equality in taxation, in regard to the defense of property, taxes should be levied on a basis of wealth, since the rich have more to lose. However, Rashi points out that those closer to the wall benefit more from its protection, so that their share of the tax should also be greater. There are, therefore, two factors involved in the allocation of such defense-related taxes: distance from the wall and the wealth at risk. The decision therefore was that those living or owning property clos-

est to the wall would pay a greater share of the tax burden than those of equal wealth farther away. At the same time, all those living in the same proximity to the wall would have their taxes levied on the basis of their wealth.[31]

Margaret Thatcher, while prime minister of England, introduced a poll tax to fund municipal services, arguing that all should pay equally for the benefits they receive. This would seem to be in accordance with the rabbinic principles of taxation. However, in the English case, no consideration of ability to pay was made, so that weaker elements with large households living in smaller quarters paid more taxes than the wealthy people with smaller families and larger homes. The inequity was so obvious that popular opinion forced Mrs. Thatcher's resignation. A mixture similar to the halakhic procedure would have prevented the inequity.

4. There is no trace in halakhic fiscal decisions of a policy aimed at the redistribution of wealth, either through discriminatory taxes or through taxes on inheritance. People, Jews and gentiles alike, have the right to bequeath their property to their heirs by Torah law, and the state is not considered an heir. There are opinions that the recipient should tithe the capital received once and then subsequently the income together with all other forms of income. However, this is an act of voluntary charity, not fiscal policy.

Even the Jubilee year in which land reverted to its original owners does not seem to fit the pattern of redistribution. The land was not redistributed equally or even proportionately to the number of souls dependent on it or in any other egalitarian fashion. What was involved was the return of land purchased to the seller, making land the subject of a forty-nine-year lease, rather than an outright sale.

5. An aspect of great importance for today's economy is the ruling of many authorities that a person is liable for taxes in the town in which he earns his livelihood.[32] In those countries, like the United States, where states and cities have their own fiscal system, the lack of such a principle has meant that the inner cities have been left in poverty, while the wealthy people live in the suburbs but earn their money in the city. Their halakhic obligation, however, to pay the social costs of the city would seem to be clear.

6. It seems doubtful whether the double corporate taxation practiced in almost all countries today, including Israel, would be halakhically acceptable. Under the accepted corporate-tax law, a corpora-

tion pays tax on its income before distribution, and then the shareholder pays again on receiving his share of the distributed profit.

7. Much of Jewish taxation is ad hoc, being levied to fund a particular purpose. This gives the public greater control over the way the tax is levied and spent, reducing the central government's excessive control over its citizens and limiting waste. The funding of major projects in the United States through state or municipal bonds voted on by the citizens is a modern parallel to the halakhic ad hoc system.

8. If it is halakhically accepted that the members have an obligation to fund the needs of the community, then the same authority requires that the funds collected be managed within the same moral framework. If tax money is a holy obligation, then the money becomes holy and needs to be treated as such, with minimum wastage and without fraud or oppression.

9. The tax authorities are considered to be mere creditors with all the legal complications arising from this status. So the halakhic tenet that "he who claims must produce evidence" also applies to the tax collector.[33] This would stand in contradiction to many countries in which the taxpayer can be called upon to prove that he has not earned more than he claims. Furthermore, halakhically, the authorities have to choose between assessment or a declaration of liability. They cannot use both methods of determining taxes.

Tax Evasion and Avoidance

The economic effect of any taxation will be the same—the transfer of wealth from the pockets of the citizens to the public purse. As a result, the after-tax income and therefore the private standard of living of the citizens will be determined, inter alia, by the tax rates and the efficiency of the tax collector. At the same time, these factors will determine the size of the state budget and the services it can provide for the citizens. All the parties concerned have to consider, therefore, the willingness of the citizens to pay the taxes levied. Ignoring this will lead to large-scale nonpayment of the taxes, limited only by the ability of the authorities to police and enforce their tax collections. Experience in many different countries and during vastly different periods of history has shown that this ability is limited wherever the taxpayer sees justification for nonpayment of taxes.

While a major cause of tax evasion, as indeed, of all economic immorality, is human greed, other factors are also at work. Sometimes these are simply rationalizations, which as the Chafetz Chaim points out, people use readily to justify their immoral actions.[34] However, in the case of tax evasion, many of them are valid and go beyond mere greed. It can be shown that governmental action to remove legitimate grievances does lead to significant reductions in tax evasion.

Academic research has shown that it is possible to summarize these additional factors as follows:

1. Tax rates: High rates of taxation, which leave the taxpayer with only a relatively small share of his income or profit, are closely linked to tax evasion. For example, countries like Italy, in which the tax rates are high, have been found to have a larger underground economy than the United States with its lower tax rates.[35] Similarly, countries that introduced tax rates of 70 percent or more found that citizens simply did not pay them.

2. Government waste: Normal, law-abiding citizens find it increasingly difficult to maintain their tax morality when it becomes obvious that part of the funds are wasted or misappropriated. While they are prepared to meet their civic responsibilities, they are not prepared to fund programs that are no longer valid, to pay for overruns in the government budget due to careless procedures or deliberate waste, or to maintain a bloated bureaucracy. Sweden, which like Italy has a high rate of taxation, does not have as large an underground economy, since its citizens do not view their public sector as corrupt or wasteful. A survey conducted by this author in Israel showed that over 80 percent of the manufacturers felt that higher tax rates were possible if the government cut its budget by at least 5 percent or its labor force by 25 percent, both indicators of excessive public spending.

3. Unfair tax basis: Whenever citizens feel that all do not share the same fiscal burden, the impetus to tax evasion becomes stronger.

4. Ideological issues: Taxes raised for an unpopular purpose or for a government budget that funds programs or activities that part of the population see as being contrary to their religious, moral, or social ideologies will, as often as not, be evaded. Such objections eradicate any guilt feelings and transform tax evasion into an achievement for whatever ideology the evader believes in.

Jews in Tzarist Russia saw the taxes of the government as part of a discriminatory policy aimed at their economic destruction. Blacks and opponents of apartheid in South Africa saw a moral duty in evading the taxes levied by the white minority government. In present-day Israel, there is a feeling among some religious sectors that since the government is a secular one, spending part of its money on irreligious or antireligious programs, tax evasion may be considered to be morally justified, or even halakhically mandatory.

Ethical Questions

Irrespective of the cause of tax evasion, the moral effects are the same. In order not to pay one's taxes, one is required to keep false records of earnings, turnover, and purchases, as well as the labor force employed. Fraudulent expenses are created in order to decrease the tax liability. The methods are limited only by the fertility of the human imagination. Lying thus becomes a normal way of life with all the resultant immorality.

Equally destructive is the effect on the pattern of consumption and standard of living. The accumulated "black money" resulting from tax evasion often cannot be used productively or invested, since this will attract the attention of the tax authorities. Therefore, these funds have to be transferred abroad and spent or invested there—once again involving deception. Alternatively, they can be spent on untraceable items such as jewelry or artwork, or consumed in ways that encourage social immorality.

Beyond the fraudulent methods of conducting business and reporting income, tax evasion needs to be considered as a form of theft, since others now have to bear a greater burden. Alternatively, and sometimes additionally, social and other services are not provided to the extent to which they would have been had all the taxes been collected. These sums have, as it were, been stolen from the potential recipients.[36]

Although tax evasion and tax avoidance are not the same, the boundaries between them are not always clear. Since the tax collector is legally a creditor, as explained above, it would seem that perhaps one would not be halakhically liable to make efforts to pay more than one is liable for, as in the case of ordinary creditors.[37] However, the gray areas that exist between the legitimate boundaries of tax avoidance and the forbidden area of evasion demand constant and careful consideration, especially in view of the potential effect on the morality of the taxpayer. For example, these areas include expenses recognized as tax deductible on the assumption that they are genuinely business related, yet in fact are actually nondividend forms of profit distribution.[38]

Moral Solutions

The effects of these unethical patterns of behavior dictated by tax evasion are not reflected only in the level of morality in that sphere. Society cannot be immoral in one aspect, in this case taxation, and moral in other aspects of human relationships. Large-scale tax evasion must, over the course of time, be reflected both in the behavior of the individual and also in the general moral fiber of society in all social aspects. Since Judaism cannot tolerate immorality and constantly and consistently seeks to create pious individuals and a godly nation, its principles must be evoked in the individual and corporate tax-related behavior.

Judaism is unequivocally opposed to deception and lying but also even to creating false impressions. So the Torah forbids bearing false witness (Exodus 20:13), "Ye shall not lie to one another" (Leviticus 19:11), and "you shall separate yourself from a false matter" (Exodus 23:7). It is interesting to note some of the relevant midrashic examples:

> A scholar told his pupil that he had lent money to Reuven but had only one witness [which halakhically would invalidate his claim]. Seeing that there could be no doubt in the student's mind regarding the truth of the teacher's claim, the latter wanted the student to be a witness. The Sages ruled that this was false evidence and forbidden. In another case a person was asked not even to give evidence—direct lying—but merely to appear before the *bet din*, thus creating the false impression that the claimant had the required two witnesses.[39]

Careful as the halakhic sources and the homiletical literature are to caution against, define, and punish theft and robbery, the injunctions against stealing from the public are even more stringent. The rationale is spiritual. Repentance for theft or robbery is repayment or return of the article to its rightful owner. However, where the damage is done to an amorphous public or to a large number of people, such compensation is impossible, meaning that the criminal can never do proper *teshuvah*: only an inferior repentance can be achieved through the giving of charity and performing righteous deeds.[40]

Even in those cases where legally improper actions may be permitted, nevertheless the Rabbis warned against being a *naval bireshut HaTorah*—evil within the limits of the law.[41] This often applies when using justified ideological arguments to sanction the theft and lying involved in tax evasion. Furthermore, it is probably humanly impossible to limit these immoral actions solely to the area for which there is ideological sanction. These actions must, sooner or later, affect other areas of economic and social conduct, until they pervade all of them. Then lying, fraud, and theft become "normal" ways of living, for which there is no sanction.[42]

It is true that often the individual or corporation is unable to find a moral way to express opposition to the high tax rates, government waste, or funding of ideologically objectional projects. In such cases, it would seem that religious leadership should provide alternatives to the easy but morally dangerous tax evasion. This is so because it has always been accepted that such leadership, rabbinical, educational, and communal, has an obligation to prevent immorality and to foster moral behavior.[43]

In this vein, Jewish communities in western Europe used their power of excommunication to prevent tax evasion either of the communal taxes or even of the discriminatory taxes levied by the gentile overlords.[44] These and many responsa militated against counterfeiters and smugglers, who by their actions were guilty of *chillul HaShem*, endangered the communities, or promoted subsequent economic immorality.

Similarly, in Israel, the religious parties and rabbinic leadership could undertake steps to rectify the causes of tax evasion described in the previous section. Pressure to reduce substantially the tax burden, both direct and indirect, and to limit the government intervention in the market, which is a major cause of that burden, would seem to be a possible legitimate religious effort. Furthermore, if indeed there is an ideological objection to the use to which tax revenues are spent, the example of the Anglican churchman Michael Scott in South Africa would seem an appropriate response. Refusing to pay his taxes for the support of an apartheid policy, he simply donated the amount owed by him to a church vocational school and sent the receipt to the tax authorities. There may be penalties and perhaps even imprisonment, but at least there would be no moral stigma attached. The Talmud tells us that "when you take something from somebody which belongs to you, do not do so secretly, but rather publicly."[45]

ECONOMIC LEGISLATION AND REGULATION

Public-sector activity in the modern world is not limited to taxation but directly affects the economic lives of its citizens through regulation and legislation and indirectly through monetary and social policies. So the discussion of Jewish perspectives on the use of wealth must, of necessity, relate to these aspects as explained in the introduction to this chapter. One major source for this perspective is the records of the autonomous Jewish communities, which provide a wealth of material on public-sector activity. Another is the halakhic decisions granted in response to these enactments or as guidelines for them, decisions that have become enshrined in the various codes of Jewish law. It is extremely difficult to extrapolate patterns of behavior from these legal and legislative forms spanning many different countries, spread over two thousand years of history, and operating within a variety of economic systems and conditions. While it is imperative that such difficulties be borne in mind, nevertheless they should not be allowed to obscure the definite pattern of regulation and behavior that emerges from these sources.

It is a pattern that, while providing for public-sector activity aimed at promoting welfare and equity, presents demands of justice that minimize the abuses of that same activity. In the following section, the problem of public-sector corruption is dealt with, while this section describes the role of the public sector in the economy. Since the regulation of corruption and prices has already been dealt with in Part I of this book, it is not necessary to repeat that discussion here. The reader is reminded, however, that such regulation forms an integral part of the Jewish economic regulation. This applies, too, to the welfare aspects discussed in the previous chapter. In this section perspectives on legislation regarding consumption, provision of public services, economic policy, and environmental regulation will be reviewed.

Limitations on Consumption

The awareness that "economics of enough" is a prerequisite for any morality, discussed in the first chapter of this book, was translated early in Jewish history into communal legislation. Communal records are rich in such legislation, and Jewish sumptuary laws have been maintained even down to the present. While the communities possessed the power to punish infringements, the efficiency of such legislation was maximized. Today, with the less formal structure and only marginal punitive powers, naturally the implementation is limited. Nevertheless, Orthodox Jewish communities still maintain relatively important means of limiting consumption and thereby affecting the pattern of economic and moral behavior. Where this is not done, the moral effects of "more is better than less" are acutely felt.

The examples of communal sumptuary laws described below actually have their roots in biblical times. All of the Prophets saw the relationship between the excessive demand for luxury, fed by spiraling standards of living, and economic immorality or oppression.

Isaiah (3:18-23) describes the luxury of the daughters of Zion as a cause of the sins that lead to destruction: "Their tinkling ornaments about their feet . . . the chains, the bracelets, the bonnets, and the ornaments . . . and the headbands and the earrings. The rings and the nose jewel. The changeable suits of clothes, and the mantles and the wimples . . . the glasses and the fine linen and the hoods, and the perfume vials. . . ." Amos links the oppression of the poor, the needy, and the righteous to the demands of "the Cows of Bashan which oppress the poor, which crush the needy; which say to their husbands, 'Bring and let us drink'" (4:1). Previously he had described the Lord's destruction of the nobles' winter houses and summer houses, and the houses of ivory. In a following chapter he describes how their houses of hewn stone were built by treading on the poor and the measures of wheat taken from them.

With this tradition, the Jewish Synod of the Rhineland in the thirteenth century ruled "that no child of the Covenant shall dress after the [extravagant] manner of the gentiles, nor wear sleeves [apparently considered an expression of luxury] nor shall have long hair."[46] In Italy in the early fifteenth century, the Synod, "in order that we may carry ourselves in modesty and humbleness before the Lord, our God, and to avoid arousing the envy of the Gentiles," placed severe restrictions on the possession of cloaks of any color other than black, while the sleeves were not to have silk linings; likewise, cloaks of sable or ermine, or of expensively dyed material were forbidden. Men's clothing, too, was restricted to less extravagant dyes and materials. The same decree came to limit the weight and type of silver ornaments worn, as well as their number. Conspicuous consumption at weddings, circumcisions, and other festive occasions was restrained by restricting the number of guests, with a fine being measured for each additional guest.[47] Other communities, such as Furth, prohibited in 1728 the serving of tea or coffee, both expensive luxury items, limited the number of musicians, and made midnight the end of festivities. Even jewelry and clothing of servants, an indication of their master's wealth and an incentive to spending, were regulated by the community of Cassel. The Lithuanian Council linked these sumptuary laws to the tax payments or assessed wealth of the members of the community when they exempted those families with a tax base of 20,000 florin or more. That same council, in a preview of modern taxes on consumption, placed fines on artisans making garments from luxurious materials or other outlawed items.[48]

Similar restrictions on festivities, on the size of apartments, and even the cost of religious articles may be found, in increasing numbers, in present-day Orthodox communities. The chasidic group of Gur has been, for many years, observing *bar mitzvahs* solely within the confines of the immediate family, and weddings are limited to 300 guests. In view of the relative expense of purchasing homes in Jerusalem, they and the Belzer *chasidim*, on the instructions of their rabbis, have been establishing communities in cheaper outlying areas. It has become a prevalent custom to buy the *arba minim*, the four species—citron, palm, willow, and myrtle—used during the Sukkot festival, in closed packages, thus eliminating expensive consumer competition.

In these and similar cases, communal action is brought to bear to reduce levels of consumption. This frees the individuals from having to maintain a lifestyle beyond their means, from onerous borrowing to finance such a lifestyle, and even from sometimes being involved in unethical business behavior to fund it. Naturally, this also reduces social friction and class conflict, making a major contribution to the individual's peace of mind and welfare.

Economic Policy

Even at the risk of some repetition, it is necessary to point out that Judaism clearly recognizes the obligation of society to enforce fair trading practices, protect consumers and producers alike, and to provide welfare in its widest sense. Furthermore, this same obligation provides the moral right for taxation in order to fund such policies. Even inflationary monetary policies that have detrimental effects on the moral fiber of society clearly come within the purview of the halakhic system. State or communal environmental legislation, limiting the scope of business activity, adding to the costs of production and distribution, or even curbing the rate of development and growth, is similarly an accepted part of Judaism's economic system. Since all of these are discussed in detail in different chapters of this book, it is unnecessary to deal with them here. However, there is an important area of present-day public economic activity that does require separate discussion here. This concerns all those policies geared toward providing employment or to prevent unemployment. Such social thinking is relatively new in economic thought and practice, so that it is difficult to refer to decisions regarding full employment in the traditional sources. At the same time, it is at least possible to provide a perspective that would allow a balanced Jewish judgment on the issue.

Judaism would seem to stand in conflict both to the schools of thought making full employment the core of an equitable economic system and to those arguing that the realignment of market forces alone will solve unemployment. The former sees such policies as an entitlement alone, and the latter perhaps ignores the human suffering occurring in the interim, while Judaism rejects both scenarios. Rather the basis is to be found in the traditional concept of charity yet provided through a public-sector agency.

Providing a person with a job or making him a partner in one's business or providing capital for him to establish his own business or even with the professional advice necessary for this is considered in all the codes to be the highest form of charity. The reasoning behind this ruling is obvious. It provides the poor, or the unemployed, with an opportunity to break the poverty cycle in which they are caught up. In the same way it prevents marginal groups or workers facing dismissal from descending into poverty. Furthermore, and no less importantly, it comes to salvage the self-respect of the unemployed and to prevent the malaise and destructive social pressures that accompany enforced idleness.

The *Arbaah Turim* and the *Shulchan Arukh* change the order described by Maimonides, so that creating a partnership in which both parties benefit is considered the pinnacle of charity, since the recipient suffers no shame. This may seem to have removed the stigma of receiving charity.[49] Nevertheless, all agree that these actions are obligations on the giver and not an entitlement of the recipient, making them definite acts of charity with all the positive and negative connotations discussed in the previous chapter.

Making such employment policies a factor of public-sector activity could possibly flow from another charity-orientated halakhic idea. This concerns the biblical ruling in Deuteronomy (21:1-9) concerning the ritual of the beheaded heifer, *eglah arufah*, to be brought by the inhabitants of the city closest to the corpse of an unknown man found cast out upon the field. As part of the ritual conducted in the presence of the Sanhedrin and the Priests, the *bet din*, the elders, had to make the following confession: "Our hands have not shed this blood nor have our eyes seen it." The Sages of the Talmud asked in amazement, "Would we ever imagine that the *bet din* were shedders of blood?" Rather what they declared was "that no one came within our jurisdiction whom we discharged without food and whom we did not see [the cognizance of his needs]."[50] "The Rabbis of yonder [Babylon] took the biblical text to refer to the slain man. No one came within our jurisdiction whom we overlooked and left without a livelihood."[51] To this the biblical commentator Malbim added that this neglect would have left the murderer without a livelihood so that he had to turn to robbery and violence.

There is in this approach recognition of the criminal and violent behavior that often results from the poverty and hopelessness accompaning long-term unemployment or subsistence-level employment. This makes public policy aimed at providing or creating employment not only a tool for promoting welfare but also for minimizing or preventing robbery and murder. It must be stressed however, that what the talmudic Sages are saying in no way justifies such behavior or removes the responsibility for criminal actions from the perpetrator. The discussion simply reflects Judaism's insistence that society, even if only indirectly, and even if only partially, is responsible for the conditions that create and stimulate violence and crime. Such responsibility requires public policy, therefore, to provide solutions to these conditions. In a similar vein, a father is required to teach his son a trade or profession; not to do so, in effect, teaches him to be a robber or a criminal.[52]

Society in Judaism is, to a large extent, free to develop whatever employment policies it sees as being efficient and desirable. Most modern societies have chosen either centralized economic planning, a mix of government subsidies and incentives, or public-sector-owned corporations. It may well be that considerations flowing from Jewish concepts of charity and morality would rather seek a direct system of assistance. This would provide funds for the unemployed or marginally employed to establish their own businesses. Such funding has been found in the past decade to be a major stimulant to new firm start-ups and to providing employment.[53]

In those cases where such policies are insufficient, the government-owned corporation would seem to the author to be preferable to subsidies to private enterprises aimed at stimulating job creation, provided such corporations are recognized for what they are—charitable institutions rather than real economic undertakings. It should be pointed out that the incentives provided in almost all Western countries today, in the form of cheap capital, fiscal benefits, or tariff protection, are also acts of communal charity, rather than viable economic decisions. This is so since the lack of employment reflects a wage level at which employers are not prepared to offer jobs. The employment incentives and the government-owned corporations are paying the worker the differential between market price for labor and what is considered necessary for an acceptable standard of living. In both cases, the worker is being paid, partially at least, not in return for real production, but rather charity to help him maintain this standard of living. Since this is the reality of the employment policy, the consideration of efficiency is secondary to the imperative of providing assistance and charity.

Direct government institutions have the advantage over the incentive system, since they can more easily be labeled as sheltered employment. They are also cheaper for the public purse, provided they are recognized as such, since their cost can be easily calculated. Rationally, they should decline over time as attrition, abhorrence of accepting charity, and improved market conditions shrink the number of recipients. In contrast, subsidized capital, employment incentives, and fiscal or tariff protection have a tendency to be perpetuated through the creation of pressure groups to obscure the real cost of providing welfare through employment, and to develop an immorality among entrepreneurs who provide nonviable economic projects, simply to benefit from them through creating jobs. The state-owned corporations in Communist countries and in Western countries became a drain on the public purse and the source of corruption, in addition to their inefficiency, primarily since their role as welfare institutions or sheltered workshops was disguised, so as to remove the stigma of charity—a stigma that rabbinic wisdom saw as the price people have to pay for public-sector assistance.

Public Works and Health Services

Even the most forceful exponents of the free market and its ability to supply equitable and moral solutions accept that there are areas that require public-sector funding and organization. Defense and public security are usually cited as two such primary areas. However, Judaism's concept of a Holy Nation and therefore of a group or communal-orientated religion cannot accept this minimalistic requirement. So there are a varied and fairly extensive range of services that the public sector is required to fund and operate. It must be stressed once more that the fact that this public sector was limited for long periods to communities and at best to supranational ones such as the medieval synods of western Europe, or the Council of Four Lands in eastern Europe, does not obscure the basic tenet—that society at large has such social obligations. Furthermore, it is clear that those obligations flow not only from the mutual benefit derived or from the economic factor that makes public-sector provision more efficient and, in many cases, the only possibility. There is also a stated declaration that morality, justice, and the spiritual elevation of man provided by Torah call for the fulfillment of these obligations.

Two thousand years ago, the *Mishnah* described the communal obligation to repair the roads and the streets from the damage caused by the winter rains, to clear the ritual baths from the fungi and mildew of winter, and to settle all other forms of repair to public amenities. These public-sector actions were continued by the Jewish communities down to their dissolution or financial bankruptcy in the eighteenth and nineteenth centuries. The *pinkas* of the Jewish Council of Padua in the sixteenth century records a decision "to add a third person to the two officers who were appointed to repair the paths and roads in the ghetto."[54] Sometimes these public works were paid for by private individuals, as was done by Mordechai Meisel in Prague in the second half of the sixteenth century. In addition to his many charitable contributions, he built the bath house, the ritual bath, a hospice for the afflicted poor, and laid stone pavements throughout the Jewish quarter.[55] However, such private philanthropy was, by and large, not a substitute for the community funding of these amenities.

The practical nature of these public works, whether publicly or privately funded, must not be allowed to disguise or distort the spiritual or moral ideas that form the basis of Jewish thinking in this regard. Not only are Jews obligated to make financial compensation for damages or crimes they commit, but they are also equally obligated to prevent such damage, caused either by their own property or in the public domain. Much of the public works—roads, drainage, street lighting, pavements, water supply—are in effect a practical expression of this prevention of damage. The public investment is simply an extension of the obligation placed on the individual by the Torah, a process that is common in Jewish law, seeing the community as an expression of the mutual interrelationship that flows from the common destiny and nationhood.

> It is a positive commandment for a man to make a fence around his roof, as it is written in the Torah (Deuteronomy 22:8) [in order to prevent somebody from falling from the roof]. He who does not make such a fence disregards this positive commandment, but is also guilty of violating the negative commandment [in the same biblical verse] "and you shall not spill blood in your house." And so it is with every obstacle [even in a public thoroughfare] that is liable to cause damage to the human body: it is a positive precept to remove it [stones, garbage, even seemingly harmless objects] and do so diligently.[56]

Maimonides points out that great scholars, Judaism's role models, were always careful to observe these laws, even though it may have been considered to be beneath their status or dignity.

The most outstanding example of the individual and communal obligation to prevent damage is to be found in regard to health care and services. All the sources, Talmud, halakhic codes and responsa, and the moralistic literature, include the discussion of health problems, nutrition, preventive medicine, and hygiene as part of the religious pattern of life. If man is created in God's image, then the care of his body, the prevention of damage, and the saving of his life must assume a major role in Jewish religious living.

A city that did not have a doctor is considered by the Talmud to be unfit for a Jew to dwell in, and a community cannot escape its obligation to provide for the medical needs of the poor. There is even a halakhic opinion that the rabbinic courts can force a doctor to treat poor patients free of charge, if there are no others available.[57]

Communal funding for the care of the sick was common, as may be seen from the 1585 decision of the council of Padua to raise funds for the medical care of Shimon Levi Ginzberg, both by the weekly collections in all of the synagogues and from the general charity funds. So too in Cracow in Poland at the same period, the community ruled that an employer had to pay the costs of hospitalization for up to a period of two weeks for the sick domestic. For a further fortnight, the costs were to be shared equally between them. After that, all costs were to be borne by the communal charitable funds.[58]

Many communities throughout the Diaspora maintained a *hekdesh*—part hospital, part inn for travelers. The enactment of the Council of Cracow mentioned previously makes reference to such a *hekdesh*. Josephus Flavius describes a synagogue in Jerusalem before 70 C.E. that also served as a hospital, and the Talmud tells of the *cheder hashayish*—the room of marble—as a place for the sick. In 1737, Samuel ben Natan HaLevi bequeathed fifty pounds to the Nuremberg *hekdesh*.[59] In the responsa of Samuel De Medina, the case of a joint hospital erected by four different communities is discussed.[60] In 1765 we know that there were eighteen patients in the Vilna *hekdesh*.[61]

The important feature of all these cases is not the existence of hospitals or medical services, but the fact that they were maintained as part of the public budget rather than through acts of private philanthropy or as part of ecclesiatical property. Furthermore, in contrast to many of the health schemes in modern economies, these public funds provided the health services without any contribution on the part of the poor and needy ill. While society has in *Halakhah* the right to decide on any system to provide such services, it cannot evade its responsibility to those who cannot afford it. At the same time, it should be borne in mind that the health services provided according to *Halakhah* are acts of charity, not entitlement.

Maimonides ruled that visiting the sick, an example of what modern medicine would describe as the support system intrinsic to communal health care, is an act of righteousness, legally binding and not just desirable. Since it is an act of *chesed* performed with one's body, it has no legal limitations in its fulfillment (in contrast to monetary charity, which the Sages have limited to 20 percent of one's wealth). It is a fulfillment of "You shall love your neighbor as yourself" (Leviticus 19: 18).[62]

This view of providing health care, hospitalization, and support services as acts of righteousness and charity, rather than entitlement, limits the overrun in costs that is such a feature of modern social medicine.

Environmental Regulation

Any economic activity represents potential damage to the environment and to the ecological welfare of society. This may take the form of pollution of the air, water, and soil, of physical damage to the human body and the animal population, or of aesthetic disfigurement. All these forms create two major problematical areas—one economic and one moral, which occur both at the individual level and between society and individuals. In this section, the discussion will center primarily on the communal aspects, even though it will be necessary to include the relationship between individuals.

Economic Issues

The economic issues flow primarily from the fact that natural resources are limited. This means that society cannot simply avail itself continuously of other resources, nor can the individual sufferer remove himself from the proximity of the disturbance or damage. In both cases, the ecological costs always have to be weighed against the benefits created by the economic activity. The individual or corporation has to consider the costs suffered by others, individually or collectively, as part of the production costs of goods and services. Society too, in the reality of life, has to compare the benefits accruing in the forms of jobs, higher standard of living, and tax receipts to the costs of pollution, quality of life, and physical damage.

Jewish law rules categorically that one who causes damages to his neighbor's body or property has to pay for them. Throughout the tractates of the Talmud—*Baba Kamma*, *Baba Metzia*, and *Baba Batra*—which are the source material for halakhic treatment of damages, it is axiomatic that people are liable for damage caused directly even without intent or even unconsiously (as in sleep), as well as that caused by their property. So too, there is responsibility for damages caused even in areas that are not private property—a pit dug in a public thoroughfare or a parked vehicle. The fact that the road does not belong to one and the damage did not occur within one's jurisdiction does not free one from responsibility. Even where the damage is caused by objects propelled by natural forces—water or wind—a person is responsible if he actually sets the object in motion (sparks from an anvil, chips from falling trees). All these apply equally to damage to the environment—air, water, soil, flora, fauna, peace of mind, and privacy.[63]

Over and above the importance of this ramified legal redress and the provision of compensation are the rabbinic sources that insist on the equal obligation to prevent damage. It may well be cheaper for the one causing the damage to pay such compensation, rather than bear the cost of removing the obstacle or operating in such a way as to reduce the environmental damage. Halakhically, there are cases in which the injured party may accept damage or environmental obstacle in return for payment, selling as it were some of his rights to a pollution-free environment. Nevertheless, it is clear that this does not release the other party from preventing the damage in the first place. Maimonides rules that one may not cause damage on the assumption that he will be able to pay for what he has caused, since it is forbidden to cause damage.[64]

It is the acceptance of this imperative to prevent damage or to enhance ecological conditions that provides the basis for the communal regulation and halakhic legislation. Both recognize that the community, whether seen as neighbors in a courtyard, citizens in a town, or people in national or international groupings, has rights that have to be protected against damage to the environment or from scenic destruction. Zoning laws and town planning are legal developments of these rights.

> It is necessary to remove the permanent threshing floors [because of the chaff], [accumulated] carcasses [in some form of refuse yard], the graveyard, and the tanneries have to be removed from the city 50 *amot*. [These are all considered to be sources of damage through smell or smoke.] Tanneries may be constructed [even beyond these limits] only on the eastern side of the town [since winds seldom come from that side. An additional yet nonphysical reason was that Jews in Babylon faced west in prayer, or because the Temple was situated on the western side of Jerusalem].[65]

This is only one example of communal power to insist on relocation or to forbid the erection of polluting industries. A different *mishnah* codified as law ruled that "one may not raise small animals [sheep and goats] in the Land of Israel [since their grazing leads to soil erosion] . . . nor may one raise a dog [who tends to bite and frighten people] . . . it is not permitted to spread nets to capture birds unless these are removed from the city [otherwise they would entrap the birds of the townspeople]."[66] The Talmud, in *Baba Batra*, also demands the removal of the mill stones used to grind wheat or barley from the neighbor's wall because of the noise and tremors. This would invite similar legislation in order to reduce the reverberations or noise projected into the ground by heavy machinery in modern plants.

One was not allowed to erect garbage plants and kilns within the city limits of Jerusalem, the former being a source of rodents and the latter a source of smoke.[67] Care was taken to prevent pollution of the water supply, whether it involved the simple act of cleansing one's soiled body or conducting any activity that would contaminate the water supply.[68] The talmudical case of an outhouse toilet that had to be distanced from a neighbor's well, whatever distance was needed to prevent such pollution,[69] would make legislation against the pouring of harmful or even merely unpleasant substances into waterways by industrial plants or by households halakhically imperative. *Sefer HaChasidim* stresses a moral and ethical aspect of protecting the water supply, seeing its pollution as an act of *lifnei iver*—putting a stumbling block in the path of the blind. After all, there are cases where others are ignorant of the pollution and can come to harm. "One who suffers from boils [or any other skin disease] is not permitted to bathe in public water. Perhaps another will later bathe in the same water and be struck by boils. For this the Torah commanded us, 'Thou shall love thy neighbor' and 'thou shall not stand on thy brother's blood.'"[70] The importance of the water supply to the health of society necessitated this halakhic ruling.

All of these zoning laws or restrictive legislation, like their modem counterparts, often clash with economic reality or with the problem of costs. The cost of introducing technical processes, zoning, and relocation to minimize or eradicate the pollution is, as it were, a tax paid for the protection of society. The Jewish perspective must, therefore, consider the financial aspects, the cost in slower growth, or sometimes even a basic threat to economic existence. It would seem that there are three major halakhic areas to be considered in the cost-benefit analysis of any environmental regulation.

1. The degree to which old established plants or industries can claim the protection of the time element: There is a recognized general commercial protection provided by *Halakhah* to the fact that one has been acting for a long period without any protest from others. However, this protection does not apply to smoke, smell, or noise, considered to be the major forms of ecological damage. Furthermore, even a basic principle of Jewish law, the sanctity of contracts, was seen to be overridden in regard to these forms of damage. The reasoning behind this was that a person is not really able to know if the odors and smoke will be bearable, so that if a contract was originally agreed upon, and then the townspeople wish to cancel it, they may do so.[71]

2. The budgetary limits that face every society require a distinction between essential protection and environmental safeguards related to exaggerated fears or the desire to provide foolproof regulations. Some sort of priority system or viable costing is required. Halakhic sources provide a concept of reasonable risk, which would place the communal legislation in a correct perspective between almost unlimited demands on the public purse and unregulated economic activity. Seeing as there are normal risks involved in living, the Rabbis freed people from the obligation to provide unlimited safety. A simple yet important example is that the fences that have to be erected on a roof in accordance with the biblical commandment to prevent "blood in your house" need only be of such a height and material as to prevent an average person leaning on it from falling off the roof.[72] This has practical application in the case of runways of airports, bridges, reduction of noise levels, and accident prevention.

3. The major area to be considered is that in which regulation conflicts with the communal economic welfare. It may be relatively easy and acceptable to force an individual or corporation to pay its taxes for environmental protection, but as a result, society may suffer economic hardship in order to enjoy aesthetic pleasure, unpolluted air and water, and a safe environment. It may well be that the cost of ecological protection is so high that employers in that area are forced to close their plants or to relocate to another area with less stringent controls. Sometimes, this may not only mean closure of one firm, but widespread unemployment, as when that firm is the sole employer or where a whole industry finds it unprofitable to operate under these regulations. Even though such controls have a legitimate halakhic basis, nevertheless, they have in the past been relaxed in order to prevent

widespread economic dislocation.[73] However, this was seen as a temporary situation forced upon the community by the fact that in exile, they did not have the power to impose the halakhic rules, which would have prevented the pollution in the first place.[74] More importantly, relaxation of the guidelines was permitted only where no danger to health existed, only discomfort or displeasure. Since men do not have the right to place themselves in danger, not only do employers not have the right to damage the health of their employees, but the latter do not have the right to accept such employment, even in return for increased wages. Naturally, this is contingent on the concept of reasonable risk. Over and above that level, it may well be that where the technological knowledge is such that an industry cannot operate without serious damage to health, that industry may not, under a Jewish economic system, be able to operate at all.

Moral Issues

The mainstay of modern economic thought in the consideration of ecological issues is in terms of costs and benefits, of responsibility for removing environmental obstacles, and of how the financial burden of preventing damages is to be determined. While this is necessary, it is in reality only the minor issue, being overshadowed by the necessity to consider the ethical and moral dimensions. Any solution to the environmental problems of the modern world is predicated by the examination of these dimensions and the society's ability to accept their implications. The ethical and moral dimensions go beyond the questions of payment for damages and even beyond the moral imperative of preventing such damage to the person or property of others or of the public. Basically, they require adjustment to the "economics of enough" and demand the recognition of the real source of all human wealth. Because of this, they place limits on economic growth and introduce spiritual elements into the mundane pursuit of material goods. Therefore, they affect the very nature of wealth creation and determine in the final resort, the parameters of such activity.

Jewish sources from the Bible down to modern mystical literature are replete with the beauty and the spiritual connotations that exist in nature. The *Midrash* tells how all the animals, birds, fishes, trees, and plants join man in praising the Lord. Throughout the Psalms natural phenomena, animals, and plants are used to describe the striving of man to merge with the spirit of the Lord, while nature's beauty is offered as an example of the spiritual contentment to which people aspire, as in Psalm 23. Similarly, the relationship between the moral and spiritual condition of man and the physical condition of nature is clearly recognized. Adam and Eve destroy the harmony that existed in Eden and are destined to live in a world in which species struggle with each other. In no way, however, must this theme of the importance of nature and all its components, together with the beauty thereof, be construed as granting the natural elements a power as a value of their own, over and above that given to them by God, their Creator. To do otherwise is to strengthen the element of idolotary present in much of the present-day environmental movements, in the notion of soul and spirit of the wind, the water, or the soil.

All the natural resources are given to man by the Creator to be used for human benefit; that is the very reason for their creation. In any conflict, therefore, between the legitimate interests of man and those of all the species of the world, those of man must predominate.

The major concern that comes to mind is the treatment of animals, birds, and fish, and the types of benefits that may be derived from them in the course of economic activity. In this regard, the guideline is the concept of *tzar baalei chaim*—the injunction not to cause pain to living creatures. This concept however must be seen in relation to the Divine blessing to mankind, first to Adam and Eve and then repeated to Noah after the flood, "and fill the earth and subdue it" (Genesis 1:28). People are given permission to use and benefit from other living creatures by God, but also limited by Him as part of the harmony established by creation. So the balance achieved by Judaism envisages permitted legitimate benefits but limited within certain halakhic parameters. These do not include wanton destruction or even killing for sport or pleasure. So fishing is permitted for food but not for recreation. Animals may be bred for meat or slaughtered for their hides and furs but not hunted as sport. A modern responsum by Rabbi Moshe Feinstein in New York forbade the pen system, whereby calves are fattened for slaughter while kept in close confines that do not permit them to move about. So, too, experimentation on animals for medical research has been permitted, but their use for trivial luxuries needs to be referred to a competent halakhic authority. This distinction is also made in regard to people, permitting surgery for health reasons, but forbidding it for merely cosmetic reasons.

Repeatedly, throughout this book, the twin strands of legislation and spiritual dimensions have been noted. These concern themselves not only with the damage done to others or their property through unethical behavior, but as importantly, with the spiritual damage caused to the perpetrator. Here too, the halakhic parameters regarding economic decisions and cruelty to animals have to be considered within the Jewish moralistic sources. These sources educate toward a moral perspective, within which the balance between avoiding cruelty and permitted use can be maintained. Before animals are slaughtered for food, a blessing is recited, just as in the performance of any other religious obligation. The blessing here is an acknowledgment that it is only through Divine permission that the animal may be killed. The first blood shed has to be covered by earth. Furthermore, kosher food requires the removal, through soaking and salting, of the blood, since we are permitted to eat the flesh but not the blood. In both instances, a respect for the blood, the essence of life itself, is cultivated. Maimonides points out that just as dogs become fierce through eating raw meat, so too people become coarsened and evil through the callous and disrespectful treatment of the blood. It is not for nothing that the Torah in Leviticus 19:26 links eating blood with superstition and soothsaying.

Animals in our care, for whatever purpose, have to be fed before satisfying our own needs. The ox may not be muzzled so that he cannot eat while threshing corn, just as the worker is allowed to eat of the food he is working with (Deuteronomy 25:4).

Torah forbids slaughtering an animal and its offspring on the same day (Leviticus 22:28) and insists on sending away the mother bird before taking the eggs of the young (Deuteronomy 22:6). Rabbinic opinion is divided between those denying that animals have maternal feelings and those who maintain that they do. Irrespective, both these biblical injunctions contribute to the development of mercy and kindness. These attitudes then spread to the interpersonal relationship and the moral improvement of the world—*tikkun ha'olam*. These merge with *tzar baalei chaim* (Exodus 3:5), the commandment to unload an overburdened animal of one's enemy; mercy to the animal is a contributing factor toward easing human conflicts. The necessity to refrain from ill-treating animals through overloading their burdens obligates one generally to assist without receiving payment. It includes the property even of the idolator, who has placed himself beyond the pale of civilization based on the Noachide laws.[75]

This balance between the rights of mankind and mercy toward all living creatures flows from the Divine source of creation and everything in it. That same source, however, also defines the legitimate interests and determines what the pinnacle of creation, man, may or may not do with the world entrusted to him.

So a man or a society may not vandalize, waste, or wantonly destroy even their own legally acquired property, let alone that of others. "He who tears his clothing, breaks his utensils, or scatters his money in anger should be in your eyes as if he has served idols."[76]

Edible fruit trees may not be destroyed in time of war (Deuteronomy 20:19). It is noteworthy that these trees belonged to the enemy. This was extended in the Talmud to include all material resources useful to man, as for example the present-day inefficient use of nonrenewable reserves of energy. This concept of *bal tashchit* is the positive injunction whereby people are supposed to prevent waste so that other people, even in future generations, may have a benefit from the resources.

Going beyond preventing waste, the Talmud tells of the old man found by Hadrian planting a fig tree. To the Roman emperor's question as to what the point was in planting a tree of whose fruit he would never eat, the Jew replied, "I eat fruit of trees my father planted, my grandchildren will eat of the fruit of my trees."[77] This is the application of the task of man placed in Eden to work and protect it.

These concepts of *bal tashchit* are only part of an educational system geared toward a correct perspective on the environment, as shown in the legal codes.

Basing himself on the biblical verse (Deuteronomy 23:13-14), Maimonides classifies the provision of proper toilet facilities, even in the volatile and unsettled army conditions, as a positive obligation—a *mitzvat aseh*—an obligation even more imperative in the orderly conditions of normal living.[78] Parallel to this injunction, we find that it is not permissible to pray in a place that is dirty, smells of urine and excreta, or that is close to a toilet or bathroom.[79] It is not permissible to greet people with *shalom*—peace—the traditional Jewish greeting, under similar conditions since it is the name of God. So too the Rabbis understood the verse "you shall not make detestable" (Leviticus 11:3,4) at the conclusion of the laws of nonkosher food to refer also to prohibiting any action or habit that is calculated to provoke disgust in others—eating from unclean plates, taking one's food with dirty hands, squashing a flea in public, or spitting in front of his fellowman.[80] This is not primarily a matter of physical hygiene but a spiritual directive. Man has to remove himself from the disgusting and repulsive. After all, the finale of the laws of kosher food is "sanctify yourselves and be holy for I am Holy." Surely this would apply to rowdy behavior, excessive noise in public places, rioting at sporting events, and any of the other manifestations of social pollution.

The spiritual dimensions of ecology find their major expression in the area of limitations on growth and the desired form of urban planning. Here the model is based on the towns of the Levites (Leviticus 25:3 and Numbers 36:1-5) that were required to have two belts surrounding their urban areas. Each town had land that was set aside for urban settlement, a belt of farmland, and a further area of open field. These were not allowed to be transformed for different purposes. The halakhic codes ruled that this plan applied to all towns in the land of Israel. It is clear that the growth of the town was thereby limited, since the farmland could not be urbanized or the open field used for farming.

The town fathers did not have the right to rezone areas in order to extend their town or to promote development, even if this meant economic progress. Such progress had to be achieved through the establishmant of new, similar small units. This would prevent the modern urban sprawl and provide, in addition to the preservation of open areas, scenic beauty, pure air, and so on, the communal benefits flowing from a closely knit society. Such a society would correct the environmental disturbances of the large urban unit, with its lack of concern for the individual, the estrangement from society, and its crime and violence.

The importance of this limitation on development goes far beyond the question of economic growth and of town planning. It is easily translatable into the use of nonpolluting forms of transport, consumer demand for nontoxic or hazardous waste products, and restrictions on products that either cannot be recycled or for which the cost of recycling is excessive. Such measures may well mean a restriction on lifestyles, less convenient patterns of consumption, and even more modest forms of recreation.

It is argued that unless this is done, the methods used to prevent ecological damage and even worse can bring in their wake moral degeneration or economic injustice. For example, concern over the destruction of the Amazon basin and its effect on global ecology morally requires financial compensation to the local inhabitants for the loss of the economic benefits otherwise gained through industrialization, logging, and large-scale farming. To demand environmental controls but leave intact the poverty, illiteracy, and squalor is an example of the injustice that flows from the desire for ecological balance without paying for it. This is not restricted to monetary payment but has implications in regard to social morality and economic immorality. In the introduction to this part of the book, sources written over two thousand years ago were presented in which the destruction of the Generation of the Flood was ascribed to their inability or unwillingness to accept restrictions on their standard of living in the interest of the environment and their search for alternative solutions. Crime and theft became a way to preserve the quality of life, nonreproductive forms of sex like homosexuality and bestiality became acceptable, as did marriage restricted only to the more superior men and women. The Rabbis taught that Er and Onan, the sons of Judah, perverted their sexual acts because they did not want to mar the beauty of Tamar through childbirth.

PUBLIC-SECTOR CORRUPTION

Judaism's acceptance of the role of the state in the economic affairs of the individual did not blind the sources to the ever-present threat to morality posed by the very existence of a public sector and the opportunities it presents for corruption. The individual greed and economic needs of civil servants, legislators, and public-sector officials are no different from that of ordinary people in the same society. It is reasonable to expect, therefore, proportions of white-collar crime, incidents of fraud and theft, and economic immorality similar to those of the general population. This is crime, and so can be dealt with in exactly the same supervisory manner and using the same policing methods as other sources of crime. The public sector, however, with its power to control and influence the lives of the citizens through welfare and through economic development introduces the wider ethical dimension of corruption. Academic research shows that such potential for corruption flows primarily from the following factors:

1. The loss of individual freedom allows for despotic government, which is thereby freed from accountability for its actions.

2. Regulations create a bureaucratic class and give it control over allocation of economic resources, allow it to determine investment and production decisions, and through taxes or tariffs, even to affect patterns of consumption. These in turn create opportunities for bribery. Economic activity may not even be possible without payments in money, goods, or even personal services to the official in charge of framing these regulations and enforcing them.

3. Wage and price policies, tax rates and the tax base, and various forms of subsidy to entrepreneurs and consumers alike can create an unethical pattern of individual behavior. Sometimes the fiscal policy is excessive or discriminatory, making for large-scale tax evasion. Wage policies, in the interest of achieving an egalitarian structure, may ignore the economic realities of supply and demand; this forces society to resort to subterfuge and lying to obtain the desired goods or services. Subsidies, as often as not, lead to waste of the goods or services included, but also to false reporting in order to obtain the subsidy.

4. The concentration of economic and political power resulting from regulation and economic legislation promotes the tidy relationships among big business, trade unions, and lobbyists, in which financial contributions flow in one direction and political favors flow in the other.

All of these factors combine to make immorality and unethical behavior normal for the majority of the population. Such behavior no longer belongs to the twilight world of individual crime, but represents the corruption of society at large.[81]

Given that power corrupts and that wealth creation and possession are major needs of humanity, economic power is probably more powerful and pervasive than other forms of state control. The greater the economic concentration and efficiency of the public sector, the greater its potential for corruption. The experience of this century, both in Socialist and Communist countries as well as in the free-market economies, provides an endless list of examples of the results of these factors on causing and spreading corruption. The scandals in Italy and Japan of the early 1990s did not flow from the special greed of those involved, but rather from the size of the public sector (some 60 percent of the Italian gross national product) or from the Japan Incorporated nature of that economy. An egalitarian wage structure in the Soviet Union and in Israel created the network of acceptable subterfuges and falsehoods needed to adjust those structures to the realities of supply and demand for labor. Countries with higher tax rates have been found to have larger underground economies, irrespective of how these are measured. The examination of the effect of subsidies, tariffs, and government incentives on the ethical behavior of corporations in Western countries is beyond our scope, but there is enough evidence of the waste—a form of corruption—and the political immorality connected with them.

It is no wonder therefore that rabbinic sources present an awareness of the corrupting influences of public-sector activity and methods of minimizing them.

Awareness of Corruption

In the Book of Leviticus, the description of the gold, copper, and other gifts brought by the Children of Israel for the construction of the Tabernacle is recorded three times. To the Sages of the *Midrash,* this superfluous repetition in the Word of God seemed strange and worthy of consideration. They explained that whenever Moses appeared in public, he heard the people discussing his health, power, and energy despite his advanced age. However, he also heard their explanation, "If you would have collected all that wealth for the Tabernacle, appointed your brother Aaron to be its high priest and your nephew Bazalel ben Hur as its architect and chief builder, you too would have looked like Moses." As soon as Moses heard this he gave a full accounting.[82] Apart from stressing the accountability necessary in handling public-sector funds, the fact that Moses, the Father of the Prophets, the lawgiver, and the man who spoke directly to God, could be suspected of corruption speaks volumes for Judaism's statement that no man, exalted and pious as he may be, can be considered or consider himself to be above temptation and corruption.

Perhaps the best illustrations of the insidiousness of public service as a temptation to corruption are the rabbinic discussions regarding two cases of inherited public position recorded in the Book of Samuel. These same illustrations show that, despite both the halakhic requirements mentioned below and the ability of society to legislate protective measures, in the final analysis, it is the spiritual dimension that defines the limitations of corruption. Chapter eight tells of the sons of Samuel, the prophet, who "walked not in his ways, but turned aside after wealth, took bribes and perverted judgment." All the commentators saw in these actions abuse of power, rather than simple bribery, thus enhancing corruption rather than minimizing it. The new judges lived in Be'er Sheva, in the south of Israel, far from the centers of population, making people travel great distances. Alternatively, they increased the judicial bureaucracy; both these pervert justice by making it expensive and cumbersome. They busied themselves in business, forcing the merchants to trade with them, presumably in expectation of favors. Their passion for wealth led them to covet and to pander. In addition, being Levites they were entitled to tithes, but used this entitlement incorrectly. By demanding their share rather than waiting for it, they denied the weaker elements of their share. Alternatively they took more than they were entitled to. Rashi, commenting on the talmudic discussion, points out that they took the tithes and also served as judges, something forbidden by *Halakhah*.[83]

This tendency to corruption in contrast to fraud or crime, inherent in any public sector, is similarly stressed in the rabbinic interpretations of the story of the sons of Eli, the High Priest, related in the same book. The text tells that they performed their ritual tasks in a manner that led to a desecration of the sacrifices and caused the women of Israel to sin. The desecration was brought about by their illegally taking the best meat or disturbing the procedures in order to benefit more than they were entitled to. Those scholars who would not accept that they actually committed adultery explained the text in Samuel 2:22–25 as referring to the fact that they neglected the dove offering of women after childbirth, since their share was small in contrast to the regular sacrifices of sheep and cattle. In this way, they delayed the women, who could not return home to their husbands, a form of sexual immorality.[84]

Restricting Corruption

This awareness of public service as a potential for corruption is summed up in the dictum "it is not the mouse who steals, but the hole." Awareness is however, on its own, insufficient, so halakhic provisions were made for accountability and for a system of preventive checks and balances. These provisions are all based on the understanding that the issues go beyond relatively simple acts of theft or white-collar crime. The power that comes with authority, the conflict between personal interests and the public service needs, and the ability to ignore public opinion make for corruption in all its manifestations. The sources recognize that good intent and operating even with the most elevated ideals are insufficient to prevent such corruption. Therefore, the Torah perspective is primarily concerned with the ideological framework, even while insisting on preventive legislation.

Early in the Common Era, public officials were considered to be above suspicion, and therefore no public accounting was needed. In the course of time, declining moral standards called for and received provisions for public-sector accounting and procedures. Even previously, temptation and external appearances were considered in regard to methods of public finance.

The recurring emphasis on appearances must not be treated lightly. Public knowledge of what officials are doing is almost always a powerful restraint on those same officials.

Collection of public funds was always to be done in pairs, while the distribution, a matter of life or death in many cases, was appropriately done by a trio, the minimum for such cases. In those days when the public sector raised its funds in currencies of different countries and areas, the officials were required to exchange them through a professional, in order to prevent mistakes or cause gossip. So too, sales or purchases of goods or services needed and the holding of funds were always to be kept separate from their private affairs. The priest who collected each day the donations and monetary offerings in the Temple in Jerusalem entered the room in which they were deposited barefooted, dressed only in a sleeveless, pocketless, shift—protection against temptation and preventing public suspicion.[85]

In all these various halakhic rulings and homiletical explanations, there is a common thread of Judaism's acceptance of the need for the public sector intertwined with the awareness of its propensity for corruption, cruelty, and immorality. They find their major expression in the rights and obligations of the king, which is the Jewish prototype of the public sector. Based on Deuteronomy (17:14-20), Maimonides, who included in his code even laws temporarily in abeyance during the Jewish exile, ruled that all are obligated to fear the king, pay his taxes, and obey his rules. The king in turn is forbidden to possess more money in his treasury than is essential for the public welfare, he may not marry many wives (in contast to the ordinary citizen, who biblically was permitted as many wives as he wished), and he may not have an excessive army. This latter limitation, linked as it is to the return to

Egypt, has led some commentators to see it as a restriction on a large standing army based on imported horses. Abarbanel, however, sees this linkage as preventing dependence on Egypt as a symbol of might and normal military success, rather than on God. Taxation in monetary and nonmonetary forms, such as to eminent domain, is limited to the needs of the public rather than including grandiose personal expenses. Above all, the king is required to have a special scroll of the Torah to be alongside him perpetually—a constant reminder that his potential power and his rights are all subject to the legal and spiritual demands of the word of God, a permanent bulwark against public-sector corruption.[86]

NOTES

INTRODUCTION

1. Adolf Hitler, *Mein Kampf* (London: Macmillan, 1968), referring to the Protocols of the Elders of Zion.

2. Karl Marx, *Early Writings*, trans. and ed. T. B. Battomore (London: Penguin, 1972).

3. Emmanuel Kant, *Religion Within the Limits of Reason Alone* (London: Routledge, 1950) (reprint) is an example of such a distortion, presenting Judaism solely as a legal framework.

4. Daniel J. Elazar and S. A. Cohen, *The Jewish Polity* (Bloomington, IN: Indiana University Press, 1985).

5. Louis Finkelstein, *Jewish Self-Government in the Middle Ages* (New York: Feldheim, 1964).

6. *Vaad Arba Aratzot*, ed. Israel Halperin (Jerusalem: Mossad Bialik, 1954).

7. Meir Tamari, *With all Your Possessions: Jewish Ethics and Economic Life* (New York: Free Press, 1987).

8. *Talmud Bavli, Baba Kamma* 30a. See also *Sefer HaChinukh, mitzvah* 330.

9. *Mishneh Torah, Hilkhot Gezeilah VeAveidah*, chap. 1, *halakhot* 1-4.

10. Rashi, Leviticus 25:36; *Mishneh Torah, Hilkhot Rotze'ach U'Shmirat HaNefesh*, chap. 12, *halakhah* 14; also *Sifra, Kedoshim; Talmud Bavli, Avodah Zarah* 6b and *Baba Metzia* 75b.

11. Genesis 33:9, 11.

12. *Mishneh Torah, Hilkhot De'ot*, chap. 5, *halakhah* 13.

Chapter 1—Uncertainty, Greed, and Business Morality

1. *Talmud Bavli, Yoma* 69b.
2. *Talmud Bavli, Berakhot* 35b.
3. Rashi, Genesis 1:31.
4. *Sifre, Devarim, VeEt'chanan.*
5. Thomas Aquinas, *Summa Theologica*, 2a.
6. William Tawney, *Christianity and the Rise of Capitalism* (London: Penguin, 1983).
7. *Avot DeRabbi Natan*, chap. 4, sec. 8.
8. Deuteronomy 11:13-17.
9. *Mishnah, Pirkei Avot*, chap. 5, *mishnah* 13.
10. *Talmud Bavli, Shabbat* 31a.
11. S. R. Hirsch, *The Pentateuch* (London: 1960), Exodus 16:2.
12. *Freedom in the World: Political Rights and Civil Liberties*, ed. Raymond D. Gostif (New York: Freedom House, 1980), pp. 40-41.
13. Edmond Lipson and C. Black, *The Economic History of England* (London: A. and C. Black, 1966), chap. 2.
14. *Mechilta, Shemot* 20:14.
15. *Shem Mi Shmuel, Parshat Shelach.*
16. *Chafetz Chaim, Sefat Chaim*, chap. 5.
17. Rashi, *Talmud Bavli, Baba Batra* 165a.
18. *Bereshit Rabbah* 41:5.
19. *Shem Mi Shmuel. Haggadah shel Pesach.*
20. Y. H. Hertz, *The Pentateuch* (London: Soncino Press, 1990), notes on Deuteronomy.
21. A. Sen, "Is Morality in Economics Worthwhile?" in *The Ethics of Business in a Global Economy*, ed. P. M. Minus, (Boston: Kluwer Academic Publishers, 1993).
22. *Sefer HaChinukh*, introduction.
23. T. Hobbes, *Leviathan* (London: Oxford University Press, 1929).
24. *Talmud Bavli, Kiddushim* 31a.
25. *Torah Temimah, Shemot* 15:26.
26. *Shem Mi Shmuel, Parshat Kedoshim.*
27. *Shem Mi Shmuel, Parshat Mishpatim.*
28. Robert North, *Sociology of the Biblical Jubilee* (Rome: Pontifical Biblical Institute, 1954).
29. *Sefer HaChinukh, mitzvah* 430.
30. A. I. HaKohen Kook, *Shabbat HaAretz.*
31. *Mishneh Torah, Hilkhot Melakhim*, chap. 9, *halakhah* 1.
32. *Techuvot Chatam Sofer*, pt. 2, no. 14.

33. Nachmanides, *Commentary on Genesis* 34:13.
34. Yalkut Yehudah, commentary on Genesis 2:16.
35. *Mishneh Torah, Hilkhot Melakhim*, chap. 9, *halakhah* 14.

Chapter 2—Clean before Man and God

1. Yaakov Kondor, *Introduction to Estimating the Underground Economy in Israel* (Tel Aviv: Mercaz Sapir, 1983) (Hebrew).
2. Leviticus 19:2.
3. *Talmud Bavli, Baba Batra* 165a.
4. *Talmud Bavli, Baba Metzia* 65b.
5. *Pit'chei Choshen*, chap. 1, sec. 1.
6. *Shulchan Arukh, Choshen Mishpat*, sec. 97, subsec. 4.
7. *Pele Yoetz, Gezel.*
8. *Vaad Arba Aratzot*, ed. Israel Halperin (Jerusalem: Mossad Bialik, 1954). See also *Be'er HaGolah, Choshen Mishpat*, sec. 388, subsec. 21, for a halakhic sanction of such bans.
9. *Teshuvot HaRivash*, sec. 452.
10. *Mishneh Torah, Hilkhot Geneivah VeAveidah*, chap. 1, *halakhot* 1-2.
11. *Mishnah, Baba Kamma*, chap. 10, *mishnah* 9.
12. *Sifra, VaYikra*, 19:36; see also *Talmud Bavli, Baba Metzia* 49b.
13. Rashi, *Talmud Bavli, Makkot* 24a and *Baba Batra* 88a.
14. *Teshuvot Beit Avi*, pt. 4, sec. 185.
15. *Mechilta Shemot* 22:27.
16. *Shulchan Arukh, Choshen Mishpat*, sec. 372, subsec. 1.
17. *Choshen Mishpat*, sec. 204, subsecs. 1-4; see also comment of HaGra.
18. *Choshen Mishpat*, sec. 231, subsec. 19, according to Meirat Einayim.
19. *Talmud Yerushalmi, Baba Metzia*, chap. 4, *halakhah* 5.
20. *Choshen Mishpat*, sec. 348.
21. *Shulchan Arukh HaRav, Hilkhot Gezeilah*, sec. 27.
22. *Talmud Yerushalmi, Baba Metzia*, chap. 4, *halakhah* 2.
23. *Talmud Bavli, Sanhedrin* 108a.
24. Genesis 6:11.
25. *Mishnah, Baba Kamma*, chap. 6, *mishnah* 4.
26. *Piskei HaRosh, Baba Metzia*, chap. 4, sec. 19.
27. *Mishneh Torah, Hilkhot Rotze'ach U'Shmirat HaNefesh*, chap. 12, *halakhah* 14.
28. *Mishnah, Baba Kamma*, chap. 10, *mishnah* 9.
29. *Mishnah, Avodah Zarah*, chap. 1, *mishnah* 7.
30. *Torat Kohanim, VaYikra* 19:14.
31. *Eduyot*, chap. 5, *mishnah* 1; comment of Rabad, Rabbi Avraham Ben David.

Chapter 3—Justice and Righteousness in the Marketplace

1. *Mishneh Torah, Hilkhot Geneivah VeAveidah*, chap. 1, *halakhah* 3; *Hilkhot Gezeilah*, chap. 1, *halakhah* 4.

2. *Talmud Bavli, Ketubot* 65b; see *Ran Nedarim* 88a; also *Shulchan Arukh, Even HaEzer*, sec. 70.

3. *Talmud Bavli, Baba Metzia* 61b.

4. *Mishneh Torah, Hilkhot Gezeilah*, chap. 1, *halakhot* 9-11.

5. *Mishneh Torah, Hilkhot Geneivah*, chap. 1, *halakhah* 4; see also *Guide to the Perplexed*, pt. 3, chap. 41.

6. *Talmud Bavli, Sanhedrin* 105b.

7. Deuteronomy 26:17.

8. *Mishneh Torah, Hilkhot Mekhirah*, introduction.

9. *Talmud Bavli, Baba Metzia* 47b and codified in the *Mishneh Torah, Hilkhot Mekhirah*, chap. 3, *halakhah* 1.

10. *Shulchan Arukh, Choshen Mishpat*, sec. 228, subsecs. 1-2.

11. *Talmud Yerushalmi, Baba Metzia*, chap. 5, *halakhah* 1.

12. *Mishneh Torah, Hilkhot Mekhirah*, chap. 13, *halakhot* 3-4.

13. *Talmud Bavli, Baba Kamma* 115a.

14. *Teshuvot Bayit Chadash*, sec. 65; see also *Mordechai, Baba Metzia* 77b, and *Shulchan Arukh, Choshen Mishpat*, sec. 227, subsec. 7.

15. *Shulchan Arukh, Choshen Mishpat*, sec. 226, subsecs. 18, 20.

16. *Mishneh Torah, Hilkhot Mekhirah*, chap. 13, *halakhot* 3-4.

17. *Piskei HaRosh, Baba Metzia*, chap. 4, *HaZahav*, sec. c.

18. *Teshuvot HaRosh* sec. 1, subsec. 7.

19. *Pit'chei Choshen*, chap. 10, sec. 1.

20. *Shoel U'Meishiv*, pt. 3, sec. 137.

21. *Mishneh Halakhot*, vol. 9, sec. 364.

22. *Mesillat Yesharim*, chap. 21.

23. *Sefer Chasidim*, sec. 925.

24. *Orchot Tzaddikim* and *Sfat Tamim*, chap. 2.

25. *Tein Emet LeYaakov*, chap. 1, sec. 78, in the name of the *Migdal Oz*; see also *Arukh HaShulchan, Orach Chaim*, sec. 156, subsec. 3.

26. *Shulchan Arukh, Choshen Mishpat*, sec. 228, subsecs. 6-9.

27. *Shulchah Arukh, Choshen Mishpat*, sec. 232, subsecs. 1-3.

28. Aharon Levine, *Free Enterprise and Jewish Law* (New York: Ktav, 1984); Yehoshua Lieberman, *Hit'charut Kalkalit BeHalakhah* (Tel Aviv: Moreshet, 1990).

29. Meir Tamari, *With All Your Possessions: Jewish Ethics and Economic Life*, (New York: Free Press, 1987).

30. *Mishnah, Baba Metzia*, chap. 4, *mishnah* 12.

31. Ephraim Kleinman, "Just Price in Talmudical Literature," *History of Political Economy* 19 (1987).

32. *HaMeiri, Beit HaBechirah, Baba Metzia*, chap. 4, *mishnah* 12.

33. Rashi, *Baba Metzia* 69a. See *Teshuvot Panim Me'irot*, pt. 1, sec. 78.

34. *Shulchan Arukh, Choshen Mishpat*, sec. 227, subsecs. 27-28.

35. *Talmud Bavli, Sanhedrin* 81a and *Makkot* 24a.

36. *Talmud Bavli, Baba Batra* 21b.

37. *Mishneh Torah, Hilkhot Sh'cheynim*, chap. 6, *halakhah* 8. Also Tur, *Shulchan Arukh, Choshen Mishpat*, sec. 156, subsec. 5.

38. *Talmud Bavli, Kiddushin* 59a, and Rashi and *Tosafot* there.

39. *Teshuvot Beit Ephraim, Choshen Mishpat*, sec. 26.

40. *Avnei Nezer, Choshen Mishpat*, sec. 17.

41. *Minchat Tzvi, S'chirat Poalim*, sec. 8.

42. *Minchat Yitzchak*, pt. 2, sec. 94.

43. *Teshuvot Chatam Sofer, Choshen Mishpat*, sec. 79.

44. *Teshuvot Chatam Sofer, Choshen Mishpat*, sec. 231.

45. Ibn Migas, *Chiddushim, Baba Batra* 21b; see also Me'iri, *Baba Metzia* 40b; also Rosh, *Baba Metzia*, sec. 16.

46. *Levushei Mordechai, Choshen Mishpat*, sec. 12.

47. *Bayit Chodash, Choshen Mishpat*, sec. 231.

48. *Talmud Bavli, Baba Batra* 8b; see also *Tosefta, Baba Metzia*, chap. 11, *halakhah* 23.

49. *Teshuvot HaRashba*, pt. 4, sec. 185; pt. 5, sec. 125.

50. *Iggrot Moshe*, pt. 2, *Choshen Mishpat*, sec. 59.

51. *Netivah, Nissan* 5693.

52. *Teshuvot HaMaharsham*, sec. 968.

53. *Teshuvot HaRashba*, pt. 5, sec. 125.

54. *Talmud Bavli, Baba Batra* 9a; see also *Tosefta, Baba Metzia*, chap. 11, *halakhah* 12.

55. *Shulchan Arukh, Choshen Mishpat*, sec. 231.

56. Rashbam, *Talmud Bavli, Baba Batra* 54; see also *Teshuvot Maharsham Choshen Mishpat*, sec. 408.

57. *Mishnah, Yoma*, chap. 3, *mishnah* 11; see *Talmud Bavli, Yoma* 38a for subsequent discussion.

58. *Shulchan Arukh HaRav (Baal HaTanya), Choshen Mishpat, Hefker VeHasagat Gevul*, sec. 3.

59. *Chavot Ya'ir*, sec. 42.

60. *Mishneh Torah, Hilkhot De'ot*, chap. 5, *halakhah* 13.

61. 2 Samuel 23:21.

62. L. Finkelstein, *Jewish Self-Government in the Middle Ages, Synod of Rabbeinu Tam* (New York: Feldheim, 1964).

63. *Avnei Nezer, Choshen Mishpat*, sec. 28.

64. *Pinkas HaKesheirim shel Kehillat Poznan*, 1621-1835 (enactments 297, 543, 554).

65. *Pit'chei Teshuvah, Shulchan Arukh, Yoreh De'ah*, sec. 236, subsec. 1.

Chapter 4—Corporate Ethical Issues

1. *Minchat Yitzchak*, pt. 3, sec. 1; pt. 4, secs. 16, 18.
2. *Iggrot Moshe, Yoreh De'ah*, pt. 3, secs. 40-41.
3. *Teshuvot Elef LeShlomo*, sec. 238.
4. *Even HaEzer, Nizkei Mamon*, chap. 1, *halakhah* 1.
5. Meir Tamari, "Equity Financing in the United Kingdom, U.S.A., Japan and Israel," *International Management Review* (Fall 1973).
6. *Iggrot Moshe, Orach Chaim*, pt. 1, no. 62, subsec. 3.
7. *Panim Me'irot*, vol. 1, no. 38.
8. *Mishneh Halakhot*, vol. 6, no. 277.
9. *Talmud Bavli, Kiddushin* 42b.
10. Edward Shils and Meir Tamari, "Ownership and Control," *Social Review* (July 1990).
11. Meir Tamari, "Non-Dividend Forms of Profit Distribution," *Economic Review* 29 (Jerusalem: Bank of Israel, 1967).
12. *Mishneh Torah, Hilkhot Mekhirah*, chap. 13, *halakhah* 4, based on *Baba Metzia* 51b.
13. *Talmud Bavli, Baba Kamma* 115a; see also *Teshuvot Bayit Chadash*, sec. 65; Rama, *Choshen Mishpat*, sec. 227, subsec. 7.
14. *Mishnah, Baba Metzia*, chap. 7, *Mishnah* 1; see also *Shulchan Arukh, Choshen Mishpat*, sec. 331, subsec. 1.
15. *Mishneh Torah, Hilkhot Geneivah*, chap. 5, *halakhah* 1; see also *Talmud Bavli, Gittin* 45a.
16. *Talmud Bavli, Kiddushin* 41-42, *Gittin* 31, *Ketubot* 38-39.
17. *Mishneh Torah, Hilkhot Gezeilah*, chap. 1, *halakhah* 4.
18. *Shulchan Arukh, Choshen Mishpat*, sec. 359, subsec. 9.
19. A. Levine, "Leveraged Buyouts," *Shma* (November 1991).
20. *Shulchan Arukh, Yoreh De'ah*, sec. 160, subsecs. 18-20.
21. *Mishneh Torah, Hilkhot Geneivah*, chap. 1, *halakhah* 3.
22. *Mishneh Torah, Hilkhot Shluchim VeShutafim*, chap. 2, *halakhah* 9.
23. *Mishneh Torah, Hilkhot Avadim*, chap. 1, *halakhah* 7.
24. *Shulchan Arukh, Choshen Mishpat*, sec. 333, subsec. 3.
25. *Teshuvot Chatam Sofer, Choshen Mishpat* 172.
26. *Mishnah, Baba Metzia*, chap. 9, *mishnah* 12.
27. *Talmud Bavli, Baba Kamma* 46a.
28. *Shulchan Arukh, Choshen Mishpat*, sec. 338, subsec. 2.
29. *Arbaah Turim, Choshen Mishpat*, sec. 337, subsec. 13.

30. *Teshuvot Maharsham*, pt. 3, sec. 54.
31. *Ruach Chaim*, sec. 333, subsec. 4.
32. *Tzemach Tzedek*, sec. 6.
33. *Mishneh Torah, Klei HaMikdash*, chap. 7, *halakhah* 14, based on *Talmud Yerushalmi, Shekalim*, chap. 5, *halakhah* 1.
34. M. Balaban, *Yaarbuch der Judisch–Literarishen Geselshaft* (Frankfurt: Kaufman, 1929), col. 11, p. 101.
35. *Mishneh Torah, Hilkhot Rotze'ach U'Shmirat HaNefesh*, chap. 11, *halakhah* 5.
36. Meir Tamari, *Small Firms in Israel* (Tel Aviv: Centre for Social Progress, 1991).
37. *Iggrot Moshe, Choshen Mishpat*, pt. 1, sec. 81.
38. Mordechai, *Talmud Bavli, Baba Metzia* 24b, sec. 257; *Bayit Chadash, Tur, Choshen Mishpat*, sec. 259, subsec. 3; sec. 12, subsec. 5.
39. *Sefer HaChinukh, mitzvah* 482.
40. *Shulchan Arukh, Choshen Mishpat,* sec. 259, subsec. 3.
41. *Piskei Batei Din HaRabbanim*, Haifa, 1963.
42. *Pit'chei Teshuvah, Choshen Mishpat*, sec. 333, subsec. 3.
43. *Mishpatei Uzziel*, pt. 3, *Choshen Mishpat*, sec. 4.
44. *Pinkas HaKesheirim Shel Kehillat Poznan*, enactment 444.
45. "Ziknei HaDayanim," *Torah VeHaMedinah*, vols. 9-10.
46. *Tzitz Eliezer*, pt. 2, sec. 26, subsec. 9.
47. *Shulchan Arukh, Yoreh De'ah*, sec. 245, subsec. 22.
48. *Tzitz Eliezer*, op. cit.

Chapter 5—When Less Is Better than More

1. Maimonides, *Guide to the Perplexed*, pt. 3, sec. 35.
2. *Mishnah, Avot*, chap. 5, *mishnah* 13.
3. *Malbim, Bereishit* 18:21.
4. *Zohar, Bereishit* 56; see also *Bereishit Rabbah* 34.
5. *Talmud Bavli, Sanhedrin* 108a.
6. *Talmud Bavli, Shabbat* 31a.
7. *Torah Temimah, VaYikra* 19:1.
8. Genesis 33:24.
9. Maharal, *Derekh Chaim Avot*, chap. 3, sec. 2.
10. *Sefer HaChinukh, mitzvah* 84.
11. Samson Raphael Hirsch, *The Pentateuch*, trans. Isaac Levy (London, 1959), Numbers 6:12-13.
12. *Mishnah, Avot*, chap. 4, *mishnah* 1.
13. *Mishneh Torah, Hilkhot De'ot,* chap. 5, *halakhot* 2, 4-13.
14. Hirsch, op. cit., Leviticus 23:22.

15. *Mishneh Torah, Nizkei Mamon*, chap. 14, *halakhah* 5.
16. Me'iri, *Baba Kamma*, chap. 6, *mishnah* 4.
17. *Mishnah, Avot*, chap. 5, *mishnah* 10.
18. *Talmud Bavli, Baba Metzia* 30b.
19. *Mishneh Torah, Hilkhot De'ot*, chap. 5, *halakhah* 13.
20. *Talmud Bavli, Baba Metzia* 30b.
21. *Arbaah Turim, Choshen Mishpat*, sec. 304, subsec. 1.
22. *Shulchan Arukh, Choshen Mishpat*, sec. 418, subsec. 11.
23. *Teshuvot HaTzemach Tzedek, Choshen Mishpat*, sec. 23.
24. *Talmud Bavli, Baba Metzia* 17b, 108a.
25. *Mishneh Torah, Nizkei Mamon*, chap. 5, *halakhah* 3, based on *Talmud Bavli*.
26. *Arukh HaShulchan, Choshen Mishpat*, sec. 175, subsec. 1.
27. *Shulchan Arukh, Choshen Mishpat*, sec. 175, subsec. 6.
28. *Mishneh Torah, Hilkhot Sh'cheinim*, chap. 12, *halakhah* 13.
29. Cited in *Sefer HaZikaron* in honor of Pachad Yitzchak (Rabbi Isaac Hutner), p. 610.
30. *Talmud Bavli, Baba Kamma* 20a.
31. *Arukh HaShulchan, Choshen Mishpat*, sec. 103, subsec. 12.
32. Ibid., sec. 175, subsec. 59.
33. *Mishneh Torah, Hilkhot Gezeilah VeAveidah*, chap. 11, *halakhah* 14.
34. *Talmud Bavli, Baba Kamma* 31a.
35. *Shulchan Arukh, Chosen Mishpat*, sec. 426, subsec. 1.
36. *Torat Cohanim VaYikra* 19, 16.
37. *Shulchan Arukh, Chosen Mishpat*, sec. 98, subsec. 1.
38. *Sefer HaChinukh, mitzvah* 68.

Chapter 6—"Thy Brother Shall Live with Thee"

1. Tur, *Choshen Mishpat, Yoreh De'ah*, sec. 247, subsec. 1.
2. *Mishnah, Avot*, chap. 5, *mishnah* 13.
3. *Malbim, Bereishit* 13;14.
4. *Talmud Bavli, Kiddushin* 20a.
5. *Torah Temimah*, Leviticus 25:13.
6. *Talmud Bavli, Baba Batra* 10a.
7. *Talmud Bavli, Sotah* 14a.
8. *Mishneh Torah, Hilkhot Mekhirah*, chap. 22, *halakhot* 15-16; see also *Issurei Mizbe'ach*, chap. 7, *halakhah* 11.
9. *Mishnah, Avot*, chap. 3, *mishnah* 18.
10. *Midrash Tanchuma, Parshat Pekudey*.
11. *Talmud Bavli, Sanhedrin* 37a.
12. Yehudah HaLevi, *The Kuzari*, pt. 2, sec. 50.

13. *Mishneh Torah, Arakhim VeCharamim*, chap. 8, *halakhah* 13.
14. *Talmud Bavli, Pesachim* 112b-113a.
15. *Talmud Bavli, Pesachim* 112b-113a.
16. *Mishneh Torah, Hilkhot Matnot Aniyim*, chap. 7, *halakhot* 1-2.
17. Vilna Gaon, *Al'im LeTrufah*.
18. *Talmud Yerushalmi, Pe'ah*, chap. 1, *halakhah* 1.
19. *Teshuvot Maharam MiRotenburg*, sec. 74; Rama, *Yoreh De'ah*, sec. 177, subsec. 25, in the name of the Mordechai; *Pnei Yehoshua, Orach Chaim*, sec. 2; *Chavot Yair*, sec. 224.
20. *Shulchan Arukh, Yoreh De'ah*, sec. 249.
21. *Midrash, Shocher Tov, Tehillim*, Psalm 1.
22. *Teshuvot Shevut Yaakov*, pt. 2, sec. 86.
23. *Arukh HaShulchan*, sec. 249, subsec. 7.
24. Meir Tamari, "Non-Dividend Forms of Profit Distribution," *Economic Review* 29 (1967).
25. *Teshuvot HaRashba*, pt. 1, nos. 664, 789; pt. 3, no. 379.
26. *Beit Dino shel Shlomo, Yoreh De'ah*, sec. 1, Moshe Sternbuch, "Ma'aser Khesufi," *Am HaTorah*, pt. 5, sec. 10; see also *Minchat Yitzchak*, pt. 5, sec. 34, subsec. 6.
27. Meir Tamari, "Profits and Profitability in Israeli Manufacturing Corporations," *Economic Review* 40 (1971).
28. *Arukh HaShulchan*, sec. 249, subsec. 7; and *Minchat Yitzchat*, pt. 5, sec. 35.
29. *Talmud Bavli, Ketubot* 50a.
30. *Arukh HaShulchan, Yoreh De'ah*, sec. 34a, subsec. 8.
31. *Iggrot Moshe, Yoreh De'ah*, pt. 1, sec. 143.
32. Moshe Sternbuch, *Am Hatorah*, pt. 5, sec. 10.
33. *Shulchan Arukh, Yoreh De'ah*, sec. 240, subsec. 5.
34. Rama, *Yoreh De'ah*, sec. 240, subsec. 5.
35. *Shulchan Arukh, Choshen Mishpat*, sec. 163, subsecs. 1-3.
36. *Shulchan Arukh, Yoreh De'ah*, sec. 249.
37. *Teshuvot HaRashba*, pt. 7, sec. 108.
38. *Mishneh Torah, Hilkhot Gezeilah VeAveidah*, chap. 5, *halakhot* 11-12; see also *Teshuvot Maharam MiRothenburg*, sec. 106; also *Shulchan Arukh, Choshen Mishpat*, sec. 369.
39. *Iggrot Moshe, Choshen Mishpat*, pt. 2, sec. 29. *Choshen Mishpat*, pt. 1, sec. 88.
40. *Sifre, Parshat VeEt'chanan*.
41. Rama, *Shulchan Arukh, Yoreh De'ah*, sec. 251, subsec. 20.
42. *Mishneh Torah, Hilkhot De'ot*, chap. 4, *halakhah* 23.
43. *Shulchan Arukh, Yoreh De'ah* sec. 249, subsec. 2.
44. *Mishneh Torah, Hilkhot Tefillah*, chap. 1, sec. 4.

45. *Talmud Bavli, Baba Metzia* 33a.
46. *Mishneh Torah, Matnot Aniyim*, chap. 7, *halakhot* 3-4.
47. Natan Hannaver, "Even Metzulah," in *The Jew in the Medieval World*, ed. J. R. Marcus (New York: Harper, 1938).
48. *Arbaah Turim, Yoreh De'ah*, sec. 251, subsec. 13.
49. *Shulchan Arukh, Yoreh De'ah*, sec. 250, subsec. 2.
50. *Mishneh Torah, Matnot Aniyim*, chap. 7, *halakhot* 5-6.
51. *Shulchan Arukh, Yoreh De'ah*, sec. 247, subsec. 7.
52. Ibid., sec. 250, subsec. 5; *Rashba*, pt. 3, sec. 140.
53. *Talmud Bavli, Baba Batra* 8b.
54. *Mishneh Torah, Matnot Aniyim*, chap. 8, *halakhah* 10.
55. *Shulchan Arukh, Yoreh De'ah*, sec. 252, subsec. 1; see Shach here and the Taz on subsec. 2.
56. *Teshuvot HaMarik*, no. 4.
57. *Mishneh Torah, Matnot Aniyim*, chap. 8, *halakhah* 13.
58. Ibid., chap. 10, *halakhot* 7-14.
59. *Shulchan Arukh, Yoreh De'ah*, sec. 251, subsec. 3.
60. *Talmud Bavli, Baba Metzia* 62a.
61. *Talmud Yerushalmi, Nedarim*, chap. 9, *halakhah* 4.
62. *Minchat Tzvi, Hilkhot Tzedakah*, sec. 5.
63. *Mishnah, Pe'ah*, chap. 8, *mishnah* 8.
64. Ibid., chap. 4, *mishnah* 5.
65. *Mishneh Torah, Matnot Aniyim*, chap. 10, *halakhah* 4.
66. *Mishnah, Avot*, chap. 1, *mishnah* 5.

Chapter 7—"Thou Shall Not Lend Thy Money at Interest"

1. *Mishneh Torah, Hilkhot Malveh U'Loveh*, chap. 4, *halakhah* 2.
2. Meir Tamari, "Analysis of Financial Accounts," *Royal Commission on Small Firms*, Report No. 17 (London: Her Majesty's Stationery Office, 1971).
3. *Mishneh Torah, Hilkhot Malveh U'Loveh*, chap. 5, *halakhah* 1.
4. *Sefer HaChinukh, mitzvah* 66.
5. *Talmud Bavli, Baba Batra* 90b.
6. Ibid.
7. *Chafetz Chaim, Sefat Tamim*, chap. 5.
8. *Mishneh Torah, Hilkhot Malveh U'Loveh*, chap. 3, *halakhah* 1.
9. *Shulchan Arukh, Baal HaTanya, Hilkhot Ribit VeHilkhot Iska, halakhah* 4.
10. *Shulchan Arukh, Yoreh De'ah*, sec. 161, subsecs. 1, 5.
11. *Mishnah, Baba Metzia*, chap. 5, *mishnah* 4.
12. *Iggrot Moshe, Yoreh De'ah*, vol. 2, sec. 63.
13. *Sho'el U'Meishiv*, vol. 3, sec. 160.

14. *Talmud Bavli, Baba Metzia* 65b.
15. *Iggrot Moshe, Yoreh De'ah*, vol. 2, sec. 62.
16. *Vayechi Yosef, Dinei Ribit LeHalakhah* (Monsey, NY: Weiss, 1984).
17. *Shulchan Arukh, Yoreh De'ah*, sec. 173, subsec. 1.
18. *Teshuvot Chatam Sofer, Yoreh De'ah*, sec. 134.
19. *Choshen Mishpat*, sec. 16.
20. *Shulchan Arukh, Yoreh De'ah*, sec. 162, subsec. 1.
21. *Arbaah Turim, Yoreh De'ah*, sec. 162, subsec. 1.
22. *Minchat Yitzchak*, vol. 6, sec. 161.
23. *Temimim Dei'im*, sec. 60.
24. *Kerem Cheimor, Sefer Hatakanot*, enactment 91.
25. *Lechem Rav*, sec. 13.
26. *Teshuvot HaRiBasson*, sec. 63.
27. Quoted in *Teshuvot Makharit*, pt. 2, sec. 40.
28. G. L. Back, "The Economic Effects of Inflation," in *Proceedings of the Academy of Political Science*, no. 31 (1975): 220-223.
29. Meir Tamari, "Taxation," in *With All Your Possessions: Jewish Ethics and Economic Life* (New York: Free Press, 1987), pp. 217-220.
30. A. J. Vidish, "Social and Political Consequences of Inflation," and S. M. Wyntes, "The Gentry's Response to Inflation in 16th Century Holland and Urecth," in *Inflation through the Ages*, ed. N. Schmuckler and E. Marcus, (New York: Columbia University Press, 1983).
31. *Shem Mi Shmuel, Parshat Noah.*
32. *Mishnah Avot,* chap. 1, *mishnah* 2.
33. *Mishneh Torah, Hilkhot Malveh U'Loveh*, chap. 1, *halakhah* 1.
34. *Sefer HaChinukh, mitzvot* 66 and 68.
35. Samson Raphael Hirsch, *The Pentateuch*, trans. Isaac Levy (London: 1959), Exodus 22:24.
36. *Talmud Bavli, Baba Metzia* 63b.
37. *Mishneh Torah, Matnot Aniyim*, chap. 10, *halakhah* 7.
38. "Company Failure and Risk Models," *Journal of Finance* 8:2 (June 1984), Special Issue.
39. *Shulchan Arukh, Choshen Mishpat*, sec. 97, subsec. 23.
40. Exodus 22:25-26.
41. *Mishneh Torah, Hilkhot Malveh U'Loveh*, chap. 3, *halakhah* 1.
42. *Mishneh Torah, Hilkhot Malveh U'Loveh*, chap. 1, *halakhah* 4.

Chapter 8—Community and Social Demands on Wealth

1. A. Wolfson, "Jewish Cultural Services for the Israeli Welfare Ideology," *Journal of Welfare and Social Security Studies* (November 1977).

2. David Ben-Gurion, *Development and Security* (Tel Aviv: Hoveret Bitachon, 1954) (Hebrew).

3. John H. Yoder, "Minority Themes," in *Religion, Economics and Social Thought*, ed. Walter Bloch and Irving Hexman (Vancouver: Fraser Institute, 1986), pp. 281-301.

4. *Mishnah, Baba Batra*, chap. 1, *mishnah* 5.

5. *Choshen Mishpat*, sec. 163, subsecs. 1-3.

6. *Shulchan Arukh, Choshen Mishpat*, sec. 155, subsec. 34.

7. *Shekalim*, chap. 1, *halakhah* 1.

8. *Teshuvot HaRashba*, pt. 3, sec. 108; see also pt. 4, sec. 175.

9. For example, Simon Dubnow, *Pinkas HaMedinah* (Berlin: Ayanot, 1925).

10. For example, Louis Finkelstein, *Jewish Self-Government in the Middle Ages* (New York: Feldheim, 1964).

11. *Mishneh Torah, Hilkhot Melakhim*, chap. 4, *halakhot* 1-7.

12. *Talmud Bavli, Sanhedrin* 20b (according to the opinion of Shmuel and not that of Rav).

13. 1 Samuel 8:11-17.

14. *Mishnah, Sanhedrin*, chap. 2, *Mishnah* 11; see also *Tosafot* 20b, *Melekh Mutar*.

15. *Tzitz Eliezer*, pt. 10, sec. 1, subsec. 3; see also *Mishpat Cohen*, sec. 148.

16. *Talmud Bavli, Baba Kamma* 113b.

17. *Mishneh Torah, Hilkhot Gezeilah VeAveidah*, chap. 5, *halakhah* 11; see also *Shulchan Arukh, Choshen Mishpat*, sec. 369, subsec. 15.

18. Ibid.

19. *Talmud Bavli, Nedarim* 28a, codified in *Teshuvot Maharsham*, sec. 457.

20. *Arukh HaShulchan, Choshen Mishpat*, sec. 163, subsec. 17; also sec. 369, subsec. 1.

21. *Teshuvot Marik*, Root 14.

22. *Shulchan Arukh, Choshen Mishpat*, sec. 369, subsec. 15.

23. *Chidushei HaRan, Nedarim* 28.

24. *Yachvei De'ah*, pt. 5, sec. 67; see also *Dovev Meisharim*, pt. 3, sec. 89.

25. Rama, *Choshen Mishpat*, sec. 176, subsec. 25, *Teshuvot HaRashba*, pt. 4, sec. 185; see also Me'iri and Rosh to *Baba Batra* 8b-9a.

26. *Teshuvot HaRashba*, pt. 5, sec. 220.

27. Ibid., pt. 1, sec. 191.

28. *Talmud Bavli, Baba Batra* 54; see comment by the Rashbam; see also *Teshuvot Maharsham, Choshen Mishpat*, sec. 408.

29. *Shulchan Arukh, Choshen Mishpat*, sec. 163, subsec. 1.

30. *Teshuvot HaRashba*, pt. 3, sec. 401.

31. *Talmud Bavli, Baba Batra* 7b. The *Chazon Ish*, following the Rama, justifies this allocation not primarily on the element of benefit, but rather on the grounds that it is the existence of these houses that caused the expansion of the city and therefore of its increased defense costs in the first place.

32. *Teshuvot HaRashba*, pt. 5, sec. 182; pt. 3, sec. 196. See however, Rama, *Choshen Mishpat*, sec. 167, who provides a different opinion.

33. *Teshuvot Maharsham, Choshen Mishpat*, sec. 442.

34. *S'fat Tamim*, chap. 5; see also Rashi, *Talmud Bavli, Baba Batra* 165a.

35. Ya'akov Kondor, *Introduction to Estimating the Size of the Underground Economy in Israel* (Tel Aviv: Merkaz Sapir, 1983) (Hebrew).

36. *Teshuvot Maharsham*, sec. 453.

37. *Talmud Bavli, Baba Kamma*, 73b.

38. Meir Tamari, "Non-Dividend Forms of Profit Distribution in Manufacturing Corporations in Israel," *Economic Review* 29 (Jerusalem, 1967).

39. *Talmud Bavli, Shevuot* 31a.

40. *Talmud Bavli, Baba Batra* 88b (Rashi); *Shulchan Arukh, Choshen Mishpat*, sec. 231, subsec. 19. See explanation of *Meirat Einiyim*.

41. *Ramban, VaYikra* 19:2.

42. Ravad, *Eduyot*, chap. 5, *mishnah* 1.

43. *Baba Batra* 89a; *Mishneh Torah, Hilkhot Mekhirah*, chap. 14, *halakhah* 12; *Shulchan Arukh, Choshen Mishpat*, sec. 349, subsec. 5; ibid., sec. 155; *Teshuvot Ruach Chaim*, pt. 7, sec. 4.

44. Louis Finkelstein, *Jewish Self-Government in the Middle Ages* (New York: Feldheim, 1964), for example, p. 261.

45. *Talmud Bavli, Baba Kamma* 7a.

46. Finkelstein, op. cit., p. 292.

47. *Pinkas HaKhesheirim shel Kehillat Poznan*, enactment 162 (Jerusalem: D. Evron, 1967).

48. Simon Dubnow, op. cit., enactment 327.

49. *Yoreh De'ah*, sec. 249, subsec. 6; see *Beit Yosef*.

50. *Talmud Yerushalmi*, chap. 9, *mishnah* 1.

51. *Talmud Bavli, Sotah* 45b-46b; see Rashi to *Sotah* 46b.

52. *Talmud Bavli, Kiddushin* 29a-30a.

53. Meir Tamari, *Small Firms in Israel* (Tel Aviv: Centre for Social Development, 1991).

54. Pinkas Padua, op. cit., enactment 1542.

55. David Gans, *Zemach David* (Prague, 1595).

56. *Shulchan Arukh, Choshen Mishpat*, sec. 427.

57. *Teshuvot Mei Ahavah*, pt. 3, *Yoreh De'ah*, secs. 336, 408.

58. M. Balaban, *Yaarbuch der Judisch–Literarishen Geselshaft* (Frankfurt: Kaufman, 1929).

59. Salo W. Baron, *The Jewish Community*, vol. 2 (Philadelphia: Jewish Publication Society, 1945), p. 329.

60. *Teshuvot Maharsham, Orach Chaim*, sec. 20; *Yoreh De'ah*, secs. 207-209.

61. Baron, op. cit., vol. 3, p. 210.

62. *Mishneh Torah, Hilkhot Eivel*, chap. 14, *halakhot* 1-5, on the basis of *Talmud Bavli, Nedarim* 40a.

63. *Shulchan Arukh, Choshen Mishpat*, sec. 155.

64. *Mishneh Torah, Hilkhot Nizkei Mamon*, chap. 5, *halakhah* 1.

65. *Mishnah, Baba Batra*, chap. 2, *mishnah* 9.

66. *Mishnah, Baba Kamma*, chap. 7, *mishnah* 7.

67. *Talmud Bavli, Baba Kamma* 82b.

68. *Tosefta, Baba Metzia,* chap. 11, *halakhah* 31.

69. *Baba Batra* 19b, codified in *Shulchan Arukh, Choshen Mishpat*, sec. 155, subsec. 21.

70. *Sefer HaChasidim*, sec. 161.

71. *Shulchan Arukh, Choshen Mishpat*, sec. 155, subsec. 36; see also sec. 156, subsec. 2. In subsec. 36, the *Shulchan Arukh* holds that such cancellation may only by made where no formal sale of the rights took place. Magen Giborim, however, holds, as do others, that even where such a sale was made, the townspeople can still cancel it.

72. *Mishneh Torah, Hilkhot Rotze'ach U'Shmirot HaNefesh*, chap. 11, *halakhah* 3.

73. *Teshuvot Maharshach*, pt. 2, subsec. 98.

74. *Shemesh Tzedakah, Choshen Mishpat*, sec. 34, subsec. 11.

75. *Talmud Bavli, Baba Metzia* 32a.

76. *Talmud Bavli, Shabbat* 105b.

77. *Midrash Tanchuma, Kedoshim.*

78. *Mishneh Torah, Hilkhot Melakhim*, chap. 6, *halakhot* 14-15.

79. *Shulchan Arukh, Orach Chaim*, secs. 76-77, 79, 83-84.

80. *Talmud Bavli, Chagigah* 5a.

81. Simchah Werner, "The Development of Public Corruption in Israel," in *Political Corruption*, ed. Arnold J. Heidenheimer, Michael Johnston, and Victor T. Levine, (New Brunswick, NJ: Transaction Publishers, 1988), pp. 251-274.

82. Bach, *Tur, Yoreh De'ah*, sec. 257, based on *Midrash Tanchuma.*

83. *Talmud Bavli, Shabbat* 56a; also *Bereishit Rabbah*, chap. 8, v. 12.

84. *Talmud Bavli, Yoma* 9a.

85. *Talmud Bavli, Baba Batra* 8b, codified in Tur, *Shulchan Arukh, Chosen Mishpat*, sec. 256.

86. *Mishneh Torah, Hilkhot Melakhim*, chap. 3, *halakhot* 1-7.

Index

About the Author

Meir Tamari is director of the Centre for Business Ethics at the Jerusalem College of Technology, consultant to the Jewish Association for Business Ethics in the United Kingdom, and dean of the American Association for Jewish Business Ethics. After making *aliyah* from South Africa to a religious kibbutz in 1950, he served in the Bank of Israel in corporate research from 1960 to 1990, achieving the position of chief economist, office of the governor. Dr. Tamari is the author of numerous books and articles—academic and rabbinic—on business ethics, small firms, risk evaluation, and entrepreneurship and is publisher of the *Business Ethics Newsletter* in Jerusalem. The pioneer of a special course on Jewish ethics and economics at Bar-Ilan University, Dr. Tamari has lectured internationally and has served as consultant to various governmental bodies in the United Kingdom, France, and the United States.